AMERICA SEES RED

AMERICA SEES RED

Anti-Communism in America

1870s to 1980s

A Guide to Issues and References

Peter H. Buckingham

REGINA BOOKS
Claremont, California

Library of Congress Cataloging in Publication Data

Buckingham, Peter H., 1948-
   America Sees Red.

   (Guides to historical issues : # 3)
   Biography: p.
   Includes index.
   1. Anti-communist movements--United States--History. **I.** Title **II.** Series.
HX83.B78 1987   335.43'0973   87-23342

ISBN 0-941690-23-7
ISBN 0-941690-22-9 (pbk.)

Regina Books
P.O. Box 280
Claremont, Ca. 91711

Manufactured in the United States of America.

For Ann and Skyler

Guides to Historical Issues

Richard Dean Burns, Editor

#1   *WHO FIRST DISCOVERED AMERICA: A Critique of Writing on*
         Pre-Columbian Voyages
         Eugene R. Fingerhut

#2   *THE MISSILE CRISIS OF OCTOBER 1962: A Review of Issues and*
         References
         Lester Brune

#3   *AMERICA SEES RED: Anti-Communism in America, 1870s to*
         1980s: A Guide to Issues and References
         Peter H. Buckingham

Contents

Introduction / xi

Part I: Anti-Communism in America, 1870s-1980s

Chapter I **Through the First Red Scare, 1870s-1920** / 1
Nineteenth Century Anti-Radicalism / 2
The Socialist Party versus the Progressives / 7
Anti-Radicalism during World War I / 11
  The Espionage Act / 12
  The War Within / 14
  The Sedition Amendment / 16
  A Watershed in American Thinking / 17
The Red Scare Begins / 19
The Palmer Raids / 24
The Scare Fades / 26
Legacies / 28

Chapter II **Anti-Bolshevism: from Normalcy to a Second Red Scare , 1921-1950** / 31
Fear and Repression in the 1920s / 33
  Anti-Red Nativists and Patriots / 34
  Government Policies / 36
The 1930s: The Myth of the Red Decade / 39
  A Revival of Fear / 40
  Extreme Anti-Communism / 42
  Roosevelt as an Anti-Communist / 43
  Congressional Anti-Communism / 45
World War II: Uneasy Partnership / 49
  A Brief Honeymoon and Renewed Hostility / 49
  Deepening Disillusion / 52
A New Red Scare / 54
  The Scare Begins / 54
  Truman Takes Control / 57
  The Election of 1948 / 59
  HCUA, Hollywood, and Hiss / 60
  The Foley Square Trial / 62
Legacies / 63

Chapter III **The Scare Deepens: McCarthyites and Other Red Hunters, 1950-1954** / 65

Joe McCarthy / 67
  McCarthy the Man / 68
  McCarthy the "Ism" / 70
Red Scare Politics / 72
  The McCarran Act / 73
  The Election of 1950 / 75
The Scare Peaks / 76
  The Rosenbergs / 78
  McCarthy and McCarranism / 80
  The 1952 Election / 84
Inquisition By Committee: "Naming Names" / 86
  Education / 87
  The Scare Returns to Hollywood / 88
The Scare Abates / 90
  Ike and Dulles at Bay / 91
  The Army-McCarthy Hearings / 93
Legacies / 98

Chapter IV **From Consensus to Travail, 1954-1968** / 101

Brief Thaw / 102
Return to Repression / 105
  The CIA / 105
  The FBI / 106
  The Anti-Communist Consensus of the 1950s / 108
Anti-Communism on the New Frontier / 110
  Persecuting a New Generation / 112
  Updating Anti-Communism / 114
Far Right Anti-Communists / 115
  Fundamentalism / 116
  The John Birch Society / 117
  The Extremist Network / 119
  The Movement in Decline / 122
Liberal Agony and Vietnam / 123
  The 1964 Election / 124
  Unintended Consequences / 125
  Red-baiting the Left / 127
  Harassing the Left / 128
  The Crusade Falters / 130
Legacies / 130

Chapter V **From an Abortive Red Scare to the New Right: America Since 1968** / 133

The Return of Richard Nixon / 135
A Near Red Scare / 138
  Hoover's Last Stand / 138
  Other Government Operations / 140
  The Pentagon Papers / 144
  The 1972 Election / 145
The Center Folds / 146
The New Right / 150
  Political Organizers / 151
  The Religious Far Right / 152
  Neoconservatives / 154
  The 1980 Election / 156
Fighting the "Evil Empire" / 158
  The New McCarthyism / 161
  The New Right Chafes / 164
  The Culture of Anti-Communism / 167
Legacies / 169

Concluding Thoughts / 171

Part II: Bibliography

References / 179
Bibliographies / 179
General Works / 180
Nineteenth Century / 183
Progressive Era / 183
World War I / 185
  The War at Home / 185
  America and the Russian Revolution / 186
The First Red Scare / 187
  General Accounts / 187
  Personalities / 188
  State and Local Studies / 189
The 1920s / 190
The "Red Decade" / 191
Labor and Anti-Communism / 193
World War II / 195
The Second Red Scare—"Trumanism" / 196
  General Accounts / 196
  The Loyalty Issue / 198
  Personalities / 199
  Regional Studies / 201

The Cold War / 201
House Committee on UnAmerican Activities (HCUA) / 204
    HCUA in Washington / 204
    HCUA and Hollywood / 205
The Alger Hiss Case / 206
McCarthyism / 208
    McCarthy-The Man / 208
    "McCarthyism" / 209
    "McCarranism" / 211
    McCarthy's Defenders / 212
    McCarthy's Critics / 212
    Victims / 213
The Media and the Red Scare / 214
    Regional Studies / 214
The Rosenbergs / 215
Anti-Communist Culture / 216
Ex-Communists / 218
The Eisenhower Years / 219
    Liberal and Leftist Anti-Communists / 219
    Conservative Anti-Communists / 221
    The Eisenhower Administration / 222
The 1960s / 222
Anti-Communist Politics / 222
    The New Left / 224
Anti-Communism and the Intelligence Agencies / 225
    General Studies / 225
    The FBI / 225
Radical Right Anti-Communism / 227
    General Accounts / 227
    The John Birch Society / 229
A Near Red Scare, 1968-1974 / 230
The New Right / 231
Religious-Based Anti-Communism / 232
Contemporary Anti-Communism / 233
Fiction / 235
    Novels About Communism / 235
    Anti-Communist Novels / 235
Author Index / 237

Subject Index / 243

Introduction

Not long ago, President Ronald Reagan dramatized the threat of communism to the world with a quotation from V.I. Lenin, leader of the Russian Revolution: "We will take Eastern Europe. We will organize the hordes of Asia. And then we will move into Latin America and we won't have to take the United States; it will fall into our outstretched hands like overripe fruit." But Lenin never said that or anything like it. The quotation came out of the imagination of Robert Welch, founder of the far right John Birch Society, a revelation which caused not a ripple in Washington or elsewhere. Many people had attributed such demonic powers to communists for so long that Lenin's extraordinary prescience made perfect sense. The incident itself only makes sense within the context of America's long battle against communism. For more than a century the United States government and many private citizens have fought leftists, foreign and domestic, real and imagined.

Twice the anti-communist struggle gave way to mass hysteria, or "red scares." It has been a factor in every presidential election since 1912 and in many congressional, state and local contests as well. Anti-communism shows up in cultural artifacts ranging from children's trading cards to advertisements to entertainment media like movies, radio, and television. Experiments by psychologists show that several million Americans stand ready at any given time to take part in a red scare. American military interventions abroad have taken place several times in the name of anti-communism, like Vietnam. Since 1945, the U.S. government has spent almost $2 trillion dollars on nuclear weapons and delivery systems (in 1985 dollars) to deter communism. It is the purpose of this study to find out how and why anti-communism has become so embedded in American politics and culture.

A few words at the outset are in order about political terminology used in this book. Originally, a "communist" was one who advocated a system whereby the community as a whole owns all property, sharing in the means of production. The most famous variation on this idea is based on the writings of Karl Marx and Friedrich Engels. The first Marxist government came into existence in Russia beginning in 1917, although the emerging Soviet system owed as much to the doctrines of Lenin, Trotsky, and Stalin as Marx himself. Most contemporary Americans have come to associate "communism" with the repressive and expansionist Soviet system and those tied to Moscow through branches of the Communist party. Since World War II local offshoots of Marxism-Leninism have taken root in China, Southeast Asia, Latin America, Africa, and Eastern Europe. The word "Left" refers to a wide variety of positions and parties, many of which are inherently anti-communist including "socialism," usually democratic in orientation and independent from foreign allegiance. "Liberal," as used in this study, denotes belief in a "mixed economy" of capitalism and the welfare state, an emphasis on civil rights, civil liberties, and the central government as an arbiter between the public and private sectors, and a universalist foreign policy based on promotion of liberal capitalism world-wide. "Conservative" in the contemporary sense is a relatively new term in American politics which alludes to those wishing to conserve traditional values of individualism and unfettered economic competition with a minimum of government, except in the area of foreign affairs.

The meanings of both liberal and conservative are still essential, if slippery, designations for the two dominant sets of attitudes at the center of American politics. All of these political labels have been misused by opponents through the years, but none more so than the pejorative "reds." Originally a reference to the traditional red flag of revolutionary socialism, red has been used at various times to mean communist, socialist, leftist, radical, liberal, or someone whose ideas the "red baiter" does not like. When enough people begin to blame communists for their problems during times of social, economic, and political dislocation, then America sees red.

PART I

Anti-Communism in America, 1870s-1980s

Chapter One

Through the First Red Scare, 1870s-1920

In the early years of the republic rapid industrialization brought profound social dislocation. As villages gave way to towns and cities, the quality of life among working people suffered. Some sought to better their lot through trade associations or unions, others joined experimental utopian crusades. To many, socialism, a system of common ownership and operation of the means of production, seemed a sound alternative to the narrow self-interest of free enterprise. Americans in the nineteenth century generally tolerated the wide variety of experiments based on socialism which bloomed briefly and then died away. The often violent class conflict between labor and capital in the 1870s and 1880s created a new fear of radicals as socialism and communism became associated with the hordes of immigrants pouring into the United States. Spurning cooperation with reform movements like the populists and evolutionary socialists, the earliest Marxist political organizations remained small and largely unappealing to the American public.

The Socialist Party of America, a coalition of leftist radicals forged just after the turn of the century, won a following among the working classes significant enough that Progressives felt compelled to counterattack with reformist legislation. Lingering fears of radicalism came to the forefront once again during the First World War when an intolerant majority sanctioned persecution of the anti-war left. Armed with the Espionage Act, the Sedition Amendment, and other laws designed to limit traditional American freedoms, the

Wilson administration, state and local officials, and patriotic vigilantes attacked domestic radicalism. The anti-radical alarm increased following the end of the war and the creation of the first communist government, Soviet Russia. Apprehension over the future, the momentum of wartime repression, renewed leftist militancy, and ambitious politicians all contributed to the collective madness of the Red Scare of 1919-1920. This time of hysteria, murder, and lawlessness left deep scars on the Left and made the country vulnerable to future episodes of irrational fear.

Nineteenth Century Anti-Radicalism

A seemingly boundless frontier and the deeply-held optimism of an energetic people provided fertile ground for nineteenth century socialist experiments. The British social reformer Robert Dale Owen pioneered the cooperative movement in New Harmony, Indiana and a dozen other communities. Followers of the French social philosopher Charles Fourier organized more than forty "phalansteries." All together, at least 178 commonwealths practiced socialism in one form or another. A few communes practiced "free love"; some demanded total sexual abstinence. There were vegetarian communes, a free black experiment, communes with economies based solely on barter, and others practicing pure communism with equal division of profits and property. In a society based on individualism, ownership of private property, and free enterprise, experiments in socialism created controversy. Josiah Warren, a disappointed Owenite, became an early critic. The practice of socialism, he believed, doomed the New Harmony commune to failure. To prove his point, Warren launched a series of "Time Stores" in which consumers bartered labor for goods. Eventually Warren founded his own town of Modern Times, New York, an anarchist experiment based solely on individualism and without any rules, regulations, or ideology.

Many of the early socialist communities flourished for only a short time; few lasted for more than ten years. Dissension often fragmented the members while the general public voiced disapproval. The experimenters themselves rather than anti-communists like Josiah Warren caused most of the experiments to lapse. Robert Dale Owen later explained that workers made too much money and land was too cheap to force the necessary spirit of sustained cooperative action.

The early utopian socialists carried on their experiments in communal living without the benefit of a central blueprint. In 1848, the chief theorist of modern communism, Karl Marx, and his collaborator Friederich Engels published the *Communist Manifesto*, the basic formulation of what came to be known as Marxism. The authors made no mention of the United States and their work was not reprinted in America until 1871. Nevertheless, Marx's writings appeared in German-American newspapers and magazines beginning in the 1850s and the *New York Tribune* carried his reports from Europe for several years. When Marx turned his attention to the United States in the last pages of *Das Kapital*, he did not seem to understand that the lack of a feudal class background (as in Europe) made America much more promising ground than elsewhere for social democracy. He did foresee a problem which American socialists would face in organizing: the lack of a permanent and oppressed proletariat. The status of wage earner, he observed in 1865, "is for a very large part of the American people but a probational state, which they are sure to leave within a longer or shorter term." Workers climbed the ladder of upward social mobility more easily in America than anywhere else, making capitalism more attractive than socialism. However, Marx had provided working class immigrants with a powerful argument which they brought with them to America.

The severe economic swings between boom and depression so characteristic of early American industrial development brought about tensions between workers (some organizing in labor unions) on the one hand and businessmen, the middle class, and government officials on the other. At the same time, Marxism and other radical teachings taking root in the working classes of Europe were changing the nature of revolution and thus altering the way Americans thought about insurrections. In struggles between the forces of monarchy and democracy, Americans sided with republican forces; but revolutions pitting class against class seemed much more frightening. The revival of revolutionary French Jacobinism in the short-lived Paris Commune (1871), which Marx hoped would signal the beginning of class warfare, aroused middle class fears in the United States. This anxiety over foreign-born revolutionaries and class conflict grew as newspapers and business leaders came to apply "communism" to activities ranging from peaceful demonstrations by the unemployed to the violent activities of a secret society of coal miners, the "Molly Maguires." The Workingmen's party of the United States was organized in Philadelphia in 1876, the second Marxist political party in the world. Renamed the Socialist Labor Party a year later, the Marxists ran candidates for local offices in several large cities and managed to elect a few. In 1877, a strike of railroad workers spread spontaneously in reaction to repeated wage cuts, raising the specter of revolutionary warfare for the first time when police and allied vigilantes clashed with laborers in a dozen cities. A New York newspaper commented darkly that the strikes were the "nearest approach we have yet had to Communism in America," thereby contributing to the myth of a "Communist" conspiracy.

Another depression in the mid-1880s added momentum to the labor movement. In May 1886, the International Working People's Association (IWPA), a militant organization of German immigrants which was both philosophically communist and anarchist joined other organizations in a general strike for the eight hour work day. At a rally in Chicago's Haymarket Square called to protest police brutality against strikers, someone threw a bomb at the advancing police, who retaliated by firing their revolvers into the crowd. The "Haymarket Riot" deepened anxiety over immigrants, radicalism and labor unions after police arrested IWPA members for the murders. Seven of the eight defendants were sentenced to the gallows, solely on the evidence that they advocated the violent overthrow of government. These spasmodic episodes of fear were harbingers of the red scares that would come in the wakes of World Wars I and II during the following century. Yet, ironically, the idea that millions of immigrants might become active politically under the socialist or communist banner was far removed from reality. Some newcomers had only one goal: to save enough money that they might return to their native land and their families with some wealth. Others went back home discouraged after failing to scale the socio-economic ladder. Many who stayed wandered from place to place in search of temporary work, failing to put down roots anywhere. This "perpetual motion" factor made most immigrants poor risks as radical recruits.

Public reaction to the violence of the 1870s and 1880s pushed the labor movement toward moderation. Three immigrant cigar makers active in the early trade union movement, Adolph Strasser, Ferdinand Laurell, and Samuel Gompers, rejected socialism in favor of concentrating on "bread and butter" issues—higher wages, shorter hours, and better working conditions. Gompers, cofounder and longtime president of the American Federation of Labor (AFL), denounced the socialists as "opponents of constructive policies," whose ideas were economically unsound, socially wrong, and industrially impossible. The majority of the AFL's craft-oriented members agreed because as skilled workers they tended to hold middle class values and since they were often Catholics, a faith which seldom opposed the status quo.

Millions of middle class Americans learned about socialism in the closing years of the nineteenth century through utopian novels. In *Looking Backward* (1888) Edward Bellamy used the future to flay contemporary capitalism. After sleeping for 113 years, Julian West awakes to find himself in the America of the year 2000, a land where government owns industry, plenty has replaced poverty and exploitation, and the people practice "fraternal co-operation." This vision of the future had little in common with that of Marx. Change would come through "evolution, not revolution, orderly progressive development...prudence and conservatism." Bellamy refused even to label his views as socialist, preferring to call them "nationalism." Soon "Nationalist Clubs" spread through the nation and his best-seller spawned many imitations. The evils of industrialism—the grimy tenements, the plummeting wages of workers, unsafe working conditions, and the oppressiveness of the impersonal city—created an audience yearning for Utopia. Within a few years, though, nationalism would be forgotten in the rush to embrace the populist crusade of the 1890s.

Bellamy's middle class socialists, Marxist immigrants, native American laborers and farmers angered by low crop prices and exploitation by railroads, unsuccessfully sought to unite behind a national organization of the discontented. All shared a fear of growing corporate power and an impatience with the prevailing laissez-faire politics of the mainstream which refused to permit government action on behalf of the victims of industrialism. For these groups, industrial capitalism caused alienation, degradation, and misery. In July 1892, they moved toward such a coalition when more than 1300 delegates met in Omaha, Nebraska to form the Populist party. The Omaha platform called for the expansion of government power "to the end that oppression, injustice and poverty shall eventually cease in the land." In addition to a graduated income tax, postal savings banks, currency reform, and a government loan program for farmers, the populists called for government reclamation of nonessential land owned by the railroads, as well as common ownership of the railroads, telegraph, and telephone companies. Populists did not advocate collective farming or socializing the means of production, ideas at the heart of socialism. But the two movements converged at enough points to frighten their conservative opponents—and the more doctrinaire of the Marxists.

The core of the American Marxist movement, the Socialist Labor Party (SLP), rejected populism. Curaçao-born Daniel DeLeon, the party's principal leader, denounced the populists as "one of the most conservative and even retrograde attempts ever recorded in the history of economic revolution." Most of DeLeon's small band of followers were immigrants, some of whom had refused to learn English out of principle. Fearful of being coopted by evolutionary socialism, the Socialist Labor Party spurned offers of cooperation, choosing to cast out party members who worked with populists and running their own candidates in the elections of 1892 and 1896. The populists responded by castigating immigrants, especially those from Eastern Europe, through resolutions calling for immigration restriction legislation. The conflict between the two parties was best exemplified at a heated meeting over campaign tactics in Illinois in 1894. When socialist

Thomas Morgan proposed a platform plank demanding that the people should own the means of production and distribution, he was hooted down. One Nebraska populist shouted: "If this is what you came to the People's party for, we don't want you. Go back from where you came with your socialism." Clearly, socialism could not become a mass movement as long as most people perceived it as un-American, that is, opposed to the "American dream" of wealth and property.

The Socialist Party Versus the Progressives

A new breed of socialists appeared at the turn of the century: men and women who put Marx into an American idiom and attracted a wider following among native-born and immigrant groups. In 1901 leftists met in Indianapolis to form the Socialist Party of America (SPA). They represented every shade of socialism save that of Daniel DeLeon, who preferred to keep the remnants of his SLP in pristine isolation. Furthest right stood Victor Berger, German-born leader of Wisconsin's highly organized socialist labor unions. Morris Hillquit, a former admirer of DeLeon, staked out the party's center. The leader of the left, Eugene V. Debs, former president of the American Railway Union, headed this coalition of Marxists, activist Christians, former populists, and militant trade unionists. The SPA also embraced William D. Haywood and the Western Federation of Miners (WFM), syndicalists advocating the reorganization of society around the workplace. As a coalition of regional leftist groups, the party's rank and file was as diverse in their interests and viewpoints as Democrats and Republicans. The SPA attracted immigrant garment workers, sharecroppers, teachers, lawyers, labor leaders, and even a few millionaires. If delegates to the 1904 national convention reflected the party as a whole, then two out of every three members were born in the United States. That such diverse groups could put aside their differences made the socialist future seem bright. "Socialism is coming," Julius Wayland wrote in his weekly newspaper *Appeal to Reason*, "It's coming like a prairie fire and nothing can stop it."

Socialists committed themselves to the SPA at a time when several reform efforts had coalesced into the loosely knit Progressive movement. The dark times of the 1890s passed, but not the fear that industrialization had brought on economic and political instability. To the predominantly upper-middle class, Anglo-Saxon, Protestant, Progressives the solution to the evils brought on by industrial progress was modification of those conditions which threatened the social and economic order—a reformation of capitalism. In order to save the old values while guiding the nation toward a more humane system of free enterprise, the Progressives set out to educate the immigrant, regulate the giant corporations, mitigate the suffering of the working classes, and broaden democracy. "We are acting in defense of property," wrote President Theodore Roosevelt in the midst of his anti-trust campaign. Roosevelt and other conservative Progressives sought to reform the "malfactors of wealth" to save the country from their folly. "As a matter of fact," Roosevelt explained, "it is these reactionaries and ultra-conservatives who are themselves most potent in increasing socialistic feeling." Americans did not support the Progressive movement simply to oppose radicalism, but there can be little doubt that anti-socialism played a key role.

Progressives became concerned with the growing socialist strength after Debs polled more than four hundred thousand votes in the 1904 presidential election, a development Roosevelt viewed as "far more ominous than any populist movement in the past." Some Progressives, including Louis D. Brandeis, came to regard conservative trade union organizations such as the American Federation of Labor as "a strong bulwark against the great wave of socialism." The National Civic Federation (NCF), an organization of businessmen and bread and butter unionists, supported labor reform and trade unionism in order to blunt the appeal of socialism among workers. In 1911, following a sweeping socialist victory in Milwaukee, the federation launched a major anti-socialist educational campaign in the National Institute Survey. Officially, the survey committee took a conciliatory line, advocating an educational campaign among workers who shared goals with the socialists; unofficially, though, members endorsed the use of mass media and education to destroy socialism. The NCF launched an informal campaign in major universities to fire socialist academics and several leftists were dropped from teaching posts. On the whole, the NCF's campaign failed. Socialism continued to grow even after President Woodrow Wilson put the capstone on the Progressive reform effort with his New Freedom program.

The socialists elected more than 1,000 officials to public office during the Progressive era. This limited success at the polls, combined with a new militancy on the part of the SPA's allies in the labor movement, brought back the old fear among conservatives that socialism was a growing threat to law and order, especially in the West. In 1905 a dynamite booby trap killed a former governor of Idaho. After obtaining evidence from a labor spy which implicated "Big Bill" Haywood's Western Federation of Miners, Idaho police kidnapped Haywood and other union officers from Denver without waiting for extradition proceedings. The incident prompted Debs to pen an angry article entitled "Arouse, Ye Slaves" for the socialist newspaper *Appeal to Reason*—a polemic which so annoyed President Roosevelt that he urged his attorney general to bar it from the mails. After languishing in prison for several months, the WFM officials obtained an acquittal, but the whole affair revealed an intolerance for unionists and leftists.

Many Americans came to feel threatened by the Industrial Workers of the World (IWW), a revolutionary industrial union founded in 1905 by Haywood, Daniel DeLeon, and Eugene Debs to supplant the craft unionism of the American Federation of Labor. Seeking to organize unskilled migratory workers, "Wobbly" officials alarmed local businessmen with firebreathing anti-capitalist rhetoric. Between 1907 and 1916, when several cities passed ordinances prohibiting IWWs from public speechmaking, the union organized free speech campaigns along the West Coast. Hundreds of unemployed Wobblies descended on targeted cities, filling the jails until the city fathers relented. Feelings ran high on both sides in 1911 after the dynamite bombing of the *Los Angeles Times* building. Even though the convicted bombers did not belong to the IWW, businessmen in

California formed vigilante committees to crush the free speech campaign. Several Wobblies and at least one sympathetic newspaper editor were kidnapped, beaten, and tarred and feathered. The terror campaign reached a climax in 1916 with the "Everett massacre," a gun battle between IWW members and a coalition of police and vigilantes which left seven dead, seven missing, and over fifty wounded. Seventy-four jailed Wobblies eventually obtained release, providing the syndicalists with another Pyrrhic victory and further poisoning the public mind against the Left as a whole.

In 1912-1913, the IWW became embroiled in two major strikes in the Northeast. When immigrant textile workers in Lawrence, Massachusetts received a reduction in pay, the Wobblies helped to organize a strike among the twenty-five different nationalities. Two months later the employers conceded wage hikes ranging from five to twenty percent. This victory encouraged workers in Paterson, New Jersey to strike after mill owners ordered a work speed up. As the work stoppage dragged on through the summer of 1913, hundreds were jailed and several violent clashes occurred between company guards and pickets. In spite of a spectacular pageant held in Madison Square Garden, the strike ended in failure, leaving the IWW no better off than before the Lawrence dispute.

After the free speech fights and the Lawrence and Paterson strikes the stereotype of the hobo Wobbly replaced the bomb throwing anarchist as the leftist bogyman. Violence did flare up when the IWW demanded the right to speak in public for higher wages for workers, but Wobblies were more frequently the victims of bloodshed than the perpetrators. While the Wobblies used violent rhetoric, they practiced passive resistance most frequently. "We have a new kind of violence," Bill Haywood noted during the Lawrence strike, "the havoc we raise with money by laying down our tools." The IWW's growing reputation for militancy coincided with a new wave of middle class nativism as more and more Americans came to feel threatened by immigrants and the implicit challenge to "WASP" (White Anglo-Saxon Protestant) values.

At the behest of powerful agricultural interests, Western governors under the leadership of Hiram Johnson pressured the

Wilson administration into an investigation of the IWW in 1915. A special agent from the Department of Justice searched for evidence of an interstate conspiracy, but he could find no violations of criminal law. Under a 1903 law, however, federal judges had the power to refuse naturalized citizenship to persons who opposed organized government, advocated political assassinations, or belonged to groups espousing such ideas. The Naturalization Act of 1906 provided that citizenship applicants had to swear that they did not oppose organized government or believe in anarchism. Beginning in 1912, judges in the Pacific Northwest began to deny IWW aliens citizenship under the naturalization law, excluding enough members to weaken the Wobblies without undercutting the source of cheap immigrant labor. Denial of citizenship was not enough for Congress, which took the anti-left campaign a step further with the passage of a new immigration law providing for deportation of alien radicals. On 5 February 1917, Congress overrode the president after Wilson had vetoed successive versions of the bill on the ground that it might exclude legitimate political exiles along with left-wing troublemakers. Federal officials did not have time to apply the new immigration law before the United States declared war on the Central Powers in April. But the government had a blueprint for action: already IWW immigrants had been denied citizenship and a vaguely worded deportation law could be applied to any and all radical aliens.

Anti-Radicalism During World War I

On 6 April 1917 the United States declared war on Germany. The next day socialist leaders gathered in St. Louis for an emergency meeting. A majority of the delegates approved a series of resolutions denouncing the conflict as imperialism and promising "continuous, active, and public opposition to the war." Moved by the idealism of Wilson ("the world must be made safe for democracy") and manipulated by his wartime propaganda machine, many Americans grew increasingly intolerant of any criticism of the government or the war. As wartime hysteria mounted, local, state, and federal officials began to curb democracy at home. President Wilson had anticipated that this might happen, telling a journalist just before the war: "Once lead this people into war and they'll forget there ever was such a thing as tolerance."

The Espionage Act

Nevertheless, socialist strength grew significantly in the spring of 1917 as millions of Americans responded favorably to the antiwar movement. Ultra-nationalists like former President Theodore Roosevelt, moral fundamentalists who viewed the conflict as a holy war, superpatriots convinced that America could do no wrong, and businessmen eager to crush the labor movement all demanded that war critics be silenced. The Wilson administration agreed. Long before the formal declaration of war, in June 1916 and again in February 1917, Attorney General Thomas Gregory attempted to persuade Congress to pass bills to curb free speech and freedom of the press and to jail suspected spies, efforts which came to nothing. After President Wilson called for Congress to give him the power to initiate "stern repression" against dissidents in his war address, Congressman Edwin Webb and Senator Charles Culbertson led a drive to push through an espionage bill which was a combination of seventeen different Justice Department proposals. Since almost everyone agreed on the need to thwart espionage, critics of the "ominopently comprehensive" legislation, as an uneasy Senator William E. Borah called it, concentrated on the proposal giving the president the authority to censor the press. While this section went down to defeat, due in large part to opposition from powerful newspaper interests, the administration could still curb the press under a clause which armed the postmaster general with the right to refuse mailing privileges to printed materials which advocated treason, insurrection, or resistance. During congressional debates, the legislators paid scant attention to a clause providing a $10,000 fine and/or twenty years in prison for anyone who would make false reports or statements designed to interfere with military operations or who "shall willfully cause or attempt to cause insubordination, disloyalty, mutiny, or refusal of duty in the military or naval forces of the United States, or shall willfully obstruct the recruiting or enlistment service of the United States...." The administration interpreted this provision of the Espionage Act, which became law on 15 June 1917, as a mandate to silence war critics.

With one out of three Americans either a first or second generation immigrant capable, in theory, of divided loyalties and tainted with foreign ideologies, there was an understandable impulse toward excessive nationalism. The zeal with which the administration and its allies carried out the subsequent campaign of repression is more difficult to comprehend. Lower level officials in Washington and in some districts of the federal court system vied with one another in their rigid compliance with the Espionage Act. Kate Richards O'Hare, a leader of the SPA, received a five year jail sentence for denouncing the war effort at a rally in North Dakota in a set speech she had delivered in other places at least seventy-five times. Others went to jail merely for attending anti-war rallies. On 28 August 1917, agents raided a socialist bookstore and party offices, arresting Charles T. Schenk, the SPA's general secretary and others for printing leaflets urging draftees to "Assert Your Rights." The U.S. Supreme Court upheld Schenk's sentence of six-months imprisonment under the Espionage Act. "The question in every case," Justice Oliver Wendell Holmes explained, "is whether the words used are used in such circumstances and are of such a nature as to create a clear and present danger that they will bring about the substantive evils that Congress has a right to prevent." In early 1918, the government indicted Victor Berger and four party comrades under the act in a move designed to knock Berger out of the close Wisconsin senatorial election. After the Armistice all the defendants received twenty-year sentences from the xenophobic Judge Kenesaw Mountain Landis. Eventually the Supreme Court set the verdicts aside and the government dropped the charges.

Postmaster General Albert Sidney Burleson moved quickly against sixty socialist newspapers by cutting off their second class mailing privileges under terms of the Espionage Act. Burleson stopped the mailing of an issue of the *Masses*, an avant garde literary magazine, because he found it offensive and then refused further mailings since it had skipped an issue! "The Cardinal" (as Wilson called him privately) banned other periodicals for such reasons as criticizing the government for deficit spending, using Thomas Jefferson's quotations to argue for Irish independence, and expressing skepticism over Britain's pledge to create an independent Jewish homeland. The Trading-With-the-Enemy Act extended the postmaster's powers of wartime censorship over foreign language magazines and newspapers. Editors of such publications had to submit translations of all stories dealing with the war for government scrutiny.

The War Within

During the World War I, the confrontation between the Left and the Right grew to such proportions as to constitute a war within the United States. State penitentiaries in Oklahoma filled to overflowing with participants from the Green Corn Rebellion, a movement of sharecroppers and tenant farmers who had vowed to force the government to stop the war. Patriotic organizations routinely broke up socialist rallies. Volunteer organizations such as the American Defense Society, the Boy Spies of America, the Sedition Slammers, and the Terrible Threateners sought to aid local, state and federal officials in ferreting out the disloyal. A quarter million Americans who joined the American Protective League (APL) received Secret Service badges from the Department of Justice. Upon first hearing of the quasi-official vigilante group, Wilson asked Attorney General Gregory "if there is any way in which we could stop it." Gregory pretended that the APL was a well-disciplined band of patriots, although historian David Kennedy has described them as "a rambunctious, unruly posse comitatus on an unprecedented national scale." Government officials and their APL deputies arrested thousands of "slackers" suspected of evading the Registration Act or urging others to do so. The APL roughed up leftists, read mail and telegrams addressed to those deemed unpatriotic, and incited others against opponents of the war.

Several states enacted criminal syndicalist laws to weaken the IWW. The Wobblies opposed the war because of its irrelevance to their struggle against exploitative employers. Anti-labor forces charged that the IWW's continued insistence on higher wages in booming wartime industries was unpatriotic. In the summer of 1917, a series of strikes brought about violent confrontations between the IWW and war supporters. Vigilantes rounded up striking miners in Jerome, Arizona and shipped them in cattle cars to California where they were jailed. In nearby Bisbee, the Citizens Protective League, working with the big mining companies and the local sheriff, incarcerated over 1,100 strikers and sympathizers at a local baseball park and then dumped them in the dessert without food or water. To the north, fifteen thousand miners walked off the job in Butte, Montana after 160 men burned to death in an Anaconda Copper Company mine. Vigilantes responded by kidnapping, torturing, and murdering Wobbly organizer Frank Little.

In August, the Wilson administration joined the anti-wobbly crusade, using the APL to open mail, follow suspected organizers, and infiltrate the union with spies. The next month, government agents raided IWW offices in 33 cities, seizing over five tons of subversive literature as a prelude to the arraignment of the entire IWW leadership. Within six months of America's entry into the war, the far left was everywhere on the run. Many Americans agreed with Theodore Roosevelt's assertion that "He who is not with us, absolutely and without reserve of any kind, is against us, and should be treated as an enemy alien."

The mounting wartime hysteria against radicalism and all things German (one-and-the-same to many) received a further boost in November 1917 when the Bolsheviks seized power in Russia. Communist demands for world revolution, the abolition of private property, and a separate peace with Germany disturbed the administration and the American people. Newspapers circulated rumors that Lenin and his associates had set up electric guillotines and forced all women to register with the "Bureau of Free Love." The government and patriotic societies concluded that Russian "Reds" were as bad as German "Huns." It was but a short step to the conclusion that Germans, Bolsheviks, American socialists, and the IWW were all part of the same conspiracy.

In the winter of 1917-1918, Wobblies came under increasing attack. Soldiers helped to break strikes in Washington state while a mob wrecked socialist and IWW printing presses in Seattle. A self-styled "home guard" searched workers for identity cards in the lumber camps of Idaho. In Oklahoma a mob whipped, tarred, and feathered a group of Wobblies suspected of bombing an oilman's home while in California authorities rounded up IWW members and charged them with violating the Espionage Act. The anti-red campaign reached a nadir in April 1918 when a mob lynched Robert Paul Prager, a German alien, because he had discussed socialism with his fellow workers.

The Sedition Amendment

Ostensibly to increase national security, several states passed sedition laws providing long prison sentences for persons convicted of criticizing the government, the Constitution, the flag, or the military. Liberals argued that the Espionage Act of 1917 had to be tightened to soothe public fears and halt the lawlessness of patriotic vigilantes. The superpatriots contended that the Espionage Act had not been effective enough in rooting out opponents of the war. A Justice Department-sponsored amendment held that false statements judged to hinder the war effort, obstruct the sale of war bonds, incite disloyalty, or obstruct enlistments were to be punishable by twenty years imprisonment and a $20,000 fine. One elastic clause made it a federal crime to utter, write, or publish "disloyal, profane, scurrilous or abusive" opinions of the American government, the Constitution, or the war effort. The postmaster general's already significant powers of censorship were to be expanded further. The amendment had little to do with espionage as Senator Henry Cabot Lodge reminded his colleagues. "To state it very broadly," he remarked, "it is aimed at certain classes of agitators who exist in different parts of the country." On 16 May 1918, President Wilson signed the Sedition amendment to the Espionage Act, a measure which put the most severe restrictions on freedom of speech and of the press in the nation's history.

Although more socialists, Wobblies, pacifists, and other opponents of the war were jailed under the new law, Eugene Debs remained free to criticize the war effort. In Canton, Ohio, after visiting some comrades in the local workhouse, he castigated those "eager to apply the brand of treason to the men who dare to even whisper their opposition to junker rule in the United States" and added his praise for the Russian Revolution. Two weeks later, the government indicted Debs on charges of attempting to incite insubordination, disloyalty, and mutiny in the armed forces, obstructing recruiting, speaking and publishing with the intent of encouraging resistance to the government, and making false statements designed to aid Germany. "I have been accused of having obstructed the war," Debs said at his trial, "I admit it. Gentlemen, I hate war." He received a ten-year prison sentence.

Meanwhile, William D. Haywood and 112 other Wobblies were charged with conspiracy against the government war program and put on trial in Chicago. Since the government found it impossible to provide direct evidence of conspiracy and difficult to prove specific violations of the law, prosecutors produced documents seized in raids in September 1917 (some of them dating from 1913) to show that the IWW as an organization constituted a conspiracy. On 30 August 1918, a jury found ninety-six of the defendants guilty on all charges after just fifty-five minutes of deliberation. Haywood and thirteen others got twenty-year sentences while the rest were given from ten years to a few days. Mass trials of IWW members in California and Kansas yielded similar results. The IWW as a whole had been put on trial and found guilty.

A Watershed in American Thinking

"To fight," Woodrow Wilson had said in the spring of 1917, "you must be brutal and ruthless, and the spirit of ruthless brutality will enter into the very fibre of our national life, infecting Congress, the courts, the policeman on the beat, the man in the street." Not only did the American people caught up in the war forget about tolerance, but so did he. Just eight months later he warned the American Federation of Labor that "the horses that kick over the traces will have to be put in the corral." Although the president issued mild protests to members of his cabinet over their excesses, he bore the ultimate responsibility for the wartime assault upon constitutional rights. Wilson, one of his biographers notes, "turned his back on civil liberties not because he loved them less but because he loved his vision of eventual peace much more." He hoped to offer the American version of democracy and liberal capitalism to the world as an alternative both to European imperialism, which had caused so much misery in the past, and to the new specter of revolutionary communism sweeping through Russia and into Eastern Europe.

The president presented his ambitious plans for the postwar world in the Fourteen Points speech of January 1918, meant to be a remedy to many prewar wrongs and a preventative for bolshevism. Wilson hoped to undercut the appeal of Lenin with promises of self-determination for the captive peoples of Central Europe, open diplomacy, and a new liberal world striving for free trade and disarmament under the aegis of a League of Nations. Wilson could go only so far in meeting the Bolshevik challenge with words; reluctantly, he agreed to participate in an Allied intervention into Russia in mid-1918. It got Soviet-American relations off to a very bad start.

The anti-red campaign at home had more success than the Allied intervention. In the government drive against dissidents, Wilson relied not only on patriotic societies but also on Samuel Gompers, president of the AFL. In return for Gompers' support of the war, Wilson gave the AFL general recognition as a legitimate interest group. Concerned with the widespread unpopularity of the war among workers, Gompers and John Spargo, a prowar socialist, created the American Alliance for Labor and Democracy. The president was so enthusiastic over the independent pro-war, anti-red organization that he told Spargo not to waste time raising money because he had "a fund that Congress has voted that is to be spent at my discretion!" Wilson's secret support of the Gompers group set a precedent for covert subsidies of anti-communist labor unions by the government during the Cold War Era.

World War I marked a watershed in American thinking about domestic radicalism. Before the war, in spite of Progressive fears, most Americans felt that socialists and syndicalists had a legitimate place within the system. Leftist opposition to the war and their support of the Bolshevik Revolution changed many minds. The profound emotionalism of the wartime crusade made Americans more fearful of dissenters. The instruments of repression created during the wartime emergency would be expanded during the Red Scare of 1919-1920.

The Red Scare Begins

America was ill-prepared for the Armistice of 11 November 1918. Government officials had given little thought to the large task of reconverting industry to a peacetime economy. Wartime contracts came to an abrupt end; with price controls lifted just as suddenly, a wave of inflation hit the country. The doughboys who won the war came home to unemployment while continuing wage controls angered labor and stimulated strikes. Industrialists yearned for a return to the times before troublesome unions and meddling Progressives had invaded their factories. Meanwhile, newspaper headlines reported the spread of bolshevism from Russia into Eastern Europe and quoted leaders of the communist Third International on the prospects of world revolution. Perhaps most frightening, the American Left seemed to be drawing fresh inspiration from the Soviet example, with Eugene V. Debs declaring "from the crown of my head to the soles of my feet I am a Bolshevik, and proud of it." So when Attorney General A. Mitchell Palmer blamed the postwar turmoil on "a disease of evil thinking" called the red movement, people listened. The announcement that he would "rid the country of red agitators" was applauded by a majority already conditioned to the menace of spies and the disloyal.

By war's end several agencies of the federal government had developed a permanent interest in the question of internal security. The Post Office possessed an elaborate index of illegal radical ideas to assist in systematic mail censorship. The U.S. Army's G-2 "negative" branch, a counterpropaganda and domestic intelligence agency, monitored radical activities in cooperation with Department of Justice attorneys, J. Edgar Hoover of the General Intelligence Division, and the Immigration and Naturalization Service. But the government could no longer prosecute radicals and unionists under terms of the Espionage and Conscription acts. That left only the Immigration Act of 1918, passed by Congress during the final days of the war, which allowed for the deportation of alien anarchists, those believing in the violent overthrow of the government, or condoning political assassinations. The law was vague enough that persons suspected of guilt by association with groups deemed subversive, and of guilt by underlying thought could be deported.

On 21 January 1919, 35,000 Seattle shipyard workers struck for shorter hours and higher pay after the Emergency Fleet Corporation refused to renegotiate a wartime agreement due to expire in two months. Representatives from other local unions in the Seattle Central Labor Council called for a general strike in support of the shipyard workers. Seattle became paralyzed on 6 February as members of 110 union affiliates walked off the job, the first general strike in American history. A Committee of Fifteen, dominated by anti-AFL radicals, allowed essential services to continue, but the strike made residents uneasy. Convinced that the general strike was a plot "to duplicate the anarchy of Russia," Seattle Mayor Ole Hanson requested and received federal troops. In the face of hostile public opinion, local affiliates of the AFL reversed themselves quickly and the strike collapsed within a few days. The brief upheaval in Seattle renewed public concern over domestic radicalism throughout the nation. Business leaders came alive to the idea of using that uneasiness to eliminate unionism, politicians saw possibilities in emulating the example of Mayor Hanson, and the press found a fresh source of exciting news stories.

Sensational newspaper headlines kept the potential red menace before the public throughout February and March. Many commended the Immigration Bureau for shipping thirty-six alien Wobblies out of Seattle on a "Red Special" train to New York for deportation. During the last days of April several public officials, including Mayor Hanson, received bombs in the mail although most were intercepted before they could reach their destinations. Radicals held rallies, meetings, and red flag parades to celebrate May Day in several cities; and violent clashes with citizens, soldiers, and sailors followed. Newspapers treated these events as a prelude to revolution, urging state and federal officials to pass anti-Bolshevik laws while cracking down on dissent.

On 2 June 1919, bombs went off in eight cities, damaging the homes of politicians and businessmen, and the Massachusetts legislature. A bomb thrower stumbled and blew himself to pieces in front of the home of Attorney General Palmer in Washington. The government responded swiftly, as a special anti-red task force headed by William J. Flynn of the U.S. Secret Service swooped down on radical meetings and arrested suspected terrorists. Although authorities never apprehended the culprits, the bombings intensified fears that bolshevism had spread to America. In reality, the danger of revolution remained remote. The Socialist Party of America was in the process of splitting into competing movements—the Communist Party, the Communist Labor Party, and remnants of the old SPA—while wartime prosecutions had reduced the Wobblies to little more than a defense organization for its jailed members. The terrifying events of 1919, including the Seattle strike, the violent May Day clashes, and isolated terrorist bombings had a cumulative effect on the public.

Several organizations formed before the war to deal with immigrants, socialists, and syndicalists advertised themselves as saviors of American values during the summer of 1919. These included the National Security League, the American Defense Society, the Ku Klux Klan, and the National Civic Federation. "Flying Squadrons" of speakers patterned after the wartime "Four Minute Men" attacked Progressive reforms such as initiative, recall, referendum, and income tax as communistic. Hundreds of thousands of former doughboys joined the American Legion to take direct action against suspected subversives. Anti-labor groups including the National Association of Manufacturers worked closely with these organizations, viewing every work stoppage as fresh evidence of radicalism.

State and federal officials investigated the problem. A U.S. Senate Judiciary subcommittee under the chairmanship of Lee S. Overman issued a 1200 page report which damned the Russian Revolution, concluding that bolshevism placed the United States in great danger. In New York, state Senator Clayton R. Lusk's committee investigated radical influence in the labor movement. Justice Department raids on the Russian Soviet Bureau and Lusk's own forays against the Socialist Rand School and the New York IWW turned up little hard evidence to support popular fears. However, Lusk concluded that radicals controlled at least 100 trade unions in his state and that the Rand School and the Soviets were conspiring to communize blacks and American labor.

The anti-labor facet of the Red Scare troubled Samuel Gompers. During the war he had supported the administration, accepting covert government funds and stumping Europe to win Allied labor over to the Fourteen Points peace program—all to gain official recognition of organized labor. Now the AFL's bread and butter unionism was being tarred with the same broad brush as the socialists and the IWW. Gompers redoubled his denunciations of the Left while supporting strikes of AFL affiliates, provided that the walkouts centered on concrete issues such as higher wages and better working conditions. The strategy did not work; for business leaders and other conservatives continued to denounce the whole union movement as a radical plot against private property. Even the police became targets of this wrath. In September of 1919, almost three-fourths of the Boston police force struck in a bid for better pay, shorter hours, and better working conditions. When the crime rate rose, newspapers pronounced the strike Bolshevik inspired. "Lenin and Trotsky are on their way," announced the *Wall Street Journal.* President Wilson called the strike "a crime against civilization," while Governor Calvin Coolidge became a popular hero after backing the mayor's decision not to rehire the strikers.

Two weeks later, the public received another jolt when 275,000 steelworkers struck for the right to organize an independent union, a raise in pay, and an eight-hour day. U.S. Steel strikebreakers and police worked in tandem beating pickets, breaking up union meetings, and stirring up racial and ethnic hatred while the press played on AFL organizer William Z. Foster's radicalism. After the strikers gave up in January 1920, Gompers initiated a purge in the AFL to save his union, but he had suffered a serious defeat. When coal miners struck under the leadership of the equally conservative John L. Lewis, it was much the same story: mine owners and government officials, including President Wilson, cried radicalism. At Attorney General Palmer's urging, Wilson invoked the Lever Act reactivating the wartime Fuel Administration, which placed the miners under government control. After a judge cited Lewis and other union officials for contempt, the miners accepted a government-sponsored offer of a modest wage hike. Once again, labor had sought the right to organize and the government and the public had seen red.

Education also came under attack during this period of smoldering hatred. "Patriotic" organizations carried out smear campaigns against school teachers, college professors, clergymen, and politicians suspected of being "parlor Reds." Even Progressives with impeccable anti-radical credentials such as Senators William E. Borah (who had prosecuted Haywood and other Wobblies twelve years earlier), and George W. Norris were denounced for suggesting that the accused had rights. Distinguished journals and magazines which expressed concern for civil liberties suddenly became suspected of pro-red sympathies. In the curious logic of 1919 blacks too became reds after racial tensions turned into riots in 25 cities, leaving 120 dead and hundreds injured.

Increasingly, through the year 1919 and into 1920 many Americans lost their sense of perspective. With the press branding all dissidents as "Reds" and "Bolsheviks," few made the intellectual effort to understand what communism meant or to distinguish radicals from liberals, or reformers from revolutionaries. "Specifically," Robert K. Murray has written, "by late 1919, a radical was anyone suspected of being pro-German, a Russian or other foreigner, a person who sent bombs through the mail, a believer in free love, a member of the IWW, a Socialist, a Bolshevist, an anarchist, a member of a labor union, a supporter of the closed shop, or anyone who did not particularly agree with you." Bolshevism had become a term which expressed people's fears about a changing world and a desire to return to simpler times. Ideology had little to do with it.

The Palmer Raids

On Armistice Day 1919, the local American Legion paraded through Centralia, Washington armed with rubber hoses, gas pipes, and revolvers. As the Legion passed the IWW hall, shots rang out. The paraders rushed the building and three of them fell dead from Wobbly bullets. When IWW member Wesley Everest tried to escape, the mob caught him at the Skookumchuck River and dragged him back to town. That night Everest was castrated, hanged, and then riddled with bullets. After several days, his corpse (with the neck stretched grotesquely) was tossed back into jail. The public mourned the legionaires while applauding Everest's murder. Further violence against the IWW followed in Tacoma, Spokane, and Oakland.

Attorney General Palmer had created the General Intelligence Division (GID) of the Justice Department under the leadership of a youthful J. Edgar Hoover to deal more effectively with domestic radicalism. Hoover developed a sophisticated card index with over two hundred thousand entries on radicals and their organizations. The GID then cranked out propaganda tying the bombings, the strikes, the demonstrations and the race riots into one massive communist conspiracy. On 7 November 1919, four days before the "Centralia Massacre," Hoover's bureau raided the offices of the Union of Russian Workers, arresting some 300 members. A. Mitchell Palmer became a very popular and powerful man. Wilson was gravely ill, suffering from the aftermath of a debilitating stroke, able only to whisper to his attorney general: "Palmer, do not let this country see red." State and local authorities throughout the country interpreted the Palmer raid as a signal to carry out their own anti-red incursions. Radical attorneys instructed their clients to say nothing, much to the annoyance of immigration officials who had planned to order deportations based on self-incriminating evidence. On 21 December, shortly after the Labor Department decided that membership in the Union of Russian Workers constituted a deportable offense in itself, 246 men and three women boarded the S.S. *Buford*, which sailed from New York to Finland. Deportees on the "Soviet Ark" (as the press dubbed it) then journied the rest of the way into Russia by train. For some, their only crime had been belief in theoretical anarchism, for others it was that they spoke Russian.

Mindful of the next dragnet, the Department of Labor ruled that aliens could see their lawyers only after "government's interests" had been preserved. Hoover also argued successfully for very high bail to keep the aliens in jail. With raiding procedures perfected, the GID and the Immigration Bureau planned swift dragnet operations, private testimony of undercover agents, seizure of tons of evidence, interrogation of aliens without lawyers, and detention under inflated bail pending deportation. As one writer described the process: "Like a pig in a Chicago packing plant, the immigrant would be caught in a moving dissembly line, stripped of all his rights, and packaged for shipment overseas—all in one efficient and uninterrupted operation."

On 2 and 6 January 1920, the Department of Justice cast wide nets over the Communist and Communist Labor parties, arresting over ten thousand persons, many without warrants. The mass arrests were not without grimly comic moments, as in New Brunswick, New Jersey, where government agents seized what was thought to be the blueprints for a bomb, presumably musical, since the plans turned out to be for a phonograph. Palmer alleged that the government had obtained documents proving Lenin and Trotsky controlled the domestic radical movement, proof which did not stand up under impartial scrutiny. Those arrested had to be guilty, the attorney general declared after an inspection tour, as they looked like "the unmistakable criminal type."

The Palmer raids touched off a new round of anti-radical activism at the state and local level. To aid in the prosecution of the IWW (now all but defunct) and other leftists, several states added strict sedition laws to their anti-syndicalist codes censoring free speech and free press. In 1919-1920, thirty-two states and Los Angeles, New Haven, and New York City made it a crime to wave a red flag in public. Over 1400 people would be jailed for violating these new laws. Congress, meanwhile, had refused to seat SPA leader Victor Berger as a representative from Wisconsin's fifth congressional district. On 19 December 1919, Berger won a special election against a fusion Democratic-Republican challenger. Three weeks later the House voted 330 to 6 to exclude him again, thus depriving the Milwaukee area of any representation until the next regular election. Berger might not have felt comfortable in Congress anyway since seventy peacetime sedition bills were under consideration. Eventually the House Judiciary Committee consolidated these efforts into the Graham-Sterling Bill, which would have made freedom of opinion a crime punishable by large fines and long prison terms. Although the bill did not pass, it mirrored America's collective state of mind in January 1920, the peak of the Red Scare.

The Scare Fades

The state legislature of New York also had a problem with socialist representatives, five of them duly elected from districts in the greater New York City area. In January they too were barred from taking their seats after a brief debate which grew so heated that one representative suggested execution as a more appropriate fate than seating the five. In a new role, many newspaper and magazine publishers who had previously leant their support to the anti-red campaign now denounced the disbarment as a blow against democracy. Conservatives such as Senator Warren G. Harding and Dean Roscoe Pound of the Harvard Law School warned that the New York assembly had gone too far. Charles Evans Hughes, a former governor of New York and Wilson's Republican presidential opponent in 1916, branded the action as "outrageous" and offered his legal services to the socialists. Governor Al Smith summarized the general feeling best, noting that "to discard the methods of representative government leads to the misdeeds of the very extremists we denounce, and serves to increase the enemies of orderly free government." Even Attorney General Palmer admitted that it was wrong to lump democratic socialists into the same category with Bolsheviks. The legislature's high-handed action marked the beginning of the end of the Red Scare.

The Palmer raids succeeded too well. With ten thousand suspected communists suddenly tossed into jail, many conservative observers realized that the government had violated fundamental due process on a massive scale. At the behest of the National Popular Government League, a panel of eminent lawyers and law professors issued a report charging the Department of Justice with using torture to force aliens to incriminate themselves and making illegal searches and arrests. The controversy alerted Secretary of Labor William B. Wilson (who had been indisposed when the warrants of arrest were signed) and Assistant Secretary Louis F. Post to actions of the Immigration Service and the covert alliance between their bureau and Palmer's. Secretary Wilson and Post reimposed control over immigration procedures from the top. When J. Edgar Hoover urged that all suspected communist aliens be deported under the Immigration Act of 1918, the Labor Department ruled that simple membership or affiliation with a communist organization did not constitute a deportable offense. The Supreme Court, which had consistently failed to protect civil liberties throughout the war years and postwar period, ruled in *Silverthorne Lumber Company v. United States* that illegally seized evidence could not be used to incriminate defendants. Assistant Secretary Post used a Montana district court's application of the ruling to cancel many of the arrest warrants. Quickly, the former partnership between the Labor and Justice Departments turned into a full-fledged bureaucratic quarrel. Palmer's supporters in Congress tried to impeach Post, but the assistant secretary's eloquent defense of his actions only made the attorney general appear foolish.

Palmer had hoped that the Red Scare would catapult him into the White House. Fewer and fewer people, however, were listening to his charges; he even found himself in the embarrassing position of having to defend the raids before skeptical congressional investigating committees. The attorney general did make headlines again when he predicted that a Bolshevik uprising would occur on May Day 1920. Newspapers ridiculed him when the communist holiday came and went without incident. Nevertheless, the Justice Department lobbied hard for the Immigration Act of June 1920 which made it a crime for aliens to possess literature deemed radical. The new law also made it illegal to use financial assistance to show sympathy and support for radical groups, a measure aimed at alien intellectuals and their "parlor Bolshevik" friends who contributed to the movement. Secretary of Labor Wilson ignored the new provisions and public opinion supported him. The deportations would continue at a dribble; eventually 591 aliens arrested in the Palmer raids were returned to their homeland.

The attorney general made one last attempt to revive the Red Scare in September 1920 after a bomb exploded in Wall Street, killing thirty-three and wounding over two hundred. The public remained calm as newspapers and magazines excoriated Palmer and other Justice Department officials for crying wolf. No one had much to say about the red menace during the 1920 presidential campaign except for Warren Harding, who noted that "too much has been said about Bolshevism in America." The fading of the Red Scare coincided with the disappearance of the profound social and economic dislocations of the post-Armistice period.

Legacies

In the early 1900s socialists and syndicalists sought to build significant political organizations which offered the working classes alternatives to the Progressive reform movement and the two entrenched and inherently conservative political parties. Progressives and businessmen battled against what they saw as the alien influences of the Socialist Party of America and the IWW. Leftist opposition to American participation in World War I was met with political repression as federal, state, and local laws discouraged dissident activities by curbing free speech and the rights of assembly. The repressive campaign did not end with the war. Anxiety over an uncertain future—the Bolshevik Revolution in Russia, and disorder and discontent at home—all led to the first

Red Scare. The federal government arrested thousands of radicals and deported hundreds of suspected leftist aliens, often disregarding due process along the way. While Congress failed to pass a peacetime sedition bill, a majority of the states adopted laws designed to suppress "reds." Once prominent conservatives began to draw back from the anti-radical crusade in 1920, the first Red Scare died out.

After the Red Scare, the American Left would never be the same again. In early 1919, even after the wartime persecution, the Socialist Party of America could boast over 109,000 members; a year later it had split into three parties and many parts with a combined membership of only 36,000. The IWW remained alive only in legend. The scare set back the cause of American labor many years and enhanced the power of big business to the point that it would dominate the 1920s. Blatant disregard for basic civil liberties guaranteed under the Constitution and the Bill of Rights did violence to the rights of all Americans as did the use of a national police for political purposes. The movement for "undiluted Americanism" survived as intolerance toward aliens, a dislike for unions, a demand for ideological conformity, a loathing of the Soviet Union, and a tendency to equate most reform ideas (including liberalism) with things foreign. The nativism which fueled the intolerance of this era did not die out; instead, it continued in campaigns for racial purity and exclusion of immigrants. Over the next thirty years, between 1920 and 1950, a pattern of fear would repeat itself in a different way. The left would make a limited comeback and have its fortunes altered dramatically by another world war, only to be persecuted again in a prolonged red scare as primitive and reactionary instincts once again came to the fore.

Chapter 2

Anti-Bolshevism:
From Normalcy to a Second Red Scare, 1921-1950

The Red Scare faded from newspaper headlines in 1921 but the aftershocks continued throughout the decade. Anti-radicalism had been institutionalized in government, business, and the public mind. "Is your washroom breeding Bolsheviks?" the Scott Paper Company asked employers in a postscare sales campaign for disposable towels. Similarly, Americans were urged to buy the Columbia Six, an automobile that "has no Bolshevistic tendencies." In the 1920s, special interest groups ranging from the American Legion to the Ford Motor Company to the Ku Klux Klan fed on the lingering fears of an unseen enemy within. Hundreds of political prisoners remained in jail as the Justice Department's Bureau of Investigation kept tabs on suspected reds. Eventually the Republican administrations freed the jailed and curbed federal surveillance without dismantling the machinery of repression.

The Republican presidents of the 1920s followed Woodrow Wilson's lead in refusing to extend diplomatic recognition to the Soviet government. They tried unsuccessfully to use the promise of American relief for starving Russian peasants to force the Bolsheviks to modify communist programs. The Department of State created special anti-communist training programs for the next generation of foreign service officers. Government officials and other politicians were quick to magnify the Soviet threat, seeing the hand of international communism at work in popular nationalist uprisings against client governments and American corporate interests in underdeveloped regions. Even at a time of relative isolationism in foreign policy, anti-communism was becoming institutionalized in government thinking.

In spite of the continued talk of the "red menace," the Left was no longer a mass movement in the 1920s. The once energetic SPA did not even run a candidate for president in 1924, merely endorsing Robert LaFollette's independent Progressive party. The communists emerged in 1921 as the legally constituted Workers Party only to find, in the words of their leadership, that they "did not exist as a factor in the class struggle." Their only major attraction, identification with the Soviet Union, turned out to be a liability since they had to spend much of their time following the bewildering factional disputes among Stalin, Trotsky, Zinoviev, and Bukharin. Attempts by the communists to broaden their popularity came to little. Their exploitation of the highly publicized alien anarchists convicted of murder, Nicola Sacco and Bartolomeo Vanzetti, won them few friends. On the labor front, the party's National Textile Workers Union organized a strike of textile workers in Passaic, New Jersey which succeeded in forcing cancellation of planned wage cuts. Encouraged, they organized fifteen major strikes of "lint head" textile workers in the Piedmont region of the South in 1929, each of them crushed brutally. By the end of the decade, the party still had less than ten thousand members. The Great Depression revived communism in the 1930s, yet with limited success came renewed public fears of radicalism. Contrary to the myth that this period was a "Red Decade," many more Americans veered to the right than to the left. A majority supported Franklin D. Roosevelt's liberal program to save capitalism. With Europe headed for war and relations between the United States and the Soviet Union deteriorating rapidly, the government resumed the surveillance of radicals. Once conflict came Congress passed the Smith Act, designed to repress the totalitarian impulse, especially the communist variety.

During World War II, many Americans discovered virtue in Stalinist Russia while some even concluded naively that the Soviets were on the road away from communism. The feelings of comradeship for domestic communists were not quite so warm, although party membership swelled to a quarter million. When it became apparent that the common enemy would be defeated, old antipathies resurfaced as the United States and the Soviet Union maneuvered for postwar advantages. Following victory, economic problems and disillusion with a less than perfect peace—key factors precipitating the first Red Scare—helped to touch off another period of anti-communist fright. Domestic politics also played a key part in the new Red Scare. Convinced of the need to launch an aggressive campaign to contain the Soviet Union abroad but lacking the consensus necessary to do so, President Harry S. Truman exaggerated the danger to national security. When Republicans tried to make the anti-communist issue their own, Truman headed them off with a loyalty-security program and a show trial of American communist leaders. Once Congress gained control of the anti-communist question following the traumatic "fall" of China, results would include a different kind of red scare, often referred to as "McCarthyism."

Fear and Repression in the 1920s

The change in presidential administrations of 1921 brought little change in policy or thinking in regard to foreign and domestic radicalism. Intolerance of leftists, ethnic and religious minorities rooted in the Progressive years continued during the exuberant 1920s. American attitudes and actions toward Soviet Russia were also consistent as three succeeding Republican administrations were content to follow Wilson's example. "I don't think you need fear any consequences of our dealing with the Bolsheviki," the president wrote in 1918, "because we do not intend to deal with them." At home, in keeping with their philosophy of limited government, the Republicans curtailed, but did not end, surveillance and harassment of radicals.

President Warren G. Harding gave little thought to the red menace—with good reason—since the Left was small and without any real leadership. Running for the White House from his jail cell in 1920, Eugene Debs had received over nine hundred thousand votes, but like the Socialist party itself, Debs was sick and tired. On

Christmas Eve 1921, Harding granted him a pardon and invited him to the White House. Over the next three years, most of those convicted under the Espionage and Sedition acts received commutations of their sentences rather than a general amnesty, which might have carried with it the implication that the convictions had been unjust.

As far as most Americans in the 1920s were concerned, socialists and communists did not have to demonstrate in the streets or lead strikes to appear to be menacing. With immigrants continuing to pour into urban areas there was always the potential for trouble. Aliens symbolized foreign ideologies and the ongoing demographic metamorphosis of the country from a land of farmers with small-town values to one of factories and big city ways. The linkage between immigrants and radicalism seemed stronger than ever with the Soviet Union sponsoring international revolutionary activities. Groups hoping to preserve the values associated with rural Protestant America felt threatened by any change in the status quo, be it posed by immigrants, labor unions or liberal intellectuals. Many saw a "communist" conspiracy lurking behind the forces changing the old way of life.

Anti-Red Nativists and Patriots

Several nativist organizations fought against what they perceived to be a conspiracy of radicals and aliens. The Ku Klux Klan, the largest group which stood for "100 percent Americanism," regarded all reform as communist and radical. Imperial Wizard Hiram Wesley Evans explained "that liberalism has come completely under the dominance of weaklings and parasites whose alien 'idealism' reaches its logical peak in the bolshevist platform of 'produce as little as you can, beg or steal from those who do produce, and kill the producer for thinking he is better than you.'" The Klan carried out terror campaigns of floggings, lynchings, and tar and feathers against radicals, blacks, Jews, Catholics and other presumed enemies of the status quo. While millions would join the Klan, the organization began to decline after 1924 when Congress passed the National Origins Act, legislation which cut immigration drastically and established a quota system against the immigration of Southern and Eastern Europeans.

Other patriotic groups flourished throughout the decade. The American Legion continued vigilante action against reds, but there was no more violence of the type that occured at Centralia because group leaders feared that the attendant bad publicity would weaken Congressional support for Legion-sponsored bonuses, pensions, and other special concessions. National headquarters instructed local posts to "keep a watchful eye on radical propagandists and use all lawful means to prevent the fulfillment of their plans." Legionaires also studied school books for evidence of subversion, commissioned the writing of their own American history text, and held annual essay contests on such themes as "Why America Should Prohibit All Immigration for Five Years." By 1927 the American Civil Liberties Union reported that the Legion had "replaced the Klan as the most active agency of intolerance and repression in the country." Parallel activities were carried on by the Daughters of the American Revolution, an organization, William Allen White noted, which "yanked the Klan out of the cow pasture and set it down in the breakfast room of respectability." Two other groups of superpatriots with roots in the Red Scare, the National Security League and the Inter-Racial Council fought against "Bolshevistic principles" among immigrant groups with foreign language propaganda to explain the benefits of loyalty to America and the pitfalls of radicalism.

In an era which worshipped the successful businessman as an American hero, the conspiracy theories of auto magnate Henry Ford gained credence. In his book *The International Jew: The World's Foremost Problem*, Ford revived the old canard of a conspiracy of international bankers and Jews to take over the world, updating it to include communists. Ford claimed that almost all Bolsheviks, including Lenin, were Jewish. Other businessmen redbaited organized labor as part of a successful anti-union campaign. The National Association of Manufacturers, the National Founders Association and other employer groups launched a crusade for the open shop, insisting that workers did not have to join unions in industries where organized labor was well entrenched. This

"American Plan" advertised itself as a bastion against radicalism and the "subversive foreign concept" (and hence "unAmerican") of labor unions. In a desperate effort to save bread and butter unionism, Samuel Gompers of the AFL, his successor William Green, John L. Lewis and other labor moderates went to great pains to disassociate themselves from any sort of radicalism. Anti-communist resolutions passed annually at AFL conventions became as fundamental a catechism as the longstanding goals of higher wages, shorter hours, and better working conditions.

Government Policies

Government officials took less and less interest in the red menace through the 1920s. Harry Daugherty, Harding's attorney general, shocked the president and his conservative cabinet in 1922 when he persuaded a sympathetic federal judge to issue a sweeping injunction against striking railroad workers on the ground that the unions were controlled by "Red Agents of the Soviet Government." Under the leadership of Daugherty's crony William J. Burns, the Justice Department's Bureau of Investigation (BI), kept watch on radical and liberal groups including the Communist Workers Party, the ACLU, and the National Association for the Advancement of Colored People. Burns saw evidence of the communist conspiracy everywhere: churches, schools, newspapers, movies, and vaudeville. To prove his point, he planned to capture the entire red hierarchy at Bridgman, Michigan, site of a Communist Party convention in the summer of 1922. Since party leaders had done nothing illegal, Burns raised the funds for his project privately. Frank P. Walsh, the ACLU lawyer representing the communists captured in the Bridgman raid, accused Burns of manufacturing evidence and shaking down businessmen in return for protection. Unrepentant, the BI chief vowed "to drive every radical out of the country and bring the parlor Bolsheviks to their senses." After Harding's death, President Coolidge appointed Harlan Fiske Stone as attorney general with a mandate to clean up the Justice Department. Although Burns went quickly (but not quietly) and his successor, J. Edgar Hoover, promised to put an end to the BI's role as a political police force, Stone's housecleaning did not go far enough for civil libertarians. Hoover's department (reorganized as the FBI in 1935) continued surveillance through paid informants of radical, liberal, and labor groups deemed "unAmerican" by the bureau.

While Harding, Coolidge, and Herbert Hoover did not match Woodrow Wilson's wartime record of anti-radical zeal, they continued his anti-communist foreign policy centering around nonrecognition of Soviet Russia. "The chief reason for withholding recognition from the Soviet regime," Secretary of State Charles Evans Hughes wrote, "lay in the subversive efforts which it had sponsored in this country. Of these, the State Department had abundant evidence." While the Soviets did sponsor world revolutionary activity, the Comintern met with little success chiefly because of the insistence that communist parties follow the Russian model without regard for local circumstances. Secretary of Commerce Herbert C. Hoover had his own ideas about how to fight bolshevism abroad. In 1921 twenty million Russians faced starvation as a result of the Tsar's unsuccessful three year fight against Germany, three years of civil war, unsuccessful Bolshevik economic policies, the Allied intervention, and a terrible drought. Two years earlier Hoover had suggested to Wilson that American food, clothing, and other supplies might be used "to stem the tide of Bolshevism," although nothing came of the idea. Now he revived the plan, quickly negotiating an agreement with the Soviets which traded food aid in return for the release of seven American political prisoners held in Russian jails and freedom of movement for American Relief Administration workers. The staunchly anti-communist Hoover hoped that the relief program might force Lenin to modify Bolshevik economic and foreign policies or, at the very least, provide an opening wedge for an American program of Russian economic reconstruction. In two years the relief association provided over seven hundred thousand tons of food, clothing, and medicine to the Russian people. Ironically, the American relief effort helped to stabilize the Bolshevik government at a time of extreme weakness.

Key career personnel in the Departments of State and Commerce played a vital role in the institutionalization of anti-communism as an axiom of American foreign policy. The Eastern European division of the State Department under the leadership of Robert F. Kelly assumed responsibility for analyzing Soviet activities and defending nonrecognition. The energetic Kelly testified before Congress on the communist conspiracy, blocked attempts by business to trade with the Russians, and cooperated closely with organizations willing to follow the department's line from the AFL to the *Washington Post*. The division chief also inaugurated a rigorous training program for his foreign service officers in Paris, the chief city of exile for anti-communist Russian refugees. It was there that an entire generation of Russian experts received an education in what one historian has called "a Russian culture which existed nowhere save in the memories of those who had fled the Bolsheviks, and the perspective that the Soviets had destroyed all that was of value in Russian life [that] was to endure in the way State Department Soviet experts approached the Soviet Union throughout their careers." One of those young trainees, Charles Bohlen (a future ambassador to Moscow) remembered that while he attended a few lectures on Marxism and Russian history, "most of our study of such subjects came from books, almost all anti-Communist." Not surprisingly, with one exception, all of Kelly's Paris-trained officers came away from their experience as hostile observers of the Soviet system, feelings intensified by the attitudes and actions of senior officials back in Washington.

State Department officials were quick to project their apprehensions over Russian communism to areas of the world where the Kremlin had little influence. When the Mexican government announced plans to take back subsoil rights granted to American petroleum and mining companies, the Coolidge administration blamed the Soviets. Secretary of State Frank B. Kellogg defended the sending of marines to Nicaragua, saying that the Soviets were developing "the international revolutionary movement in the New World." This line of reasoning, based less on reality than on distorted fears and stereotypes, would be subsequently repeated many times.

The 1930s: The Myth of the Red Decade

The Great Depression offered the Left a chance for a new beginning. Communists and socialists no longer had to make potential followers dissatisfied with the status quo; millions of the hungry, the homeless, and the unemployed were ready to listen. Liberals, intellectuals, and trade unionists, outgroups since the Progressive Era, took a second look at the example of the Soviet Union and found much to admire. In the 1932 presidential election, the Left garnered almost a million votes. Upton Sinclair won the Democratic nomination for governor of California in 1934 on a watered-down socialist platform. In the Pacific Northwest, the left-leaning Cooperative Commonwealth Federation gained widespread popularity as did similar organizations in the Midwest. After 1935, communists abandoned overt revolutionary activity, joining the New Deal as part of a "popular front" strategy against fascism, a move which made them more acceptable than before. Yet, the period of the 1930s can hardly be seen as a "Red Decade" as some writers have claimed. Soviet foreign policy and Comintern machinations, the continuing popularity of right-wing groups, congressional investigations, and repressive legislation all help to explain why the Left did not capitalize on hard economic times. Assessing the Left's failure in the 1930s, the Socialist party's perennial presidential candidate Norman Thomas could only conclude that "it was Roosevelt in a word." More important than the popular and effective FDR, or any other factor, was the continuing faith of the overwhelming majority in the resilience of liberal capitalism.

In the early 1930s, communists enjoyed some successes in organizing mine workers in Kentucky, agricultural workers in California, and poor whites and blacks in the South. Militant communists organized riots of the unemployed, the hungry, and the evicted, welcoming the inevitable confrontations with police. A wave of radical-led strikes by taxi drivers (New York and Philadelphia), streetcar operators (Milwaukee), truck drivers (Minneapolis), textile workers (twenty states), and farm laborers (many locales) shook the nation in 1934. San Francisco dockworkers under the leadership of Australian-born communist

Harry Bridges launched a general strike, yet another example of the depth of class conflict felt at the time. Yet communist activities were dwarfed by the efforts of political moderates who controlled most of organized labor. While Communist Party (CP) leaders could boast that their ranks had increased from 7,500 to 30,000 (the majority of which were native born) between 1930 and 1935, membership in labor unions rose during the 1930s from less than 3 million to almost 9 million. "I'll work with anyone who'll work with me," promised John L. Lewis, president of the new Congress of Industrial Organizations (CIO), a policy which gave communists the opportunity to take control of 12 to 15 of the 40 international CIO unions. The wily Lewis, whose own United Mine Workers Union barred communists from membership, prized the Marxists as tough, dedicated organizers used to obeying orders. In the late 1930s, the CP became an important power in the CIO, but only by deferring to anti-communist labor leaders and supporting the general foreign and domestic policies of the New Deal.

A Revival of Fear

Communist activities aroused a frightened majority to the point that Congressman Emanuel Celler of New York observed "a general hysteria of fear gripping the nation against communism." In response to the unrest, several states passed new sedition statutes while Illinois revised its anti-radical code and other states dusted off anti-red laws, seldom used since the first Red Scare. States also jailed strikers and communist organizers under criminal syndicalist laws. To fight labor unrest in Texas, the Department of Labor urged legislators to pass anti-syndicalist legislation and outlaw the Communist Party. Georgia prosecuted twenty-five persons on the basis of antebellum statutes devised to discourage slave revolts. The Immigration Service began once again to deport alien radicals deemed a menace to society.

The most notorious anti-radical incident of the early Depression years occurred in Washington, D.C. in July 1932, when some 22,000 World War I veterans of the Bonus Expeditionary Force (BEF) camped out with their families to encourage their legislators to vote a special payment for wartime service. Five thousand left the city when Congress offered them a loan to get back home instead of a bonus; the others stayed, having already lost everything. President Hoover ordered the Army to surround occupied government buildings and turn the BEF protesters over to police. But Army Intelligence had reported to Chief of Staff General Douglas MacArthur that "the first bloodshed by the Bonus Army at Washington is to be the signal for a Communist uprising in all large cities, thus initiating a revolution." Exceeding his authority, the general ordered his forces to follow the tear-gassed veterans into their shanty town at Anacosta Flats, where they burned the huts down. Hoover backed MacArthur's action, announcing that the BEF had been made up of "Communists and persons with criminal records." A subsequent government investigation revealed no evidence of a communist conspiracy; on the contrary, the BEF had run suspected communists out of their encampment. Undaunted, Secretary of War Patrick Hurley urged the president to send troops to key cities to thwart further plans of "reds and possible communists."

Congress had already begun a series of investigations on the extent of communist activities. In 1930 a special House committee chaired by Representative Hamilton Fish spent six months interviewing 275 witnesses in 25 cities from New York to Gastonia to Los Angeles. The committee issued a final report linking communists, blacks, aliens, and advocates of free love to the Kremlin along with such "closely affiliated" liberal organizations as the American Civil Liberties Union. The committee defended the role of law enforcement officials in breaking up rallies and labor meetings, noting that "Communist women and children insult and spit on the police and scratch and bite them. There has been too much denunciation of the police for alleged brutality by 'pinks' and metropolitan papers." Several bills growing out of the committee's recommendation to deport alien communists failed to pass Congress. One was introduced by Martin Dies, a young Texan who would chair a standing committee to investigate "subversive and un-American propaganda" beginning in 1938.

Extreme Anti-Communism

In the 1930s, many writers and intellectuals found the appeal of communism to be irresistible—at least for a short time—but there was much more power, money, and influence at the other end of the political spectrum. At least one hundred and perhaps as many as eight hundred nativist, fascist, and conservative groups of anti-communists gained significant followings during the "Red Decade." Former Klansmen made up the bulk of the Black Legion, the largest of the nativist groups. Black-robed members swore an oath to preserve "the secrets of the order and to support God, the United States Constitution, and the Black Legion in its holy war against Catholics, Jews, Communists, Negroes and aliens." The Legion murdered two auto workers suspected of communist activity and terrorized leftists in Indiana, Michigan, and Ohio.

Fascist-style demagogues attracted at least ten times as many adherents as the communists. The undisputed "Kingfish" of Louisiana, Senator Huey Long, was no Adolf Hitler ("Don't liken me to that sonofabitch," he said) but he appeared close enough to the real thing with his "Share Our Wealth" plan for Franklin Roosevelt to brand him as "the most dangerous man in America." Long debated Norman Thomas in New York City to prove that his plan to redistribute income, provide old age pensions, veterans's bonuses, cheap food, free homesteads, cars, radios, and washing machines was not socialism and the cheering audience agreed. So did Lawrence Dennis, the leading intellectual of the far right, who praised the Kingfish as "the nearest approach to a national fascist leader." After Long's assassination in 1935, Father Charles Coughlin and Gerald L.K. Smith carried on the struggle against communism and liberalism. As early as 1929, Coughlin told millions of his radio listeners that the world must accept either "Christ or the Red Fog." In 1935, the radio priest broke with the New Deal, helping to found the Union party along with Smith and Francis Townsend, an advocate of old age pensions. A vote for Roosevelt, Coughlin noted, was a vote for "the Communists, the socialists, the Russian lovers, the Mexican lovers, and the kick-me-downers." Just before election day in 1936, Coughlin warned his followers that America faced a crossroads: "One road leads toward fascism, the other toward Communism. I take the road to fascism." The anti-Semitic Smith, inheritor of Long's movement, praised the Union party as "this new force against Communism."

Wealthy conservatives preferred to work through the Liberty League, an organization formed in 1934, as a retired Dupont Corporation executive explained, "to protect society from the sufferings which it is bound to endure if we allow communistic elements to lead the people to believe all businessmen are crooks." Like the Union Party, which could muster only 892,000 out of an expected ten million votes in 1936, the Liberty League's membership of 124,000 fell far short of their goal of four million. Both organizations discovered too late that they simply did not have the appeal of liberal anti-communist Franklin D. Roosevelt.

Roosevelt as an Anti-Communist

Manipulating the media as no president ever has and pushing his New Deal through Congress, FDR resuscitated the American capitalist system with haphazard and moderate reforms. While his public rhetoric revealed a certain enmity toward the business elite, Roosevelt was, as he put it, "the best friend the profit system ever had." The New Deal expanded federal government, strengthened the presidency, extended social welfare programs, and limited some rights of property. FDR coopted a few popular ideas from the socialists, but he did not carry out the Socialist party platform, Norman Thomas observed, except on a stretcher. As the exponent of a systematic ideology, Thomas recognized what the president's critics on the right refused to see, that New Deal liberalism was essentially an effort to conserve.

"I am fighting communism, Huey Longism, Coughlinism, Townsendism," Roosevelt told a Hearst reporter in 1935, "I want to save our system—the capitalist system; to save it is to give some heed to world thought of today...." The president used the deep-seated fear of communism to gain the cooperation of reluctant business groups. He warned mine owners that failure to support the National Industrial Recovery Act would only benefit the communists, an argument repeated during debate over the Wagner Bill. For their part, the communists heaped scorn on the New Deal initially, labeling it "social fascism." That all changed in 1935 when Joseph Stalin ordered communist parties to cooperate with Progressive reformers and socialists in a united front against fascism, a policy which would keep the Soviets from facing Nazi Germany in isolation.   The abrupt about-face shocked some Communist Party leaders; others welcomed the opportunity to work within the American system. The party adjusted to the new situation quickly, supporting the New Deal on opportunistic grounds. When an old friend told FDR that "the Communist Party has decided to pat you on the head," the president roared with laughter, greatly amused by an old enemy's sudden support.

Roosevelt found much less to laugh about in regard to the world situation.   The trend toward authoritarianism coupled with aggression by authoritarian regimes in Europe and Asia fueled renewed fears of foreign ideologies. Diplomatic relations between the United States and the Soviet Union, which the president had inaugurated in 1933, soured quickly when the Soviets discovered that old debts and continued isolation interested the Americans more than new credits and possible aid against an increasingly bellicose Japan. For their part, the Americans grew tired of Russian hedging on the debt question and of continued Comintern agitation.

On 24 August 1936, Roosevelt summoned FBI Director J. Edgar Hoover to the White House for a general discussion of national security. Hoover opened the conference with a report on communist activities in labor unions and New Deal agencies along with tidbits on the activities of Father Coughlin. When the president expressed an interest in expanding intelligence on "subversive activities in the United States, particularly Fascism and Communism," the director reminded him of the limitations placed on the bureau by Attorney General Stone in 1924—and that the Department of State had the authority to request such an investigation. At a meeting the next day, FDR observed "that [American] Communism particularly was directed from Moscow, and that there had been certain indications that [Soviet Consul] Oumansky,...was a leading figure in some of the activities in this country," a situation which clearly merited State Department interest. When Secretary of State Cordell Hull agreed with this analysis,

Roosevelt gave Hoover an oral directive "that investigations be made of subversive activities" and that they be made "quite confidentially." Hoover took the president's vague order to mean that his bureau once again had carte blanche to spy on the left.

Congressional Anti-Communism

By 1938 the growth of the Communist Party and the Popular Front strategy of working with the New Deal instead of against it worried many members of Congress, especially those like Martin Dies who had never cared for Roosevelt's reforms. The House allocated $25,000 for Dies to chair a special Committee on Un-American Activities (HCUA) for the purpose of investigating "subversive and un-American propaganda." Beginning in August the committee heard a parade of witnesses denounce 640 organizations, 483 newspapers, and 280 labor unions as communistic including several Catholic groups, the Boy Scouts, and the Camp Fire Girls. Joseph Brown Mathews, a reformed fellow-traveler (communist sympathizer), explained that many movie stars, even Shirley Temple, had lent their names to leftist organizations, a remark which led Secretary of the Interior Harold Ickes to ridicule Dies as "a burly Congressman leading a posse comitatus in a raid upon Shirley Temple's nursery to collect her dolls as evidence of her implication in a Red Plot."

The committee seemed especially interested in establishing connections between the New Deal, communist front organizations, and the CIO. No hard evidence unmasking the New Deal as a red stratagem was forthcoming; still, the committee smelled conspiracy. "It is not the open and undisguised activity of the Communists that we need fear," a report of January 1939 noted, "It is not their direct influence which should occasion alarm. It is rather the subversive and insidious way in which they go about their destructive work...." While Dies later admitted that some "screwball witnesses" had "smeared" some decent Americans, HCUA did strike a responsive chord: seventy-four percent of Americans who had heard of the committee favored further investigations. The House gave Dies $100,000 to continue to sniff out the conspiracy and the publicity-hungry chairman did so in a manner which alarmed many of his conservative allies. Popularizing snappy slogans, whoary myths, and using guilt by association techniques, Dies charged that the Communist Party "has been permitted to entrench itself deep in our body politic."

Congress passed a series of laws in 1938-1939 which reflected the new concern over domestic radicalism. The Foreign Agents Registration Act (the McCormack Act) required agents of foreign governments to register with the government in order to expose sources of alien propaganda. House Committee staff members investigating communist influence on the Works Progress Administration produced evidence of "Red propaganda" which they had planted at the New York City Writers Project offices. Congress then banned radicals from receiving welfare funds. Expanding on this principle, the Hatch Act of 1939 barred from federal employment persons who belonged to any organization advocating the overthrow of the government.

With the exception of the Great Depression, no event meant more to Americans in the era between the world wars than the Spanish Civil War of 1936-1939. This conflict pitted a Loyalist coalition of socialists, communists, anarchists, liberals, and moderates assisted by the Soviet Union against a fascist-style Nationalist movement backed by Germany and Italy. Communists played an important role in organizing committees, and also, conventions of support and the international military brigades which fought alongside the Loyalists of the Republic. The cause attracted Americans because Spain appeared to be the last hope for democracy and pluralism in an area of the world that was lurching toward militant fascism. Most newspapers, popular magazines, and the financial press either took a pro-Loyalist stance or remained nonpartisan, although Hearst publications, the *Chicago Tribune*, and the *Washington Times* regularly denounced the "Reds in Spain" and their American comrades. Opinion polls revealed only nine percent of Protestants and two percent of Jews sympathized with General Francisco Franco's Nationalists. However, Catholics favored Franco over the Loyalists 39 percent to 30 percent.

American Catholic leaders were outspoken in their support of the Spanish Catholic church, which had lost significant power as a result of the separation of church and state and other secular liberal reforms. Fearing that the long battle against anti-Catholic prejudice in the United States might be dealt a severe setback, American Catholic leaders and the Catholic press compared Franco to the Founding Fathers and attacked the Republic as "Red Communism." The need to express solidarity with the Spanish church dovetailed nicely with the 1937 papal encyclical criticizing atheistic communism and the American church's growing misgivings that the New Deal was socialistic. Anti-communism, Catholics discovered, could provide a special sense of security, a reaffirmation of allegiance to the mother church, and to their Protestant and secular homeland. "As nothing was more Catholic than anti-communism," scholar David O'Brien notes, "so there was nothing more fully American." Having found common ground between faith and patriotism, Catholic leaders used anti-communism to inspire the laity and further the objective of acceptance in a pluralistic society. The church scored an immediate victory in the campaign against the Spanish Republic. The Roosevelt administration maintained a policy of nonintervention in the Spanish Civil War for a variety of reasons, among them the influence of British foreign policy and the mood of political isolationism. None was more important than the Catholic church's political pressure on the Democratic Party, power it would not hesitate to use against leftists closer to home in the future.

Events abroad continued to exacerbate fears at home. In August 1939 Stalin, despairing of cooperation with the West against Hitler, carried out his own version of appeasement with the signing of the Nazi-Soviet Pact of Non-Aggression, paving the way for Germany to attack Poland. The pact disgusted American liberals and progressives who had admired the Soviet Union as an anti-fascist ally of the Spanish Republic. The Popular Front split apart with American communists denouncing Roosevelt and most liberals vowing never again to trust Stalinists. Overnight the Communist Party discovered the virtues of isolationism. Communist-controlled labor unions fomented strikes, especially in defense-related industries. Retaliation came quickly from both liberals and conservatives. The ACLU purged communist leader Elizabeth Gurley Flynn from its board of directors. Over three hundred

Communist Party members were arrested on various charges in thirteen states while the federal government indicted the party chairman for traveling on false passports. The House voted to deport Harry Bridges and came within three votes of denying the American Ambassador to Russia his salary. The mood of the House was such, one congressman remarked, "that if you brought in the Ten Commandments today and asked for their repeal and attached to that request an alien law, you could get it." In June of 1940 Congress passed the Alien Registration Act (the Smith Act), an amalgamation of anti-alien and anti-radical bills compelling aliens to register with the government and making it illegal to "knowingly or willfully advocate, abet, advise, or teach the duty, necessity, desirability or propriety of overthrowing or destroying any government in the United States by force or violence, or by the assassination of any officer of any such government." Here was the peacetime sedition act Palmer could not get in the wake of the first Red Scare, the first such law since 1798.

Stalin's actions following the Nazi-Soviet Pact intensified the American distrust of communism. The Red Army occupied almost half of Poland under the secret terms of the agreement with Hitler. The Soviets returned the Baltic states of Estonia, Latvia, and Lithuania to Russian control and when Finland resisted granting similar concessions to Moscow, Stalin ordered an invasion. According to an opinion poll, ninety-nine percent of Americans wanted the Finns to win. In January 1941, President Roosevelt asked Congress to support Lend-Lease as part of his campaign to aid Britain with everything short of war in its lonely fight against the Nazis. FDR insisted that the bill include a provision which would allow assistance to any country resisting fascism. Significant sentiment gathered in Congress to specifically ban aid to the Soviet Union, but the president remained adamant. He had secret information which indicated that Hitler was planning to attack his troublesome partner sometime in the future. By June 1941, relations between Washington and Moscow had reached a nadir. American communists were more reviled than at any time since the Red Scare.

World War II: Uneasy Partnership

On 25 June 1941, three days after Hitler launched "Operation Barbarossa" against the Soviet Union, the *Wall Street Journal* editorialized that "the American people know that the principal difference between Mr. Hitler and Mr. Stalin is the size of their respective mustaches." Desperate to keep the country out of the World War, American isolationists continued to see little difference between fascism and communism. The Roosevelt-led interventionists, convinced that the United States would become involved, advocated aid for the Russians to keep the Red Army going against Hitler. A Gallup opinion poll taken in July showed that seventy-two percent hoped for a Soviet victory while only four percent wanted Germany to win. A subsequent *Fortune* magazine poll reflected more clearly the deep ambivalence most Americans felt: 35 percent viewed Germany and Russia as equally bad and 32 percent saw the Soviets as only slightly better. Even after Pearl Harbor and Hitler's subsequent declaration of war made the United States and the Soviet Union allies, Americans never lost what had come to be a compulsive distrust of communism.

A Brief Honeymoon and Renewed Hostility

The new Popular Front alliance of the war years between the American mainstream and the communists was stronger than the coalition of the late 1930s. Giving the war absolute priority, the government encouraged the public to accept the Soviet Union. Jailed communists, including a group serving time for contempt of the California legislature and CP chief Browder received pardons. The party's support of the war and the alliance with the Soviets gave it a new prestige. Communists in labor unions agitated against strikes and on occasion broke them enthusiastically. "Any strike," the *Daily Worker* explained, "is bound to prove a hindrance to the war effort." The party advocated incentive pay plans and piece-work schemes damned for years by labor moderates as worker exploitation. The sharp turn to the right made the party attractive enough that membership approached an all time high of one hundred thousand. This phenomenal growth was misleading as the party did not ask recruits to carry out revolutionary deeds and or even to be active politically; by 1944 the party no longer required members to believe in Marxism! Irving Howe described wartime CP locals as "far closer in spirit to a high-powered fraternal lodge or a businessmen's lunch club than to a radical party." Browder became so enamored of the party's new prestige and respect that he envisioned the spirit of national unity and class collaboration lasting long after the end of the war.

In some minds, the valiant Soviet struggle against the Nazi juggernaut made them acceptable allies. Americans also wanted to believe that the war might cause the Soviets to forsake, or substantially modify, their communism. A few select events seemed to bear this hope out. The Comintern had not met for years; during the war, Stalin ordered it dissolved as a gesture of goodwill. The Soviet leader approved a cautious truce with the Russian Orthodox Church. With Moscow besieged, Stalin inspired millions by invoking the names of Russia's greatest historic heroes of the past: Alexander Nevsky, who defeated the Teutonic Knights seven centuries earlier and Marshall Kutuzov, Napoleon's arch-nemisis. Americans of all shades of political opinion, from General MacArthur to Vice President Henry Wallace to theologian Reinhold Niebuhr exercised wishful thinking about a new Russia. Opinion polls taken early in the alliance period revealed that only about twenty percent of Americans believed the Soviets would be uncooperative in the postwar world. Hollywood made twenty-five major films depicting the Soviet Union in a positive light. In March 1943, *Life* magazine found Russians to be "one hell of a people...[who] to a remarkable degree...look like Americans, dress like Americans and think like Americans." Opinion makers, including the *New York Times*, reported that Russia seemed to be headed away from communism and toward capitalism and democracy. While these fantasies helped the the majority to accept an old ideological enemy as a partner, there was bound to be anger and disappointment when the Soviets turned out not to be changing their political system after all.

The mental gymnastics which transformed Stalin from a Russian Hitler into "Uncle Joe" did not carry over on to the homefront: most

Americans continued to distrust domestic radicalism in spite of the Popular Front. Before Pearl Harbor, Roosevelt paid off a political debt to the Teamsters Union, ordering his attorney general to prosecute union dissidents belonging to the Trotskyite Socialist Workers Party. Eighteen were convicted of violating the Smith Act and a Civil War-era conspiracy law as the Stalinist CP applauded, aware that the Grand Alliance with Moscow would keep them out of jail. But the FBI kept close tabs on CP members throughout the war. Hoover's bureau infiltrated the party so thoroughly that informants attended all official functions. The bureau managed to bug a secret meeting of the top leadership when the CP chieftains were foolish enough to gather in a recording studio. Unofficial counterintelligence operations included the breaking up of a marriage between party official Gus Hall and the daughter of a wealthy publisher. In Washington, the House Committee on Un-American Activities continued its search for links among communists, the CIO, and the New Deal, although operating under steadily diminishing budgets.

Many ex-radicals, liberals, and intellectuals who had abandoned the CP after the Nazi-Soviet Pact saw no reason to modify their feelings toward the Soviet Union. After the war turned against the Axis in 1943, they rallied together to protest against *Mission to Moscow*, a truly awful pro-Soviet film based on former Ambassador Joseph Davies' best-seller. Anti-Stalinists Max Eastman, James T. Farrell, Sidney Hook, A. Philip Randolph, Norman Thomas, Edmund Wilson and many others complained that the movie brought to this country "the kind of historical falsifications which have hitherto been characteristic of totalitarian propaganda." Critical studies of the Soviet Union began to reappear after a hiatus of three years. William L. White's *Report on Russia* exposed the Soviet labor camp system. William C. Bullitt wrote a long article for *Life* warning that the Soviets planned to take over Eastern Europe.

The growing suspicion of communism was reflected in the political arena as well. To upgrade its image, the American Communist Party dissolved, resurfacing as the supposedly nonpartisan Communist Political Association, which endorsed

Roosevelt for a fourth term. Republican presidential candidate Thomas Dewey tried to make the most out of the connection, charging in the final days of the campaign that "now the Communists are seizing control of the New Deal, through which they aim to control the Government of the United States." A few hours later, he warned of "the threat of monarchy in the United States." Roosevelt, who had long since repudiated the communist endorsement, simply placed the contradictory charges side-by-side, making Dewey look foolish. The two candidates agreed that their hostility toward American communism did not signify disrespect for Stalinist Russia. In the end, the unwelcome communist support for the president neither hurt nor helped the Democrats and the voters gave FDR a fourth term.

Deepening Disillusionment

Conflicting political goals also put strains on the alliance. In 1941 the Soviets needed a second military front in Europe as soon as possible. FDR rashly promised Soviet Foreign Minister V. M. Molotov that one would be opened on the continent by the end of 1942, but military considerations forced the president to renege. By the time of the second front in France in June 1944, the Red Army had pushed the bulk of the German Wehrmacht out of Russia and Stalin had begun to rationalize that since his country had carried the burden of fighting it should have a proportionate share of the spoils. The Soviets, victims of three major invasions from the West (France once and Germany twice) in 130 years, wanted to control parts of Eastern Europe as a buffer zone and to effect a reconstruction of the former Russian empire. Even before Pearl Harbor, Stalin made it clear that "all we ask for is to restore our country to its former frontiers," meaning that the Soviets intended to take and keep half of pre-war Poland, the Baltic states, and parts of Finland and Rumania, all within the domain of the pre-1914 Russian empire.

The Americans, however, had very different priorities. Determined at all costs to avoid another Great Depression, they hoped to see world markets and sources of raw materials open to all comers on an equal opportunity basis. This strategy required that all of Europe, reconstructed on the solid political base of self-determination, remain open to American trade and investments. Obviously Europe could not be both open, as the Americans wanted, and closed, as the Soviets hoped. Roosevelt recognized that Stalin had legitimate security concerns in Eastern Europe. Roosevelt strived consistently to keep the alliance together, believing that a permanently weakened Germany and the collective security apparatus of the proposed United Nations might make Stalin secure enough to keep the door to Eastern Europe open.

By 1945, with Germany reeling back on two fronts, Italy knocked out of the war and Japan's empire shrinking rapidly, the Big Three of the Grand Alliance met at Yalta to hammer out their differences. Roosevelt came away from the conference pleased. As Secretary of State Edward Stettinius remarked: "the Soviet Union made greater concessions at Yalta to the United States and Great Britain than were made to the Soviets." Although the president and Churchill understood the Soviet need to have Poland and Eastern Europe in "friendly" hands, they were also eager that the liberated nations of Europe be allowed to practice self-determination. The Big Three promised that free elections would be held in Eastern Europe, but in all probability Stalin interpreted the agreement as tacit approval of a Soviet sphere in that region.

Within a few weeks the differing interpretations of the Yalta accords became apparent as the Soviets pressured Rumania to install a pro-Soviet regime while pressing the Soviet reorganization of the Polish government. Roosevelt's death on 12 April 1945 brought Harry S. Truman to the presidency. Inexperienced in foreign affairs, Truman vowed to continue FDR's basic policies. He paid close attention to a group of inherited advisers who emphasized that the Soviets could not be counted on to cooperate after the war. The American ambassador to the Soviet Union, Averell Harriman, argued that Stalin's need for aid from the United States would lead to acceptance of a harder American line. Within two weeks of becoming president, Truman had become convinced that if the Soviets did not agree with the American interpretation of the Yalta agreement on the United Nations "they could go to hell." The president scolded Foreign Minister Molotov over Soviet policy in Poland. Truman was not alone in his concern; for many Americans, especially the six million of Polish ancestry, Poland had become a symbol of Soviet intentions. Public opinion polls showed a steady increase in the number of Americans who felt the Russians could not be trusted.

A New Red Scare

The Cold War between the United States and the Soviet Union which developed rapidly after World War II fed upon mistrust. Emerging with unprecedented power and strength, both nations regarded the other as a global bully. Stalin compared the United States and its allies to the Nazis; Americans spoke of the threat of "red fascism." At the same time, there was a special sense of exhilaration in the United States after the war, a heady feeling that peace and prosperity could be had largely on American terms. But only bad news seemed to follow. Domestic economic problems, Soviet intransigence in Europe, Russian spies, an obnoxious new Communist Party, and red-baiting by Republicans and conservative interest groups, all contributed to President Truman's taking a hard line against communism at home and abroad. This new brand of militant anti-communism spawned a second Red Scare, one which opened the way for the strident demagoguery practiced by the McCarthyites of the 1950s.

The Scare Begins

Postwar economic problems irritated Americans no end. The cost of living rose following the expiration of price controls. Workers demanding higher wages in key industries walked off their jobs, making 1946 the most strike-plagued year in history. Businessmen, conservative politicians, and the American Legion fought back, just as they had in 1919-1920, with charges of communism in labor unions. The U.S. Chamber of Commerce spearheaded the campaign with a series of reports and speeches on the Soviet menace. To avoid being taken over by communists, a Chamber official warned, "we will have to set up some firing squads in every good sized city and town in the country and . . . liquidate the Red and Pink Benedict Arnolds." Using documents leaked by the FBI and HCUA, Father John F. Cronin issued a series of reports for the Chamber charging that a communist fifth column had not only penetrated the American labor movement but the government as well, including the State Department, which was in the process of delivering China and Eastern Europe to the Kremlin.

Many Americans agreed with the Chamber of Commerce. In China, Mao Tse-tung's communist forces were besting those of Chiang Kai-shek. At the same time, Stalin tightened his grip on the Soviet sphere in Eastern Europe, installing satellite governments which threw religious leaders into jail. Roman Catholic leaders who had energetically supported General Franco against international communism in the late 1930s became obsessed with the communist menace at home. Francis Cardinal Spellman charged that red subversion made "tools and fools" of Americans. Bishop Fulton J. Sheen denounced "the fellow travelers in the United States and those whose hearts bleed for Red Fascism." The Knights of Columbus, a Catholic fraternal group, launched an anti-communist educational campaign with a series of radio broadcasts and town meetings. The Catholic War Veterans concentrated on holding classes in the art of detecting radicalism while the Association of Catholic Trade Unionists fought to eliminate communist influence in American labor. Catholics, especially those of Polish ancestry, defected from the Fair Deal coalition because the Truman administration did not seem to be tough enough against the Soviets.

Spy scandals added to the growing climate of fear and mistrust. In March 1945, agents of the Office of Strategic Services (OSS) raided the offices of a leftist magazine, *Amerasia*, where they found thousands of classified government reports, dealing mostly with such subjects as rice yields and livestock figures in China. A few months later the FBI seized the material and arrested six people on charges of espionage, although the cases were dropped on the grounds that the OSS had failed to obtain a search warrant. The next year Canadian authorities broke up a major spy ring which had passed more significant secrets on to the Russians. The fact that these spies collaborated with Canadian communists led jittery Americans to believe that the same thing was happening in the

United States, where the newly reconstituted Communist Party, USA (CPUSA) under the leadership of William Z. Foster had returned to the militant anti-capitalist rhetoric of the early 1930s.

After the war conservatives damned Roosevelt and Truman for being too soft on communism. FDR had, in their eyes, foolishly and immorally allowed himself to be duped into selling out Eastern Europe at Yalta. Truman continued to appease the communists with a passive foreign policy and by his failure to suppress the conspiracy at home. J. Edgar Hoover warned that the forces of "red fascism" had penetrated organized labor, the media, churches, colleges, public schools, fraternal groups, and, of course, government. Proportionately there were more communists in the United States, he noted darkly, than in Russia at the time of the Bolshevik Revolution. After the breakup of the Canadian spy ring, the FBI chief reported to President Truman that the Bureau had stepped up investigations of Soviet and CPUSA espionage based on information from two former communists, Whittaker Chambers and Elizabeth Bentley. In the summer of 1946, Truman reapproved Roosevelt's 1940 directive giving the FBI the power to wiretap groups suspected of "subversive activities" and Hoover quickly broadened political intelligence gathering operations. He also continued to leak information to favorites in Congress, especially members of HCUA and to conservative political groups. The Chamber of Commerce used FBI material in a report of October 1946, which reiterated Hoover's charges of pervasive communist influence in America, recommending an aggressive campaign against subversives.

Truman Takes Control

On the eve of the 1946 congressional elections, Truman was being criticized by many liberals, including Walter Lippmann, Albert Einstein, Henry Morgenthau, Jr., Joseph Davies, and Elliott Roosevelt, for abandoning Roosevelt's policy of accommodation with the Soviet Union. Socialists and communists blamed him for the Cold War. He had fired Secretary of Commerce Henry Wallace for criticizing administration foreign policy. "The Reds, phonies and 'parlor pinks' seem to be banded together," Truman confided to his diary, "and are becoming a national danger. I am afraid they are a sabotage front for Uncle Joe Stalin." In spite of his hard line policy against Moscow, conservative intellectuals and politicians, the U.S. Chamber of Commerce, the Catholic Church, and many newspapers continued to castigate the president for not doing enough. According to a July 1945 Gallup poll, 87 percent of the people approved of the president's policies; a little more than a year later, less than one-third rated his performance as even adequate. Republicans plastered the countryside with billboards asking "Had enough?" For the first time since the 1920s, the GOP took both houses of Congress. Republicans employed the anti-communist issue, but also promised significant tax cuts, a pledge which did not augur well for a program of massive economic aid to rebuild western European nations into solid trading partners capable of resisting the communist impulse.

As a political centrist and party regular, Truman abhorred the reactionary anti-New Deal red-baiters, yet he believed that the international communist challenge had to be met forcefully. "Really," he wrote to his mother in November 1946, "there is no difference between the government which Mr. Molotov represents and the one the Czar represented—or the one Hitler spoke for." Like his right-wing critics, then, Truman regarded communism as "red fascism," a movement which only understood the language of force. While the president knew there was nothing to fear from the American Communist Party, he could not afford to ignore Republican charges that the administration was not fighting home grown reds hard enough at a time when national security seemed threatened from abroad. To undercut his critics, the president followed a suggestion of the House Civil Service Subcommittee by appointing a Temporary Commission on Employee Loyalty to investigate current national security measures against suspected communists in government.

On 21 February 1947, the British informed Undersecretary of State Dean Acheson that they could no longer underwrite security in Greece and Turkey. Acheson convinced a bipartisan congressional delegation of the necessity for American aid to keep the Soviets from dominating the region, a questionable assumption since Stalin had stayed out of the civil war raging in Greece and showed little inclination to move against the troublesome Turks. Truman appeared before Congress on 12 March to ask for help in the worldwide struggle against communism, portraying the situation dramatically in terms of an ideological battle "between alternative ways of life." In essence the "Truman Doctrine" challenged Congress to accept a Cold War foreign policy rooted in the fear of foreign and domestic communism.

Nine days later, the president announced the implementation of a new program to weed out possible security risks in the government. He based Executive Order (EO) 9835 on the recommendations of the Temporary Commission on Loyalty, a group which came to its conclusions largely on the testimony of FBI and military intelligence investigators who urged vigilance against communists and New Deal reformers. As one G-2 officer put it, "A liberal is only a hop, skip, and a jump from a Communist. A Communist starts as a liberal." Had the president heard this ominous tautology he might have thought twice about a program which declared open season on former Roosevelt and present Truman administration personnel. Under terms of EO 9835 the attorney general was to draw up a list of organizations deemed "totalitarian, Fascist, Communist, or subversive." Past or present membership or "sympathetic association" with such groups triggered an investigation of government employees and job applicants by security officers working for agency and Civil Service Loyalty Boards. Suspected disloyalty was considered "reasonable grounds" for dismissal with scant constitutional safeguards for the accused. Vague loyalty standards forced the boards to anticipate the potential for future fealty to the government. Board members poked and probed those summoned about family activities, reports that they owned communist books or art, rumors about Negroes visiting their homes, their reading habits, and even what kinds of clothes they wore. All information, substantiated and unsubstantiated, went into a permanent file and stayed there to be passed from agency to agency for further scrutiny. Over twelve hundred government workers were fired and about six thousand more resigned during the Truman administration. Many had become victims of a system biased against any form of dissent. The attorney general's list affected not only government employees, but all Americans suspected of belonging to or associating with suspected subversive organizations. This domestic counterpart to the Truman Doctrine, the most repressive anti-red government campaign since the Palmer raids, can be said to have marked the beginning of a new red scare. Ironically, Truman's program backfired on him; instead of soothing fears about communist infiltration of government, the loyalty drive heightened the climate of fear and attracted the further interest of Congress, especially members of the House Committee on UnAmerican Activities.

The Election of 1948

Truman continued his middle-of-the-road approach to the Cold War as he geared up for a tough presidential election campaign in 1948. In foreign policy, the president took George Kennan's advice from the previous year when the diplomat (writing under the pen name "Mr. X") had called publicly for "long-term, patient but firm and vigilant containment of Russian expansive tendencies." Communist containment moved ahead on the homefront as well. Early in 1948, the Justice Department arrested alien leaders of the CPUSA for deportation. This strategy did not satisfy members of HCUA, who favored the prosecution of the entire communist leadership under terms of the Smith Act. In March, the president prodded a dawdling Congress into passing the Marshall Plan, a massive program for rebuilding Western Europe and Japan into strong, anti-communist trading partners. He came out strongly against HCUA's Mundt-Nixon Bill, which would have required all CPUSA members to register, on reasoning that it violated civil liberties. This was a move widely applauded by liberal anti-communist organizations such as Americans for Democratic Action and unions like the CIO then engaged in its own purge of CP members. As an alternative to the Mundt-Nixon Bill, the Justice Department gave approval to Federal Grand Jury indictments charging the National Board of the Communist Party with organizing a political movement to teach and advocate the overthrow of the government in violation of the Smith Act. On 20 July, the

FBI conducted a raid on the party's national headquarters, arresting its entire leadership. Truman had cleverly undercut his Republican critics on the right, isolated Henry Wallace's Progressive party coalition of leftists and disaffected liberals, and staked out the center for himself. Truman and his liberal allies pulled off a razor-thin victory by red-baiting Wallace shamelessly and branding Republican opponent Thomas Dewey "a fascist." The president succeeded, albeit temporarily, in regaining control of the anti-communist issue.

HCUA, Hollywood, and Hiss

Renewed concern over communism in the postwar period brought HCUA back into the public spotlight. In late 1946, committee counsel Ernie Adamson issued a report claiming the existence of a massive communist plot to bring the American economy down with a general strike. The Library of Congress had become, he charged, "a haven for aliens and foreign-minded Americans." One of his staff members even smelled a conspiracy in Kreml hair tonic since it closely resembled the word "Kremlin." The committee later disavowed these wild charges, but found happier hunting grounds in Hollywood where accusations of communist influence had cropped up during a lengthy and bitter strike against several major studios. Working from the assumption that the Screen Actors Guild was "lousy with communists," HCUA Chairman J. Parnell Thomas set out to prove that "the government had wielded the iron fist in order to get the companies to put on certain Communist propaganda." A subcommittee heard testimony from producers and movie stars, including Gary Cooper, who volunteered, that when it came to communism, "From what I hear, I don't like it because it isn't on the level." Others, guild President Ronald Reagan among them, minimized the communist issue, emphasizing instead the importance of safeguarding democratic principles. A group of ten, all longtime communist activists, refused to testify at all and eventually received jail sentences for contempt of Congress. While Thomas could point to wartime pro-Soviet films like *Mission to Moscow*, he could find no direct links to the New Deal. Still Hollywood had felt the heat; on 26 November 1947, Eric Johnston of the Motion Picture Producers

Association announced that none of the "Hollywood Ten" would be employed again "until such time as he is acquitted or has purged himself of contempt and declares under oath that he is not a Communist." To save the motion picture industry from HCUA and adverse public reaction, the producers created a blacklist which would grow in time to include at least 250 writers, directors, and actors. Further covering themselves, Hollywood studios began to crank out anti-communist films where reds plotted diabolically, aided by naive liberal dupes, thus breathing life into the unreal and stereotypical characters that made up the red nightmare.

The House Committee on Un-American Activities scored its greatest political triumph in 1948, hearing testimony from Whittaker Chambers accusing several former government employees, including Alger Hiss, of being communists. Hiss was no small fish: he had served in the Department of State and helped to organize the Dumbarton Oaks Conference, the Yalta meeting, and the United Nations. The suave Ivy Leaguer's eloquent denials under oath impressed President Truman (who branded the whole business as a "red herring") and several members of HCUA. Only young California Congressman Richard Nixon wanted to pursue the case further. On 17 August, Hiss and Chambers faced one another in the Hotel Commodore under committee auspices. Hiss dared his accuser to repeat the charges away from the witness chair where he would not be protected by congressional immunity. Armed with a steady diet of FBI briefings, Nixon and other committee members pushed Hiss hard on details at a subsequent hearing, forcing him to qualify his answers again and again with phrases like "to the best of my recollection." When Chambers finally accepted Hiss' challenge, the former New Dealer sued for libel. In response to a lawyer's call for any correspondence between the two men, Chambers upped the stakes to espionage, producing State Depart-ment documents and memoranda he said Hiss had purloined, including a roll of microfilm Chambers had recently hidden inside a pumpkin on his Maryland farm. The statute of limitations on espionage had expired, but a grand jury indicted Hiss on perjury charges and he was convicted at a second trial in early 1950.

The Hiss case took on an importance far beyond the question of whether the dapper Ivy Leaguer or Whittaker Chambers was lying, an issue scholars still debate today. To HCUA and other conservative groups, Hiss became a symbol of the privileged Eastern establishment, liberal internationalism, and the New Deal, tangible proof—at least to some on the Right—that the Democratic party harbored red traitors. The HCUA hearings, Hiss' lawsuit, and the two perjury trials kept the case in the headlines through 1949, allowing the Republicans to flay the administration with the communist issue. New and disquieting events added more fuel to the Red Scare. A more tangible espionage case broke in March when the FBI arrested Judith Coplon, a Justice Department official, for passing secrets to the Russians. In September the Soviet Union shocked Americans with the explosion of their own nuclear bomb.

The Foley Square Trial

The executive branch also helped to keep the Red Scare going through 1949 with the most sensational and expensive political trial up to that point in American history, the prosecution of the CPUSA hierarchy under the Smith Act at Foley Square courthouse in New York. Since the prosecution could not point to revolutionary deeds or even proof of incitement to violence, the government concentrated on attacking the party as a conspiracy. Books and articles by Marx, Engels, Lenin, and Stalin were the best evidence that government lawyers could muster. Former party member Louis Budenz, who had become a professional anti-communist witness, writer, and speaker, played a key role, explaining to the jury the CPUSA's covert commitment to the violent overthrow of the government. A procession of government informants proved less effective than hoped. Attorneys for the eleven defendants bored the jury with the introduction of additional Marxist materials in order to "educate the masses." All attempts to turn the trial into a communist propaganda victory backfired on those charged. Judge Harold Medina sided with the government most often, allowing prosecutors to discredit defense witnesses by demanding that they "name names" of Communist Party members. To no one's surprise, the jury found all eleven guilty of violating the Smith Act and Medina sentenced them to prison. The real purpose of the trial had been, as the *Washington Post* noted, "not so much the protection and security of the state as the exploitation of justice for the purpose of propaganda." In this sense, the Truman administration used the Foley Square Trial to answer Republican charges that the government was coddling communists.

But Truman had already lost control of the communist issue by late 1949. In December, Chiang Kai-shek fled across the Straits of Taiwan with the remnants of his Nationalist army leaving China to Mao Tse-tung and the communists. Many Americans joined with the highly vocal "China Lobby" to blame the administration for "losing" China, as if the world's most populous country had belonged to the United States. Truman's comment that "we picked a bad horse" came closer to the truth since the United States had spent three billion dollars and sent a host of military advisers and diplomatic missions in an attempt to save Chiang's venal regime from collapsing. In the temper of the times, the charge of "losing China" made sense for it had the virtue of being less traumatic than the reality that American power was limited.

Legacies

In early 1921, at a time when the government was still pursuing radicals in the aftermath of the first Red Scare, the eminent Harvard Law School professor Zechariah Chafee, Jr., warned that "unless the methods used by the Department of Justice are severely condemned by Congress and the American people they will be repeated in future emergencies." Few took Professor Chafee seriously at the time, but his jeremiad turned out to be prophetic. The Republicans called a halt to the harassment without taking steps adequate to insure the rights of dissidents in the event of another scare. A period of relative tolerance followed in the years between the wars, although congressional committees and several right-wing groups searched for evidence of communists in high places. By the late 1930s fearsome events overseas revived the general mistrust of communists. At the behest of the White House, the FBI resumed its watch on the left while Congress passed laws designed to curb "alien influences." The cynical Hitler-Stalin pact intensified the enmity many felt toward the Soviets, leaving a lingering impression that fascists and communists were part of the same satanic conspiracy. The uneasy period of wartime cooperation between the United States and the Soviet Union gave way to a new period of anti-communist hysteria. Diplomatic and economic disappointments coupled with spy scandals and a Republican willingness to ride the anti-communist issue caused Americans to see red everywhere from Hollywood to the White House. Not to be outdone, Truman seized control of the second Red Scare in Washington, using it to push through an expensive program of communist containment in foreign policy, to persecute the left at home, and to get elected as president in his own right.

A new red scare had been under way for three years when Senator Joseph McCarthy burst upon the scene in February 1950. By that time, the Truman administration's energetic, if questionable, crusade had largely contained the Soviet Union, purged the government of the few communist sympathizers left over from the Popular Front era, and broken the American Communist Party. Parallel efforts by HCUA, the FBI, and conservative political groups contributed substantially to the postwar anti-communist hysteria. When Congress wrestled the Red Scare issue away from the president again, Truman's liberal anti-communism yielded to a conservative Red Scare presided over by the likes of Democrat Pat McCarran and Republican Joe McCarthy.

Chapter 3

The Scare Deepens:
McCarthy and the Other Red Hunters, 1950-1954

On 9 February 1950, the junior senator from Wisconsin, Joseph Raymond McCarthy, spoke before the Ohio County Women's Republican Club in Wheeling, West Virginia on the issue of the communist threat. Lifting material from a recent speech by Congressman Richard Nixon, McCarthy charged that the United States was losing the struggle against atheistic communism because the State Department harbored traitors. "While I cannot take the time," McCarthy said, after tossing off a few names, "to name all of the men in the State Department who have been named as members of the Communist Party and members of a spy ring, I have here in my hand a list of 205...a list of names that were known to the Secretary of State and who nevertheless are still working and shaping the policy of the State Department." At first, McCarthy's tough partisan rhetoric, delivered far from the centers of power, attracted scant attention. But when he continued to make the charges, changing the figures as he went, his fellow politicians, the media, and the public began to take notice. Before long, the junior senator became a center of attention for four of the noisiest and most frightening years in American history.

Historians agree that a red scare occurred in 1919-1920, but there is considerable disagreement over the period 1947-1954. Those who regard Truman's anti-communist crusade as necessary and proper lean toward the interpretation that another red scare did not begin until 1950 or that, if it did begin earlier, HCUA had more to do with it than the Truman administration. Other writers, seeing the difference between Truman and McCarthy as one of degrees (and eager to condemn both) tend to treat the period as one "Great Fear" as David Caute put it. Neither of these explanations is completely satisfactory. Certainly, the periods 1919-1920 and 1947-1950 had this in common: liberal Democratic presidential administrations, reacting to political pressures brought on by postwar unrest, turned to direct state repression of the Left. During the first Red Scare, victims included communists, socialists, anarchists, syndicalists, and "parlor Bolsheviks," that is, liberals and Progressives who had strayed too far to the Left. Under Truman, the Communist Party was targeted as were those who had joined communist fronts along with some "fellow travelers," again many of them liberals or Progressives. There were many differences between these two red scares as well, such as length of time and levels of violence, but none was more important than the way each one ended. Conservatives called a halt to the first scare once it became apparent that continuing mass hysteria posed more of a threat to order and civil liberties than the scattered remnants of the American Left. They behaved very differently in 1950.

After three years of red scare under Truman, conservatives were angry. The growth of Soviet power, the rise of "red" China, the end of the American nuclear monopoly, and revelations of communist espionage led them to conclude that national security remained in mortal jeopardy. Under these circumstances, they found the conduct of Republican Senator Joseph McCarthy and his allies in the Democratic Party like Pat McCarran to be useful politically. This phase of the second Red Scare, which at the national level consisted chiefly of congressional bullying of the powerless—and of respected liberals and moderates—pushed the country to the right. Once Dwight Eisenhower became president and McCarthy began attacking powerful institutions such as the Army, he became a nuisance, more of a threat to order than the perceived enemies of conservatism. The second Red Scare then began to fade, leaving behind bitter legacies and a lingering mass psychosis which transformed anti-communism into America's invisible ideology.

This Red Scare did not belong to Senator McCarthy any more than the first Red Scare belonged to Woodrow Wilson and A. Mitchell Palmer. These men were products of their times, riding short-lived waves of hysteria until cast aside in ruins. McCarthy the man was not as important as "McCarthyism," the practice of making wild and often unprovable accusations in the name of anti-communism. Furthermore, there were many practitioners of McCarthyism at the national, state, and local levels and in both the Republican and Democratic parties. Timing was everything; under Truman, the Cold War and the hunt for domestic subversives had fed upon one another to create an environment of fear and suspicion conducive to McCarthyism. The breakdown of Truman's artfully crafted bipartisanship, continuing revelations concerning Soviet espionage, a stalled war against communism in Korea, and the seemingly ineffectual response to the Soviets by two successive presidents all contributed to the deepening Red Scare at least as much as did McCarthy.

Joe McCarthy

Historians have not treated Joseph McCarthy kindly. He emerges from the pages of many biographies and textbooks as a kind of fiend representing the darker side of the American character who discovered anti-communism in 1950 and presided over a reign of terror until exorcised four years later. Such a simple and self-serving explanation absolves liberals and moderate conservatives in politics, business, education, and the media (and "the system" itself) from sharing in the blame for the ruined lives and the mental and legal repression of the "McCarthy era." The raw materials of history—McCarthy's rambling, inarticulate speeches and the kinescopes of him in action—reveal not the devil, but a disorganized, opportunistic, frequently desperate, alcoholic politician blundering and bullying his way through election campaigns and hearings. His career prior to 1950 illustrates that McCarthy was a complex man, part cynic and part idealist, both gifted and troubled.

McCarthy the Man

After working his way through school during the Great Depression, Joe McCarthy practiced law in rural Wisconsin, where he exhibited disregard for community standards, often appearing personally and professionally disheveled. As a judge, he quickly gained a reputation for playing fast and loose with the law while showing genuine compassion and imagination in many of his decisions. Ennui and patriotism led McCarthy to enlist in the Marines after Pearl Harbor. He spent most of the war as an intelligence officer debriefing pilots on Bougainville in the South Pacific. Anxious for a return to politics, the restless McCarthy publicized himself back in Wisconsin as a war hero. Stories began to appear about the exploits of "Tailgunner Joe," the fighting leatherneck who fired more bullets during one mission than anyone else. In 1944, McCarthy boasted that he flew fourteen bombing missions, but three years later he said it had been seventeen; by 1951 the number rose to thirty-two. In fact, he had flown twelve times, blazing away at coconut trees in undefended areas, a common practice among bored desk-bound officers. After the war, "Tailgunner Joe" claimed to have about "ten pounds of shrapnel" in his leg. Actually, his only war-related injury resulted from a hazing incident. While McCarthy's falsehoods may be dismissed as typical exaggerations of a proud veteran, they do reveal a disrespect for the truth and, more significantly, a difficulty in distinguishing between reality and fiction.

McCarthy did not wait for the end of the war to reenter the political fray. Taking a leave of absence, he finished a surprising second in the Wisconsin Republican Senate primary of 1944 in spite of having been a Democrat only six years earlier. In 1946, McCarthy squeaked past vulnerable incumbent Senator Robert LaFollette, Jr. to capture the GOP nomination. Like so many Republican candidates that year, McCarthy redbaited his Democratic opponent as "communistically inclined." A member of the staunchly conservative, anti-New Deal "class of '46," Senator McCarthy continued to denounce the communist menace with regularity in his first years as a senator, although he did break ranks by supporting President Truman's foreign policy.

Some senators found his behavior disturbing. To cover his gambling losses, McCarthy accepted a substantial loan from a Pepsi-Cola lobbyist interested in a bill to decontrol sugar. Passage of this measure would have meant large profits for soft-drink manufacturers, sugar companies, and sugar producers, including sugar beet farmers back in Wisconsin. Violating the unwritten rules of the Senate club, McCarthy (nicknamed "the Pepsi-Cola kid") attacked opponents of the bill personally and consistently misrepresented facts in his decontrol campaign. He became a leader in the fight against public housing, calling it "a breeding ground for communism." Realtors paid him high fees to speak at their conventions, although at least one organizer regretted inviting McCarthy to Columbus, Ohio where he became intoxicated, borrowed money to shoot craps, and cavorted openly with prostitutes. The senator also sold an article on public housing, which he did not write, for $10,000 to the Lustron Corporation, a manufacturer of prefabricated homes having an obvious interest in McCarthy's efforts to limit government housing.

Halfway through his freshman term, Joe McCarthy had done little to warrant his reelection and he knew it. To head off mounting opposition back home, he attacked the *Madison Capital-Times*, a liberal newspaper which had published several unflattering stories on McCarthy's judicial career. City Editor Cedric Parker, the senator charged, was "a known communist" of the "red mouthpiece" in Wisconsin. While Parker did belong to communist front organizations before World War II, this could hardly be considered proof that his paper pushed the communist line. The increasingly frigid atmosphere of the Cold War made McCarthy's accusations newsworthy and gave him the publicity he needed. Touring the state in a "personal campaign against communism" during the last months of 1949, McCarthy expanded his attacks to include the State Department as a government agency "honeycombed and run by Communists." He repeated this charge several more times in speeches on and off the Senate floor. Seeking to explain McCarthy's famous attack on the Department of State made at Wheeling, West Virginia, some writers have created a myth that he became converted to anti-communism suddenly at a dinner meeting on 7 January 1950. But McCarthy had already discovered the political capital to be made from flaying the Truman administration's loyalty program. The Wheeling address of 9 February was just another effort by one Republican among many who hoped to use the issue of subversives in government for partisan purposes.

McCarthy had no list of 205 "members of the Communist Party and members of a spy ring" that night in Wheeling. In all likelihood he picked up the number 205 from a four-year-old report from the secretary of state to Congress indicating that loyalty checks on 3,000 government employees had turned up adverse reports on 284 persons and resulted in 79 dismissals. Therefore, McCarthy must have reasoned, the other 205 might still be hatching communist plots at the State Department. His subsequent charge, made in Salt Lake City the next day, that he had the names of 57 "card-carrying members of the Communist Party" working for Secretary of State Dean Acheson, came from a 1948 House Appropriations Committee probe which had cleared 108 individuals suspected of inefficiency, 57 of whom still worked for the State Department. McCarthy had obtained a lot of publicity for himself by twisting two outdated reports and using a little arithmetic. People in Washington were talking about McCarthy—and demanding hard evidence. The senator seemed pleased with the controversy he had raised, telling skeptical reporters back home: "I've got a sockful of shit and I know how to use it."

McCarthy the "Ism"

On 20 February, McCarthy took the floor of the Senate to discuss his allegations. Twisting outdated information from the House Appropriations Committee's "Lee List," the senator launched into a five hour dissertation on the communist tendencies of eighty-one former and present State Department employees, changing an "active fellow traveler" into an "active communist" and so on down through the list. Robert Taft, leader of the Republican right, found it to be "a perfectly reckless performance," yet also potentially useful politically. Confident that they could make McCarthy and the Republicans look foolish, Democrats turned the matter over to a special subcommittee chaired by Millard Tydings, a shrewd conservative Democrat.

The Tydings Committee hearings transformed Joe McCarthy from an obscure junior senator into a premier red hunter. Candidly admitting in private that he had a great issue and no evidence, McCarthy assembled a staff of experts. J. Edgar Hoover contributed much information and a former agent. Richard Nixon fed him data from HCUA's massive records. Reporter Jack Anderson combed columnist Drew Pearson's files for leads, while publisher William Randolph Hearst lent a couple of crackerjack reporters. As money rolled in from wealthy right-wing sources, McCarthy began to attract a whole host of professional anti-communists, including J.B. Mathews, former chief investigator for Martin Dies, who brought with him the precious "Appendix Nine" list of over twenty thousand suspected reds and pinks.

McCarthy gave public testimony for four days, naming familiar names without providing any proof that the State Department still employed communists. Subsequently he charged that China expert Owen Lattimore was "the top Russian espionage agent in this country." An angry Harry Truman denounced the accusation as silly, noting that "the greatest asset the Kremlin has is Senator McCarthy." For all intents and purposes, Truman's comment marked the end of foreign policy bipartisanship during his presidency. When McCarthy could not come up with evidence against Lattimore, he recanted the spy charge. Lattimore's eloquent defense of his career set the senator's cause back further, but testimony by Louis Budenz (another old HCUA favorite) vaguely supporting the Republican canard of a conspiracy to sell Chiang Kai-shek out to the communists gave McCarthy enough credibility to keep the hearings going.

To divert attention from the embarrassing failure to prove his allegations, McCarthy attacked "the Reds, their minions, and their egg-sucking phony liberals" for smearing him. He included those newspaper reporters "who would hold sacrosanct those communists and queers who have sold 400 million Asiatic people into atheistic slavery." The hearings dragged on, degenerating into bitter partisan bickering. Convinced that "Joe had the Senate paralyzed with fear,"

Senator Margaret Chase Smith presented a "Declaration of Conscience" signed by seven liberal Republicans attacking McCarthy and the right-wing of the party. Most of the Senate GOP gave McCarthy its support out of a belief that the Truman administration was losing the Cold War and that the junior senator from Wisconsin had significant popular support which might be parlayed into election victories. A few Democrats came out against him, but the majority of them, Southern and conservative, loathed McCarthy's snobbish, Eastern, intellectual victims and so said little. The Tydings Committee's lengthy final report of 17 July denouncing McCarthy's case as "a fraud and a hoax" touched off another vicious verbal brawl. That same day, FBI Director Hoover announced the arrest of Julius Rosenberg on charges of atomic espionage. Other arrests would follow. Furthermore, the United States had become involved in a shooting war against communism in Korea. Although the Senate voted to accept the Tydings report, the highly-charged political atmosphere allowed McCarthy to thrive.

Red Scare Politics

In early 1950, smarting from Republican criticism of his internal security policy and the unexpected Soviet acquisition of the atomic bomb, President Truman asked the National Security Council to take a fresh look at the Cold War. The resulting study, NSC-68, proceeded from the twin assumptions that the world had divided into two camps, one slave and one free, and that the United States faced an adversary with a master blueprint of world conquest. Eschewing a policy of negotiating with the Soviet Union, the council recommended a massive rearmament program, the building of the hydrogen bomb, tax hikes, a government campaign to rally the people behind the effort, a system of American-led regional alliances, and a program to weaken the Soviets internally. In time of peace, there was little real chance that Congress would vote for the huge appropriations necessary to carry out such an ambitious program. Truman and Acheson needed to show the Republicans that they were as willing to contain communism in Asia as they had in Europe.

On 25 June 1950, North Korea launched an attack into the south. Truman acted at once, gaining support from the United Nations (which the Soviets were boycotting), sending supplies to South Korea, and positioning the Seventh Fleet between China and Taiwan. The president extended the Truman Doctrine to Asia with pledges to aid the French against communists in Indochina, to fight communism in general, and to support the Filipino government's struggle against Huk rebels. When the South Korean army and the U.S. Air Force failed to repel the invaders, American ground troops were sent in under UN auspices, although General Douglas MacArthur took his orders from Washington.

For a time, the whole country rallied around Truman. The Bowman Gum company rushed into print sets of "Fight the Red Menace" trading cards for youth (subtitled "Children's Crusade Against Communism") featuring drawings of soldiers in Korea, a saluting General MacArthur, Russians in slave labor camps, portraits of diabolical communist leaders (with faces colored green), and frightening renditions of nuclear war. "All over the world," one card explained, "agents of the Red Menace seek chances to make trouble. They even fool well meaning people into helping them do their dirty work." The Korean war muted Truman's domestic critics—at least for a time—while pushing the country further to the right. "My only forum is page one," Senator McCarthy noted, "I don't have that now, so I'll keep quiet."

The McCarran Act

The subversives issue came back into the headlines during the summer of 1950 with the arrest of Julius and Ethel Rosenberg on charges of spying for the Soviet Union. Day after day the war in Asia, a Soviet atom-spy ring, and McCarthy's renewed charges of "highly placed Red counselors" in government monopolized media attention. Congress reconsidered the Mundt-Nixon Bill, which had failed two years earlier. This bill required the registration of communist political organizations. Democratic Senator Pat McCarran of Nevada took control of the legislative effort. A long-time opponent of Roosevelt and Truman—who he claimed had abandoned China to communism—the conservative Democrat put together an internal security proposal that included Mundt-Nixon and five other sedition and anti-alien bills. Since a companion omnibus measure had already sailed through the House, worried Senate liberals offered an alternative to the McCarran Bill which would give the president the power to declare an "internal security emergency," and the attorney general the authority to arrest and detain suspected subversives in special facilities. In the end, Democratic leaders agreed to add the "concentration camp" bill to McCarran's package as liberals and conservatives vied with one another to strengthen their anti-communist credentials before the November elections.

President Truman vetoed the Internal Security Act because he felt it would stifle basic civil liberties. At the same time, the president claimed, the anti-communist bill "would actually weaken our existing internal security measures and would seriously hamper the Federal Bureau of Investigation and other security agencies...and give aid and comfort to the enemy who would destroy us." This curious rationale did not win over the Congress, which voted promptly to override the veto. The Internal Security (McCarran) Act made it a crime to "combine, conspire or agree with any other persons to perform any act which would substantially contribute to the establishment in the United States of a totalitarian dictatorship." The act created a Subversive Activities Control Board with the power to order communist organizations and fronts to register with the Justice Department. Members of such groups could not hold government or defense-related jobs or use passports. They would be sent to concentration camps in the event of war or revolution with most of their constitutional rights suspended. Aliens with past or present connections with foreign or domestic communist groups were subject to deportation or denial of admittance to the United States. Naturalized citizens would be denaturalized if they joined organizations deemed subversive. The McCarran Act struck the most serious blows against free speech and free association since the Sedition and Espionage Acts of World War I—at least on paper. No communist organizations actually registered with the government; no individuals went to jail for conspiring to create a totalitarian state; and six concentration camps built in the early 1950s remained empty. The law did keep out leftist immigrants and visitors, but surely not communist spies. This exercise in "McCarranism" was McCarthyism translated into action, a reflection of the impulse in times of stress to confuse dissent with treason.

The Election of 1950

Republicans hoped to make political gains in Congress by red-baiting their opponents in the 1950 elections just as they had four years earlier, a difficult task considering the anti-communist credentials of most conservative Democrats and many liberals, including the president. The strategy yielded meager results. Senator McCarthy played only a minor role in the campaign. Many office seekers practiced McCarthyism in the year of Korea and the Rosenbergs, but anti-communism was only a secondary issue in many races.

Conservative Southern and Western Democrats were the first to use communism as a campaign issue in 1950 during the spring primaries. George Smathers, a conservative Florida congressman, attacked liberal incumbent Senator Claude Pepper for supporting Truman's "socialist" Fair Deal and meeting with Stalin five years earlier. "He likes Joe," Smathers said of "Red" Pepper, "and Joe likes him." In addition, Smathers resorted to traditional racial demagoguery, charging that his opponent supported civil rights for Florida blacks, an issue at least as significant in Pepper's defeat as red-baiting. The same held true in North Carolina where conservative Willis Smith defeated liberal Frank P. Graham by exploiting white racial fears and stirring up anti-radicalism for good measure. Democratic primaries in California and Idaho featured conservative red-baiting of prominent incumbent liberals. For a time Democrats hoped that the war in Korea would rally voters around the party, but mounting casualties cast a pall over the country in the final weeks of the campaign. To make political hay from the Korean stalemate, the Republicans did not have to criticize this new and frustrating form of limited war; merely mentioning the subject usually sufficed.

Senator McCarthy spoke in fifteen states on behalf of Republican candidates during the fall campaign. To defeat Millard Tydings in retaliation for standing up to him, McCarthy virtually took over the campaign of political novice John Marshall Butler, providing money (from Texas oilmen and the McCormick newspapers), political gossip, and an office staff. Working with a conservative Washington newspaper, campaign aides put together a pamphlet full of McCarthyite charges against the "commiecrat" senator, complete with two separate photos of former CPUSA chief Earl Browder and Tydings pasted together to look as though the two were chatting amiably. After Butler won the election, the media credited the victory to McCarthy, ignoring evidence that Tydings had lost favor with Maryland voters for other reasons. Many also gave him credit for Everett Dirksen's upset of Majority Leader Scott Lucas in Illinois, although corruption in the Democratic party probably played a more important role than the issue of communism.

Elsewhere, McCarthy had less impact. California Congressman Richard Nixon discouraged McCarthy's presence in his successful race against liberal Helen Gahagan Douglas. He came anyway, but so did Gerald L. K. Smith in order to "help Richard Nixon get rid of the Jew-Communists." Nixon chose to pattern his campaign after that of Democrat George Smathers—only instead of "Red" Pepper, Mrs. Douglas became "the Pink Lady"—with equally rewarding results. In the end, Republicans picked up only five seats in the Senate and twenty-eight in the House, hardly the sweeping victory they had hoped for in an unexceptional off-year campaign. The theme that liberals were "soft on communism" reaped dividends for conservatives in both parties, yet state issues often predominated.

The Scare Peaks

A month after his re-election, Pat McCarran, the already powerful chairman of the Senate Judiciary Committee, took charge of the new Senate Internal Security Subcommittee (SISS), meaning to make it the Senate's version of HCUA. Joseph McCarthy emerged from the campaign with the unwarranted reputation of a slayer of pink Goliaths, a distortion which continued to make him a force to be reckoned with in Washington. Their power and prestige coincided with the peak of the Red Scare in 1951-1952 as the Rosenbergs went on trial for "the crime of the century" and most of the news from Korea was bad.

During the first four months of the Korean war, General MacArthur orchestrated the brilliant landing at Inchon that allowed UN forces to recapture South Korea and carry the war into North Korea. Dismissing warnings that China would enter the conflict rather than see North Korea destroyed, MacArthur pressed his advantage, even after skirmishes with Chinese "volunteers" in late October 1950. A month later, with North Korea on the verge of defeat, two hundred thousand Chinese soldiers attacked the exposed center of the U.N. forces, sending them into headlong retreat. The normally optimistic MacArthur predicted disaster unless the war could be carried into China. President Truman and the Joint Chiefs of Staff disagreed; conflict with China would have been, General Omar Bradley later testified, "the wrong war, at the wrong place, at the wrong time, and with the wrong enemy."

When the Korean war was stabilized close to the prewar border between north and south in March 1951, the administration prepared to negotiate a cease-fire, an opportunity which was lost when the openly defiant MacArthur crossed the 38th parallel to taunt the Chinese. On 5 April, House Minority Leader Joe Martin read into the record a letter from the general calling for the reunification of Korea, sponsorship of an invasion of China by Chiang Kai-shek and an Asia-first priority in the Cold War. "If we lose the war to Communism in Asia," MacArthur opined, "the fall of Europe is inevitable; win it and Europe most probably would avoid war and yet preserve freedom.... There is no substitute for victory." Immediately, Truman dismissed the general for insubordination, thus touching off a great public debate over the nature of the anti-communist crusade.

MacArthur questioned not only the administration's Europe-first policy but the whole notion of merely containing communism rather than rolling back the Iron/Bamboo Curtain. Containment was frustrating for a people addicted to problem solving. It meant following a policy of restraint and negotiation rather than "victory." And, of course, containment cost money. Small wonder that sixty-nine percent of voters sided with MacArthur according to a Gallup poll. The Right protested against the dismissal in the hope of turning the incident into a political triumph. "This country today," Senator William Jenner of Indiana cried, "is in the hands of a secret inner coterie...directed by agents of the Soviet Union." McCarthy charged that red conspirators had plied Truman with "bourbon and benedictine" to get him to commit treason. MacArthur had been fired, Senator Nixon said, "simply because he had the good sense and patriotism to ask that the hands of our fighting men in Korea be untied." The general received the welcome of a conquering hero, addressing a joint session of Congress, several conservative groups, and a special Senate investigative committee, where he defended his stance of "no compromise with atheistic communism—no halfway in the preservation of freedom and religion. It must be all or nothing."

President Truman told reporters that it would take six weeks for the "fuss" over MacArthur to die down—and it did. The same Gallup polls which showed most people taking the general's side revealed also that the public was divided over expanding the Korean war into China and that less than one in three favored helping Chiang Kai-shek retake the mainland. Truman prevailed over the vain MacArthur but the debate revealed that while millions of Americans wanted to roll back communism they did not relish the price of victory.

The Rosenbergs

On 19 June 1953 Julius and Ethel Rosenberg died in the electric chair at Sing Sing prison. They and several others had been arrested in 1950 as accomplices of Klaus Fuchs in the theft of secret information on the atomic bomb for the Soviet Union. Fuchs implicated Harry Gold as a courier to the Russians; Gold, in turn, implicated a machinist at the Los Alamos nuclear project, David Greenglass; and Greenglass gave the FBI the names of his sister and brother-in-law, the Rosenbergs. In March 1951, Julius, Ethel, and a third defendant, Morton Sobell, went on trial for conspiracy to commit espionage, a strategy U.S. Attorney Irving Saypol chose because second-hand or hearsay evidence was admissible in the prosecution of conspiracy and the government's case was not strong. During World War II, the prosecution said, the Rosenbergs convinced David Greenglass to help them steal atomic secrets for the Soviets. Greenglass, who had already been found guilty but not yet sentenced for espionage activities, provided damaging testimony (along with his wife Ruth) against his in-laws. Max Elitcher, another key prosecution witness facing a possible jail sentence, claimed that his former friends Sobell and Julius Rosenberg tried to involve him in the conspiracy. The Rosenbergs steadfastly claimed innocence throughout the trial and until the end of their lives. After the jury found the defendants guilty as charged, Judge Irving Kaufman passed sentences of death on the Rosenbergs and 30 years in prison for Sobell. An unsuccessful appeal process delayed their electrocution by two years.

The Rosenberg case ranks as one of the most controversial in American history. Most leftists accepted their innocence as a matter of faith, believing that the couple was framed in a government conspiracy to frighten Cold War critics. How, they asked, could Julius Rosenberg (who graduated near the bottom of his college class), Ethel (a high school dropout), and her brother, David Greenglass (a barely competent machinist), possibly have stolen the secret of the atomic bomb and run a Soviet spy ring for so long? The right believed that justice triumphed and that the death sentence was appropriate. The Rosenbergs' crimes, Judge Kaufman observed during the sentencing, were "worse than murder." Delivering the bomb to Stalin "has already caused, in my opinion, the communist aggression in Korea, with the resultant casualties exceeding 50,000 and who knows what that millions more innocent people may pay the price of your treason." The judge spoke for many Americans when he blamed the Korean situation and the end of the American nuclear monopoly on the defendants, agents of the communist conspiracy.

There can be little doubt that Julius Rosenberg was a talented amateur spy who dreamed of doing something useful for the Soviet Union and the Marxist-Leninist cause. David Greenglass stole atomic secrets, but the Rosenberg ring did not commit what J. Edgar Hoover called "the crime of the century." Like so much of Hoover's rhetoric, that comment was for public and congressional consumption; privately, he told his agents that the Soviets had not learned much "solely through the operations of the Rosenberg espionage network in this country." The government went all out against the Rosenbergs because Julius might have provided information about other espionage operations. Furthermore, communists and fellow travelers might also be discouraged from spying for the cause if they knew what fate awaited them. The case against Ethel Rosenberg appeared much less clear cut, for the government prosecuted her, in large part, to prod Julius into confessing. "[P]roceeding against his wife," Hoover told the attorney general in 1950, "might serve as a lever in this matter." The FBI never gave up hope that one or the other of them might break down and confess, even after being strapped into the electric chair. The Bureau had a team of agents standing by during the last hours, just in case, complete with a list of questions for Julius Rosenberg, including "Was your wife cognizant of your activities?" Even the FBI did not seem sure that Ethel was guilty. But the Rosenbergs had decided to die rather than compromise themselves. The Left and the Right each then claimed victory for having unmasked a wicked conspiracy.

McCarthy and McCarranism

The Rosenberg trial did not ease American fears of communist subversion in government. Truman's Loyalty Review Board had been the subject of much criticism from Republicans and right-wing Democrats on the one hand for being too soft on the State Department and from libertarians on the other for being too inquisitorial. On 28 April 1951, President Truman issued Executive Order 10241 establishing new standards for determining loyalty. "Reasonable doubt" of innocence replaced "reasonable grounds" for a belief in guilt as the criterion for dismissal, meaning that civil servants would have to prove their innocence rather than the board having to demonstrate their guilt.

The Review Board then took another look at hundreds of cases where the employee had received clearance under the old rules only on appeal, including that of John Stewart Service. A State Department expert on the Far East, Service had been critical of Chiang Kai-shek's government and advised American neutrality in the Chinese civil war. His association with the leftist journal *Amerasia* also made his loyalties suspect to administration investigators and conspiracy theorists such as Senator McCarthy. Although six loyalty/security checks and three hearings had cleared Service, the Loyalty Review Board recommended dismissal under the revised 1951 criteria. But the new rules did not redound to Truman's benefit; on the contrary, they served to intensify the perception of earlier loyalty programs as inadequate. Instead of undercutting his critics with a tougher program, the president merely strengthened the right-wingers.

On 14 June 1951, Joseph McCarthy launched a sustained attack in the Senate against General George C. Marshall, army chief of staff during World War II, former ambassador to China, the author (as secretary of state) of the European Recovery Program which bore his name, and current secretary of defense. The senator put Marshall at the center of "a conspiracy so immense and an infamy so black as to dwarf any previous venture in the history of man." Specifically, the general had stood "side by side" with Stalin, selling out Poland and China in the process. Although McCarthy took credit for writing the polemic, the real author was Forrest Davis, a right-wing journalist who had given a manuscript on communists in government to the senator at a party during a fit of alcohol-induced generosity. McCarthy later had Davis' work published under his own name as *America's Retreat From Victory, The Story of George Catlett Marshall*. There was nothing in the senator's speech that he and others on the Republican right had not said before; Marshall had become a favorite target for the conspiracy-minded since his ill-fated attempt to put together a coalition government of Chiang Kai-shek and Mao Tse-tung.

On 6 August, shortly after a Senate subcommittee issued a report critical of the 1950 Republican campaign against Millard Tydings in Maryland, Senator William Benton asked the Rules Committee to investigate McCarthy's conduct to see if he should be expelled. President Truman went on the offensive against McCarthy as well, telling a lukewarm American Legion audience that Americans should rise up against "scaremongers and hatemongers." The president sent his secretary of labor to a convention of the Veterans of Foreign Wars with a similar message, but the delegates seemed to reserve most of their enthusiasm for McCarthy's appearance. As Senator Guy Gillette's Subcommittee on Privileges and Elections prepared to investigate Benton's charges, McCarthy appeared before a subcommittee of the Foreign Relations Committee which was considering the nomination of Philip C. Jessup as a United Nations delegate. A distinguished attorney, author, professor, and public servant, Jessup had become another symbol to the Right of what was wrong with Truman's foreign policy since he had edited the *China White Paper*, helped to get MacArthur fired, and counted Dean Acheson and Alger Hiss as friends. McCarthy repeated charges he had made against Jessup in previous hearings regarding affiliation with communist fronts, accusations which had been proven false to the satisfaction of almost everyone, except the McCarthyites. He could only complain about "the Commiecrat Party" when Senators John J. Sparkman and William J. Fulbright (both Southern Democrats) questioned his proof. Fulbright unnerved McCarthy with his close questioning, sarcasm, and ridicule to the point where the latter could only sputter that "I am dealing with too many of these slimy creatures to keep all the details of each in my mind."

McCarthy claimed victory when the subcommittee voted down the Jessup nomination, but the senator's standing in public opinion polls went down in the fall of 1951 as several newspapers and *Time* magazine ran unflattering stories. Never one to back away from a fight with the media (even attacking columnist Drew Pearson physically at a party), McCarthy labeled his critics as communist dupes and degenerates. He forced *Time*'s Henry Luce to back down by organizing a campaign urging corporations not to advertise in his magazines. To avoid the adverse political fallout, McCarthy's fellow Republicans in the Senate worked to sidetrack the Gillette subcommittee investigation while, at the same time, putting some distance between themselves and their erratic colleague. To keep the anti-McCarthy query going, Truman issued an executive order giving the subcommittee access to tax returns. When the senator retaliated with charges that Truman's special assistant on minority problems had once been a communist, the president characterized McCarthy as "pathological" and "a character assassin." The subcommittee could not produce solid proof of McCarthy's early dalliances with Pepsi Cola and Lustron or the pocketing of funds meant for the anti-communist crusade. In mid-1952, he defended himself on the floor of the Senate in typical fashion, attacking Senator Benton at length. As election day approached and McCarthy's threats increased, subcommittee members lost interest in the probe.

"McCarranism," more than anything else, saved McCarthy from isolation and disgrace during the Gillette investigation. In December 1950, the Senate authorized Judiciary Committee Chairman Pat McCarran to take another look at Truman's internal security policy. The Nevada Democrat packed his Senate Internal Security Subcommittee with ultra-conservatives from both parties, men who disapproved of the president's foreign policy as too soft on communism, admired Chiang Kai-shek, and were convinced that the State Department had sold China out. McCarran wanted desperately to prove the China conspiracy McCarthy had talked about so much since Wheeling. For his part, the junior senator from Wisconsin, who had been buttering up the powerful McCarran for months, lent members of his staff to the committee gladly. On 10 February 1951, the SISS swooped down on a favorite target of the far right, the Institute of Pacific Relations (IPR), a left-leaning organization dedicated to the study of the Orient, carting off files from a storage barn in rural Massachusetts. Ironically, many IPR files had already been purloined by members of McCarthy's staff (including the ubiquitous J. B. Mathews), but investigators from a jealous HCUA (which had fallen on hard times without Richard Nixon) forced their return in time for the SISS raid. McCarran's hearings on the IPR opened in July and lasted for almost a year with the SISS also investigating along the way subversive aliens, communist influence on youth, radio, television, movies and the telegraph industry, and red espionage. The committee's final report of July 1952 claimed that the IPR's purpose was "to serve international Communist interests and to affect adversely the interests of the United States." Pinpointing the conspiracy to sell out Chiang, the report concluded that "but for the machinations of the small group that controlled [the IPR], China would be free." In retrospect, it seems obvious their conclusion that a group of obscure scholars caused the communist takeover of China was nonsense, but at the time many newspapers and magazines accepted it uncritically.

The 1952 Election

Korea, administration corruption, and the exploiters of the second Red Scare such as McCarthy and McCarran drove the Democrats out of the presidency. Truman seized on the communist issue in 1947, but the far right took it back again in early 1950 and kept the Red Scare going. For the next two and a half years, "Give 'em Hell Harry" engaged in personal attacks on the McCarthyites, yet the more he talked the more publicity his critics received. And the more people came to believe in the conspiracy. Sensing a presidential victory for the first time since the high 1920s, the Republicans nominated Dwight D. Eisenhower, war hero and political novice. While pledged to purge government of "Communistic, subversive, or pinkish influence," "Ike" was a political moderate when compared with other leading lights of the GOP, including Generals Douglas MacArthur and Patrick Hurley, Joseph McCarthy, Robert Taft, and Styles Bridges. To placate the party's strong right-wing, Eisenhower chose Senator Richard Nixon as his running mate. Campaigning on the theme of "$K_1 C_2$"—Korea, communism, and corruption—Ike concentrated on the crooks and left the "commies" to his running mate, a strategy which worked well. Nixon played his role to the hilt, slashing away at Democratic presidential nominee Adlai Stevenson as "Adlai the appeaser," a man who "carries a Ph.D. from Dean Acheson's Cowardly College of Communist Containment." Eisenhower also pandered to the far right at times. In an appearance before the American Legion, he argued for "liberation" of communist countries, while Stevenson denounced McCarthy and McCarthyism before the same audience. Ike despised McCarthy and William Jenner for attacking General Marshall as a traitor, but it was impossible to snub them completely. After the Indiana Republican Jenner embraced him at a campaign rally, Eisenhower commented privately that "I felt dirty from the touch of the man." The general decided to make a swing through McCarthy's home state, in part, to make amends to Marshall. When McCarthy got wind of the plan, he confronted the candidate only to be blistered by a rare outburst of Eisenhower temper. However, the offending paragraph of praise for Marshall, war hero and staunch anti-communist, was excised in the name of a higher cause—ending "twenty years of treason."

McCarthy campaigned in ten states on behalf of his friends, including Connecticut, where William Benton faced a tough fight. A week before the election, the Wisconsin senator purchased time on network television and radio to attack Adlai Stevenson. Waving documents before the cameras in a manner perfected in hundreds of performances since Wheeling, McCarthy accused the Democratic nominee of trying to force communism on Italy, defending Alger Hiss, membership in various left-wing organizations, and surrounding himself with equally soft liberal advisers. The audience especially enjoyed the senator's repeated (and quite deliberate) "Alger—I mean Adlai" slips of the tongue. McCarthy did not campaign in the Massachusetts Senate contest between incumbent Henry Cabot Lodge and Democratic challenger John F. Kennedy. After hearing rumors that the Massachusetts Republican was conspiring against him, McCarthy vowed "to teach that bastard of a Lodge to suck eggs." A hefty contribution to McCarthy's re-election campaign from Joseph P. Kennedy did not hurt either. Besides, the Kennedy family had solid anti-communist credentials; Congressman Kennedy had denounced the China experts, Yalta, and General Marshall long before McCarthy's speech at Wheeling. After the election, McCarthy would give young Bobby Kennedy a job on his staff.

The 1952 campaign featured plenty of red-baiting all around. In Washington state, for example, incumbent Republican Senator Harry P. Cain and challenger Henry Jackson, both hardliners, charged each other with being soft on communism. Eisenhower alternately bemoaned the "witch-hunts" for communists and denounced the Yalta agreements as a betrayal. After pollsters revealed that Korea was the most important issue to the voters, Ike became a critic of the war, vowing to go there personally if elected. Democrats, including President Truman, denounced the general for stating in 1945 that the Russians desired friendship with the United States. To counter charges that he was "soft on communism" Adlai Stevenson endorsed the Smith Act, Truman's loyalty program, and the firing of communist teachers. He fought back against Nixon's vacuous alliterations with the charge that Eisenhower and his foreign policy adviser John Foster Dulles had closer ties to Alger Hiss than he, hence their guilt of "spiritual treason."

A record voter turnout gave Ike fifty-five percent of the popular vote and thirty-nine of the forty-eight states. Republicans gained control of both houses of Congress, but just barely, a clear indication that the Eisenhower grin meant more to the voters than McCarthy's rhetoric. The people of Wisconsin gave Senator McCarthy a second term, although he ran behind every other Republican on the ballot. Of the ten Republicans outside Wisconsin who received his help, six won their contests, including William A. Purtell, whose defeat of William Benton added to McCarthy's legend. Yet, because all six Democratic losers ran well ahead of Adlai Stevenson, Senator McCarthy probably hurt his friends more than he helped them. Such analysis might have sobered the jubilant senator momentarily, for he was not nearly as powerful as he thought.

Inquisition By Committee: "Naming Names"

McCarthyism may have dominated Washington politics during the early 1950s, in the sense that "Trumanism" prevailed during the late 1940s, but as the election results of 1950 and 1952 showed, Senator McCarthy was hardly a national powerhouse. The anti-communist hysteria of this period took many forms below the national level. State laws often followed the example of the federal government. Truman's loyalty program led to a majority of the states pushing through similar programs between 1947 and 1954.

After Congress passed the McCarran Act, nine states followed with omnibus anti-communist laws, some going so far as to outlaw the CPUSA altogether. Sometimes, the states copied legislation from each other to establish state loyalty boards, outlaw "subversive organizations," ban members of such groups from elective office, and create special task forces to compel obedience. The California legislature was especially fond of loyalty oaths, requiring them for every state employee, public housing residents, and all organizations requesting tax-exempt status. Nine hundred state employees refused to sign the Levering Oath which stated that the signer would not support groups "that advocate the overthrow of the Government of the U.S. or California by force or violence or other unlawful means." The resisters, none of them spies or saboteurs, were fired and blacklisted from their professions. Real Stalinist spies, of course, would not hesitate to sign oaths. Some states had their own versions of the House Committee on Un-American Activities and, like HCUA, they ignored the rights of accused subversives as they accumulated thousands of dossiers.

Education

Educators received the attentions of legislative committees during the Truman and McCarthy red scare, just as they had during World War I and the days of the Palmer raids. In the late 1940s, there were at most about fifteen hundred teachers and professors (out of one million) in the United States who at one time or another had either joined the CPUSA or sympathized with the party. With school boards, regents, trustees, and politicians bringing heavy pressure to bear on principals and college presidents to purge their schools of "reducators," the profession surrendered. The National Education Association rationalized that because communists had given up the right to think as individuals that they no longer had the privilege of teaching others. Professor Sidney Hook, a former Marxist, provided a more detailed argument for casting his former comrades out of the classroom. In "Heresey, Yes—But Conspiracy, No," Hook reasoned that purveyors of unpopular ideas should be protected under the First Amendment. Communists, however, as part of a conspiracy to overthrow the Constitution did not qualify for protection under law.

In 1952-53, Senator McCarran began hauling teachers and professors before his SISS.   Over one hundred subpoenaed witnesses took the Fifth Amendment rather than answer questions about their pasts and, as a result, many never taught again.   The California state legislature's Un-American Activities Committee put a liaison agent on every major university campus to collect data and monitor appointments.   They had plenty of company: the FBI, the Central Intelligence Agency, and the Civil Service all had their own investigators checking names.   The political purges took the jobs of at least six hundred educators, more than half of them in New York City, a relatively small number to be sure, but the cleansing process cost more than can be measured.   In such an atmosphere, many teachers and professors steered away from controversial subjects and radical readings.   A sterile, unblinking conformity settled over American schools for an entire generation.

The Scare Returns to Hollywood

Communist influence in entertainment intrigued the political vigilantes almost as much as education.   HCUA's 1947 investigation of communists in Hollywood had created panic among movie producers, who responded with a growing blacklist and anti-communist films.   All communists, according to the movies of this genre, engaged in espionage and the violent overthrow of the government. Reds did not look normal; they were either overweight or underweight, too well-dressed (indicating hypocrisy) or sloppy. They never laughed, always lied, and often killed in cold blood. Many of the films rewrote World War II history to reflect Cold War opinions; thus in *Operation Secret* (1952) the prime villain was not Hitler, but a French communist resistance fighter.   *My Son John* (1952) celebrated chauvinism and virulent anti-intellectualism. Slight and dark, John was led down the garden path to communism because he chose college and civilian government employment, unlike his football playing brothers who enlisted in the military.   But American values win in the end as John repents his sins just before being machine gunned gangster-style at the Lincoln Memorial.   *Big*

Jim McClain (1952) seemed to bring Hollywood full circle around with John Wayne (who also produced the film) as an HCUA process server battling reds in Hawaii. There was no happy ending in this film, for the communists hid behind the Fifth Amendment, just like the Hollywood Ten. The anti-communist message even crept into science fiction movies such as *Them* (1954), an allegorical thriller pitting giant mutant ants (the reds) against the FBI, the Los Angeles police, and the armed forces. Ironically, these films became victims of the capitalist market place as most of them lost money.

HCUA helped Hollywood producers prove the patriotism and fidelity of their employees. Beginning in 1951, the House committee began subpoenaing actors, writers, and directors, not to provide new information about the communist conspiracy in Hollywood, but to "name names." The committee already knew who had signed what petition and joined what red fronts back in the 1930s and 1940s. Movie people were called upon to betray their friends as an act of purification and as the price for avoiding various blacklists. Hollywood witnesses had three choices: invoke the First Amendment (freedom of speech and association) and risk jail (like the Hollywood 10), invoke the Fifth Amendment (against self-incrimination) and face the blacklists, or name names and hope to continue working. One witness in three chose to name names; the others refused. Nonprofit, patriotic organizations such as the American Legion, the Catholic War Veterans, and the Motion Picture Alliance for the Preservation of American Ideals began their own blacklists while others did it on a professional basis. Almost overnight, a network of collaborators developed: lawyers, doctors, religious figures, and even gossip columnists who counseled subpoenaed clients to cooperate and helped to clear their names.

The second Red Scare did much damage to Hollywood. Blacklisted writers sometimes continued their work under different names for a fraction of the pay. Actors and actresses, though, could not change their faces. A few killed themselves rather than face poverty and social ostracism; others went to Europe or to Broadway, which had no blacklist. Many got out of show business completely. The Hollywood social scene changed since friends no longer trusted one another. Life was not much better for those who chose to go through the degradation ceremony before HCUA. Most (not all) worked again, although they sometimes had to testify again and again before other committees. Edward G. Robinson got his name off the blacklist after five HCUA appearances and agreeing to have a ghost written article entitled "How the Reds Made a Sucker Out of Me" published under his name in *American Legion Magazine.* Years later, after the blacklists had finally been broken, Dalton Trumbo, one of the original Hollywood Ten could only conclude that "it will do no good to search for villains or heroes or saints or devils because there were none; there were only victims." Anyone, regardless of how they chose to answer, Trumbo argued, became a victim because they were asked. Even those who asked the questions sometimes became victims themselves, Senator McCarthy included.

The Scare Abates

Joe McCarthy had every reason to be optimistic as Truman yielded the White House to Dwight Eisenhower in early 1953. Leaders on both side of the senatorial aisle did not seem inclined to challenge him. Quickly putting together a staff for his new Permanent Subcommittee on Investigations, McCarthy helped to hammer out an agreement with rival anti-communist hunters, SISS and HCUA, so that the three would not be in direct competition. In spite of the unpleasant flap over General Marshall during the campaign, Joe liked Ike and the new secretary of state, John Foster Dulles. The honeymoon did not last. Soon, the junior senator would speak ominously of "twenty-one years of treason." Eisenhower, vowing that "I just will not—I refuse—to get into the gutter with that guy," dispatched the vice president to do the job for him. The president's strategy, McCarthy's irrational behavior, and a partial thaw in the Cold War all came together to bring the Red Scare to a close by the end of 1954.

Ike and Dulles at Bay

To appease right-wing Republicans who demanded that Ike "clean out" the Department of State, the president asked Congress to create the watchdog post of under secretary of state for administration and operations. The job went to the president of Quaker Oats, Donald B. Lourie (who was as politically innocent as the friendly fellow on the Quaker Oats box), while real power lay in the hands of his chief security officer, Scott McLeod, a close associate of Senator McCarthy. In his first three weeks on the job, McLeod sacked twenty-one career personnel for suspected homosexuality. The security chief and his agents snooped in desks and filing cabinets at all hours of the day and night in search of evidence. Foreign service officers stationed overseas found that their private letters had been steamed open. McLeod tapped telephones and subjected State Department people to lie detector tests. By the end of the year, almost five hundred had been let go, none with a hearing.

Morale plummeted as the atmosphere at Foggy Bottom came to resemble Stalin's foreign service. Secretary of State John Foster Dulles permitted McCarthy's surrogate to ride roughshod because he feared becoming a whipping boy for the Right—the way his friend Dean Acheson had during the Truman years. Dulles also felt vulnerable because, like Acheson, he had been close at one time to Alger Hiss. The Wisconsin senator opposed the confirmation of Harvard President James B. Conant to the High Commission of West Germany because the educator resisted congressional committees investigating alleged subversion on his campus. Conant's quick confirmation did not deter McCarthy and others on the far right from going after Charles E. Bohlen, Eisenhower's choice as ambassador to the Soviet Union. A distinguished career foreign service officer, Bohlen had served as Franklin Roosevelt's translator and adviser at the Yalta Conference. At his confirmation hearing, Republicans tried to trap Bohlen into admitting what many right-wingers took for granted: that Roosevelt had sold out Poland and China to the Communists. "I am going to oppose the nomination," McCarthy announced, "on ground that Bohlen was too important a part of the old Acheson machine in the State Department." When the appointment went before the full Senate, McCarthy suggested that Dulles was covering up derogatory information and that Bohlen should be subjected to a lie detector test. This strategy alienated Robert Taft and Majority Leader William Knowland, deeply conservative men who had long given Joe their support. Only thirteen senators voted against Bohlen, eleven Republicans, Pat McCarran, and one other Democrat. Eisenhower refused to criticize McCarthy in public; for as he confided to his diary on 1 April "that nothing will be so effective in combatting McCarthy's particular kind of troublemaking as to ignore him. This he cannot stand."

In the spring of 1953, HCUA turned its attention to communist infiltration of education and entertainment while SISS (chaired by McCarthy's friend William Jenner) searched for reds in schools and the United Nations. McCarthy decided to probe "mismanagement, subversion, and kickbacks" at the Voice of America. Created during World War II to broadcast anti-fascist propaganda, the VOA became an instrument of Truman's anti-communist foreign policy under the International Information Agency (IIA). When the subcommittee's investigation began to drag, McCarthy turned his attention to the IIA's Overseas Library Program, which had included a few books by Marxists but none considered overtly anti-American or pro-Soviet. The senator charged that the libraries contained over thirty thousand pro-communist books out of some two million volumes, a figure he derived by padding the list with anti-communist authors such as Arthur Schlesinger, Jr., John Dewey, Stephen Vincent Benet, moderate civil rights leader Walter White, Foster Rhea Dulles (a cousin of the secretary of state), and Whittaker Chambers. Panicky IIA librarians pulled the offending volumes and a few were consigned to flames. Two of McCarthy's youthful aides, Roy Cohn and David Schine, took the investigation to Europe where they intimidated IIA employes, ran up large hotel bills, and, on one occasion, swatted one another with rolled-up newspapers in front of startled onlookers. After hearing testimony from thirty-three witnesses, McCarthy could find no evidence of conspiracy, but from his point of view the investigation had been a success, once again garnering the spotlight.

President Eisenhower hoped to cut McCarthy down to size by ignoring him in public, winning away his allies in the Senate, and taking command of the subversives issue. On 27 April 1953, he issued Executive Order 10450 which gave every federal agency the power to conduct personnel evaluations. Derogatory information was to be forwarded to the FBI. The order specified that the attorney general was to keep the lists of subversive organizations up to date and provide the lists to the bureaucracies. Whereas Truman's program concentrated on "loyalty risks" (persons with possibly subversive beliefs and associations), Ike's plan centered on rooting out "security risks," a much broader term that included persons suspected of disloyalty, incompetence, dishonesty, disgraceful behavior, or immorality. By October, the president could boast that 1456 people had been fired under the new system, although only 342 were branded as security risks. The next month, in an exercise of vintage McCarthyism, Attorney General Herbert Brownell released an FBI report showing that President Truman had dismissed information that Assistant Secretary of the Treasury Harry Dexter White was a communist fellow traveler. After an angry Truman denounced the Eisenhower administration for stooping to McCarthy-style tactics, the senator demanded and received television time for reply. McCarthy spent most of his free air time attacking the president and secretary of state for failing to break with the "whining, whimpering appeasement" of their Democratic predecessors. Why, he asked, did the administration permit American allies to trade with China, an enemy holding American prisoners-of-war. Ike and Dulles issued indignant replies; so did McCarthy. The president had not fared very well in the power struggle against McCarthy by the end of 1953, when polls revealed that fifty percent of people rated McCarthy favorably, compared to thirty-two percent at mid-year and only twenty percent in the spring.

The Army-McCarthy Hearings

But McCarthy had already begun to dig his political grave. Members of both parties disliked the verbal assaults against the

Eisenhower administration and the ungentlemanly personal attacks on powerful Southern Democrats. Administration officials moved to discipline the maverick Republican by orchestrating the ouster of J.B. Mathews for writing an article in *American Mercury* charging that seven thousand Protestant clergymen supported "the Communist apparatus." In an unprecedented protest against his domineering chairmanship, Democrats boycotted McCarthy's subcommittee. Only the personal intercession of Vice President Nixon kept him from launching an embarrassing investigation of the Central Intelligence Agency. When McCarthy got wind of security problems at American military bases, including Fort Monmouth, New Jersey, he held hearings (as a subcommittee of one) without uncovering much in late 1953. Alarmed Army brass launched their own purge, dismissing civilian employees for such subversive acts as living with a radical father and joining the Young Pioneers at the age of twelve in 1933.

In December, McCarthy and his chief counsel, Roy Cohn, received a tip from General Ralph W. Zwicker on the case of Irving Peress, a dentist in the U.S. Army Reserves who had been ordered to active duty and promoted to Major in spite of having claimed "federal constitutional privilege" on loyalty forms in regard to membership in subversive groups. Determined to pursue the case as a symbol of bureaucratic incompetence, McCarthy hauled General Zwicker before the subcommittee. When the general attempted to avoid answering one of McCarthy's hypotheticals, the senator remarked that "anyone with the brains of a five-year-old child can understand that question." Zwicker's subsequent answer did not please McCarthy, who raged that he "is not fit to wear that uniform." The bullying cross-examination led Secretary of the Army Robert Stevens to forbid other officers from testifying before McCarthy's panel.

To keep the investigation going while a truce was arranged with the administration, Senator McCarthy presented a new "Red link": Annie Lee Moss, a Pentagon clerk tied by the FBI to the CPUSA, although the black mother of four was sent home until her health improved. With Robert Stevens scheduled to appear next, Republicans Karl Mundt, Everett Dirksen, and McCarthy met with the army secretary at lunch to arrange an armistice. In the chicken luncheon "Memorandum of Understanding," Stevens agreed to cooperate fully with the subcommittee, a statement the press interpreted as an abject surrender to McCarthy. President Eisenhower became angry enough to persuade Dirksen to revise the memorandum. At a news conference on 3 March, the president defended Stevens and his old comrade Zwicker without mentioning McCarthy by name, although he did concede that the Peress case had been botched. Responding to rumors that the president planned to denounce him at the news conference, McCarthy had a biting reply ready for reporters which turned out to be completely inappropriate to Ike's mild comments. One of the senator's closest friends in the media, Willard Edwards, later remembered the incident as "the day McCarthy died."

Hostility toward McCarthy continued to mount in March 1953. The Senate's "quiet man," Republican Ralph Flanders of Vermont, heaped scorn on his colleague for having nothing to show except "the scalp of a pink Army dentist" in a speech eliciting public praise from Eisenhower. Edward R. Murrow's television program "See It Now" on CBS showed clips of McCarthy in action, browbeating witnesses, making misstatements, burping, laughing at his own crude political jokes, and picking his nose. Murrow, who had presented previous programs on the injustices of the security screening process, the Harry Dexter White case, and the conflict between the ACLU and the American Legion in Indianapolis, had become incensed when one of McCarthy's aides threatened to expose the broadcaster as an "anti-anti-communist" unless he kept quiet. Many journalists had preceded Murrow in denouncing McCarthy including the Alsop brothers, Walter Lippmann, Quincy Howe, and Elmer Davis, but Murrow brought the senator into the American home through the power of television and refuted many of his charges systematically. "The terror," Murrow had commented, pointing toward a television viewing screen, "is right here in this room." When Annie Lee Moss returned to a subcommittee hearing well enough to testify, Americans shared her terror.

On 11 March, the same day as the Moss hearing, the White House released the "Adams Chronology," a report alleging that

Senator McCarthy and his staff had joined Roy Cohn in demanding that the Army give preferential treatment to G. David Schine, one of the senator's young consultants. To cover themselves, McCarthy, Cohn, and others manufactured eleven interoffice memoranda which suggested that the Army was using Schine as a hostage to thwart the Monmouth probe. A televised reply by Vice President Nixon to Adlai Stevenson's criticism of the Republican party as "half McCarthy and half Eisenhower" made it clear that the White House supported the Army and not McCarthy. Opinion pollsters found McCarthy's popular support to be fading. Even his hard-core supporters back in rural Wisconsin reportedly were unhappy with him for being that too preoccupied to help them battle against falling farm prices. Friends worried that McCarthy had become utterly dependent on alcohol and Roy Cohn.

On 16 March, the subcommittee decided to conduct public hearings into the Army-McCarthy controversy with Karl Mundt serving as chairman, although McCarthy retained the right of cross-examination. There was much more to the televised hearing than the privileges of Private Schine. Joseph McCarthy, who boasted in better days that "I don't answer accusations, I make them," was himself on trial. Just minutes after the hearing began, McCarthy interrupted with "Point of order, Mr. Chairman," a device he used hundreds of times to make personal comments. Before the hearings ended, professional and barroom comedians would be imitating him and people would laugh; the fear and respect were fading. The senator, Roy Cohn, and subcommittee counsel Ray Jenkins met their match in Joseph Welch, the counsel for the Army. When Jenkins introduced a photograph of Schine and Stevens standing together, Welch showed how the picture had been cropped, bringing back recollections of the doctored Tydings/Browder composite of four years earlier. During his testimony, McCarthy further irritated President Eisenhower with his call for two million government employees "to give us any information which they have." Convinced that McCarthy was wilting under the pressure, Ike would have no part of a Republican movement to take the Army-McCarthy hearing off television.

The most famous single incident in the hearing took place on 9 June, two weeks into Roy Cohn's testimony. After Welch had questioned Cohn about his draft status during the Korean War, the two men had come to an understanding whereby nothing further would be said about it in return for the subcommittee team keeping the name of Fred Fisher out of the proceedings. Originally Fisher had been part of Welch's team, but had been dropped after the revelation that that he belonged to the National Lawyers Guild, a group HCUA considered subversive. During Cohn's testimony, McCarthy interrupted to bring the Fisher matter up as a way of smearing Welch. "Until this moment, Senator," Welch then commented, "I think I never really gauged your cruelty or your recklessness." The Army counsel went on to explain the circumstances surrounding the young lawyer's dismissal. When McCarthy attempted to retake the offensive, Welch cut him off, saying "Let us not assassinate this lad further, Senator. You have done enough. Have you no decency, sir, at long last? Have you left no sense of decency?" Again, the Wisconsin senator resumed his attack, but Welch would have none of it and the spectators applauded him. Shortly thereafter, as the hearing recessed, a dazed McCarthy could only ask "What did I do? What did I do?"

The exchange over Fred Fisher did not finish McCarthy; neither did any other single incident. It was his behavior as a whole which repelled people. Republicans came to see McCarthy as a political liability. The hearings dragged on until 17 June, by which time Senator Flanders had introduced a resolution demanding that McCarthy be stripped of his chairmanships. When he ran into opposition from Republican leaders and Southern Democrats, Flanders substituted a resolution of censure for conduct unbecoming a senator. McCarthy lost a powerful defender in September with the death of Pat McCarran. On 2 December 1954, after much political maneuvering, the Senate voted 67-22 to "condemn" McCarthy for abusing the Gillette-Hennings Committee (which had investigated him in 1951-1952) and the current Watkins Committee (investigating him in 1954). The Eisenhowers took the McCarthys off their guest list. With the media all but ignoring him, McCarthy lost interest in political issues. He died on 2 May 1957, from the effects of chronic alcoholism at the age of 48.

In August 1954, the Senate passed the Communist Control Act, a law branding the CPUSA as "the agency of a hostile foreign power" which should be outlawed. During the congressional election campaign that fall, Republicans followed a strategy of "McCarthyism without McCarthy," with Vice President Nixon red-baiting Democrats in 30 states. Adlai Stevenson called it "McCarthyism in a white collar." This tactic, which the GOP had followed faithfully since the 1946 sweep did not work particularly well. The Democrats regained control of both houses in another unexceptional off-year campaign where local and economic issues and personalities took precedence.

The Senate condemnation of McCarthy made no difference to millions who remained faithful to him, among them the Catholic War Veterans, and those who believed what they read in the *Chicago Tribune, U.S. News and World Report,* and the Hearst syndicate. Many continued to follow the fictional exploits of another anti-communist tough-guy: Mickey Spillane's Mike Hammer, who waged a one-man war against "Red sons-of-bitches who should have died long ago." Kids kept reading comic books where the heroes beat up, ran over, burned, lynched, and fed to the sharks Commie agents of evil; men taking the law into their own hands, the reasoning went, because Washington was too permissive. Such echoes of the second Red Scare continued to be heard for years afterwards.

Legacies

"What did I do?" McCarthy had asked after his exchange with Joseph Welch. It is a question scholars are still asking about him. What McCarthy did was to provide Americans with a simplistic solution to the riddle of why the world's most powerful nation could not always have its way—because of a conspiracy of Soviet communists abroad and government officials at home. He was a little rough, some people thought, but the country needed him. He had files, charts, and graphs and he named names. The Senate caucus room where McCarthy's subcommittee did its work, journalist William S. White wrote, "stank with the odor of fear and the odor of monstrous silliness." McCarthy turned out to be a fraud. He never found a single communist spy, never provided the information which led to an indictment for treason, and never even uncovered one communist working on a classified defense project. He hurt the lives and careers of hundreds of people, demoralized the federal bureaucracy and the armed forces, and harmed the country's reputation in the world. Senator McCarthy held two presidents at bay and paralyzed the Senate. He was only one of many who sought to exploit fear of communism for political ends, but he was unhampered by any sense of restraint or propriety.

Truman, Eisenhower, Nixon, McCarran, J. Edgar Hoover and others contributed to the post-World War II Red Scare—this period of anxiety which fed on loathing of the Soviet Union, anger over the "loss" of China, confusion in regard to the stalemate in Korea and the battle for political power. During the second Red Scare, anti-communism had become virtually synonymous with American patriotism. The communist personified evil; the anti-communist American embodied goodness. According to this simplistic equation, the communists and their dupes were responsible for most all of the world's problems. The threat of communism seemed so pervasive, so monstrous, that opposition to it had become a reflex response. In America, a French journalist noted during this period, "a man can get away with saying absolutely anything, no matter how trivial, preposterous, obscene, or even treasonable, providing he begins and ends by saying 'I hate Communism.'" As politicians were anti-communist first and liberal or conservative second, anti-communism came to constitute an "invisible ideology."

Chapter 4

From Consensus to Travail, 1954-1968

The second Red Scare tapered off through the middle 1950s as the Cold War settled into an uneasy, nuclear-tipped stalemate and the conservative course of the Eisenhower administration reassured most Americans that the reds had been cleaned out of Washington and academia. In 1955, political scientist Samuel Stouffer concluded that less than one percent of the population seemed worried about the threat of communism in the United States, noting that "a picture of the average American as a person with the jitters, trembling lest he find a Red under the bed, is clearly nonsense." Government informers lost some of their glamor. The Supreme Court began to chip away at repressive laws and practices designed to contain domestic communism at the expense of individual civil liberties. A frank exchange of views between President Eisenhower and the post-Stalin leadership of the Soviet Union led to the "spirit of Geneva"—a new optimism that peaceful coexistence was possible.

The thaw did not last either at home or abroad. In 1956 twin crises in Eastern Europe and the Middle East heated up the Cold War. Demands for black civil rights and concern over intelligence gathering capabilities led the FBI to step up J. Edgar Hoover's obsessive crusade against the American Left. The High Court retreated in the face of increasing criticism. Extreme right-wing groups came into existence: the John Birch Society, the Minutemen, the American Nazi party, and several competing branches of the Ku Klux Klan. The liberal administrations of John F. Kennedy and

Lyndon B. Johnson were no less committed to anti-communism than Eisenhower. For all their differences, these three presidents shared a common failure: they did not come to terms with the momentous changes taking place in the underdeveloped areas of the world, especially Asia. The invisible ideology of anti-communism pushed the country into the Vietnam quagmire. The war, in turn, touched off a prolonged internal crisis which threatened to tear the country apart, rekindling leftist activism and, ultimately, repression.

Brief Thaw

The Senate condemnation of Joe McCarthy and the negative response to Republican red-baiting in the 1954 congressional elections wound down the Red Scare. Early in the following year, Harvey Matusow, a celebrated ex-communist informer responsible for naming over 200 names before congressional committees, confessed that he had fabricated testimony in a number of government cases. He went to jail in spite of SISS claims that it was all just another communist plot. At about the same time, former Republican Senator Harry Cain of the Subversive Activities Control Board (created by the McCarran Act) began a one-man campaign against the loyalty programs of Truman and Eisenhower, charging that they had gone too far and that the Attorney General's list of subversive organizations caused "distrust, suspicion and misgivings." Senate and House committees held hearings on the abuses of civil liberties which had taken place during the late hysteria. Congress cut maintenance costs out of the budget for the emergency detention centers set up under the McCarran Act.

Events abroad lessened Cold War fears as well. President Eisenhower brought about an armistice in Korea with veiled threats of nuclear force. He refused to send American troops to Southeast Asia to save French Indochina, although he worried about the long term effects of Vietnamese communism. After the death of Joseph Stalin in March 1953, Eisenhower took the opportunity to try a series of cautious peace initiatives which culminated in a Russian-American summit at Geneva in 1955, the first such affair in ten years.

There were limits to the thaw. Eisenhower, Secretary of State John Foster Dulles, and his brother Allen, chief of the Central Intelligence Agency, saw the Soviet Union behind every revolutionary and reformist movement in the world, no matter how autonomous or neutralist it claimed to be. John Foster Dulles regarded neutrality in the Cold War as an "immoral and shortsighted conception" but one step removed from communism. The Eisenhower-Dulles team did not hesitate to act when they thought they perceived the hand of Moscow at work. Ike authorized the CIA to orchestrate the overthrow the government of Iranian Prime Minister Muhammad Mossadegh, an ardent nationalist (and anti-communist) who had seized the vast oil holdings of the foreign-owned Anglo-Iranian Oil Company. After Iran, Ike and the Dulles brothers turned their attention to Guatemala, where a troublesome democratic regime under the leadership of Colonel Jacobo Arbenz Guzman nationalized huge, unused tracts of land from the United Fruit Company as part of a land reform program. On 18 June 1954, American airplanes bombed the capital and several towns with explosives and Coca-Cola bottles while a CIA-trained Guatemalan force marched over the border from Honduras. In keeping with the post Red Scare thaw, Eisenhower kept the interventions small and quiet. He understood the limits of American power and had little enthusiasm for a direct challenge of Soviet power.

The Supreme Court had not distinguished itself in defending the rights of radicals during the red scares. Oliver W. Holmes, Jr.'s opinion in *Schenck v. U.S.* (1919) that "the question in every case is whether the words used...create a clear and present danger" served as a rationalizing device for jailing "Reds" with unpopular opinions. Historian David Caute has described the high court during the second Red Scare under Chief Justice Fred Vinson as "a compliant instrument of administrative persecution and Congressional inquisition." The appointment of Earl Warren as chief justice and William J. Brennan as an associate brought about a signal period of judicial activism which, for a time, threatened to halt the worst abuses of Trumanism and McCarthyism. Ironically, as a young district attorney, Earl Warrren had prosecuted members of the Communist Labor Party for violating California syndicalism statutes during the first Red Scare. In *Peters v. Hobby* (1955) the court reversed the dismissal of a government employee on the technical ground that the Loyalty Review Board did not have authority to review the case. The next year, forty percent of the cases the high court agreed to hear involved subversion or communism. A college professor could not be fired, the court said in *Slochower v. Board of Regents,* solely because he had taken the Fifth Amendment before a Senate committee. In *Pennsylvania v. Nelson,* the court ruled that the Smith Act superceded state sedition laws, which made them null and void.

The court continued to dismantle the vehicles of repression in 1957. The informer system of the FBI received a body blow in *Jencks v. United States,* when the court ruled that witnesses' statements had to be made available to criminal defendants. On June 17, 1957 ("Red Monday" to a growing chorus of critics) the Supreme Court handed down four more decisions involving the Red Scares. *Service v. Dulles* reversed the dismissal of foreign service officer John Stewart Service by Secretary of State Dean Acheson on narrow grounds. *Yates v. United States* overturned the convictions of fourteen leading members of the CPUSA under the Smith Act and made further prosecutions under the omnibus legislation less likely. The Court took on HCUA in *Watkins v. United States,* ruling that the House committee had an obligation to inform witnesses in regard to the relevance of their questions. While the grounds were narrow again, the chief justice included a warning against abuses of congressional investigative powers. The *Sweezy v. New Hampshire* decision also contained a lecture for government, this time the state of New Hampshire, for "an invasion of petitioner's liberties in the areas of academic freedom and political expression." In these decisions and others in 1956-1957, all the high court had done, Earl Warren later wrote, was to prevent "rabid congressional committees from 'exposing for the sake of exposure,' from establishing 'guilt by association,' and from compelling witnesses to implicate themselves without regard to Fifth Amendment protection against self-incrimination." Congress could still probe subversive activities, and the executive branch still had the Smith Act and the loyalty program as anti-subversive tools.

Return to Repression

The court's decisions limiting congressional and executive witch hunting infuriated the president, leading him to comment on several occasions that his appointment of Earl Warren "was the biggest damn fool thing I ever did." Years later, Ike would tell Warren that "those Communist cases" proved that the chief justice had not been as conservative as he had hoped, adding that if he could have his way with American reds "I would kill the S.O.B.'s." Congressman Donald Jackson of HCUA charged that the Warren Court had made his committee and SISS "innocuous as two kittens in a cageful of rabid dogs." Senator James Eastland, chairman of SISS, issued a report implying that the court had given aid and comfort to the enemy. The backlash against the rulings spawned over 170 bills, most designed to curb court power in the area of subversion control. Southerners, outraged by the court's *Brown v. Board of Education* (1954) desegregation decision, forged a coalition with Northern anti-communists in the name of states' rights. Only the adroit political maneuvering of Senate Majority Leader Lyndon Johnson kept the Senate from passing several bills which had already sailed through the House. One bill restricting the impact of *Jencks v. United States* on FBI information did pass. By 1958 an alarmed Supreme Court began to retreat from libertarianism, upholding the firings of a Philadelphia school teacher and a New York subway conductor for refusing to answer questions about shady past associations. Subsequent decisions were also more in line with the anti-communist consensus.

The CIA

The brief thaw in the Cold War did not include the FBI and the CIA, shield bearers of the invisible ideology. Acting under a vaguely worded section in the National Security Act (1947), the CIA began undertaking covert actions in foreign nations to counter communist intrigue. No one questioned the legality—or the morality—of secret psychological, political, paramilitary, and economic operations the agency carried out in forty-eight countries between 1947 and 1954. A special commission chaired by former

President Herbert Hoover advised Eisenhower, in effect, that the ends justified the means in the Cold War struggle. "Hitherto acceptable norms of human conduct do not apply," the report continued. "If the United States is to survive, long-standing American concepts of 'fair play' must be reconsidered." The overthrow of governments in Iran and Guatemala represented only the tip of the iceberg. In underdeveloped nations, the CIA extended financial support to politicians and statesmen of every political stripe, save the extreme left, to foster stability. In smaller countries, the agency could buy the support of key political and military elites for less than a million dollars, a small price to pay for the avoidance of "another China."

Closer to home, the CIA began looking at Americans' mail in 1952, intercepting over 28 million items over the next twenty years. Communist "brainwashing" experiments on prisoners-of-war during the Korean conflict led the intelligence agency to conduct its own tests. In "Operation Midnight Climax" (1955) CIA-hired prostitutes in San Francisco gave their customers the hallucinatory drug LSD and other potent concoctions while agents observed the results behind one-way mirrors. Between 1957 and 1961, a highly respected psychiatrist, working under CIA contract in Montreal, gave unwitting mental patients LSD daily for months along with severe shock treatments in an effort to "de-pattern" personality traits. Although the National Security Act forbade the CIA from operating inside the United States, the agency ignored the will of Congress in the name of a higher law, national security against communism.

The FBI

The FBI did at home what the CIA did overseas; it gathered intelligence on individuals and groups deemed subversive and harassed them covertly. The bureau investigated every member of the Communist Party as well as other groups which the reds might be using as fronts. The FBI watched every group deemed "left of center" under the COMINFIL program. Because the CPUSA and several black organizations shared an interest in civil rights, the bureau considered them as potential fronts. Trusted in opinion polls above all others (including Eisenhower) to deal with the communist problem, J. Edgar Hoover had increased his power and prestige by frequently issuing dire warnings about the strength of the communist movement. Although CPUSA's membership had declined rapidly after 1948, the bureau had almost 1,600 agents and 5,000 "subversive informants" to keep tabs on the party and other subversive groups.

For Hoover, the Supreme Court's concern over civil liberties could not have come at a worse time. The successful Montgomery, Alabama bus boycott threatened to make the cause of civil rights a mass movement, potentially exploitable by communists. The high court had emasculated the Smith Act, reduced the power of such reliable Hoover allies as HCUA and the Subversive Activities Control Board, and required bureau agents to make pretrial testimony available to defense lawyers. Consequently, in August 1956, the FBI developed a secret counter-intelligence program (COINTELPRO) which formalized the long-standing program of harassing remnants of CPUSA. In this massive operation, which one critic dubbed "underground McCarthyism," the bureau created material to foment party dissent, leaked tips to the news media, kept federal, state, and local government authorities posted on members' movements, and informed employers anonymously of "radical or immoral activity." Hoover's agency also used "dirty tricks" against CPUSA, creating chaos at rallies, meetings, and press conferences by phoning in rental hall cancellations, infiltrating the party with troublemakers, packing meetings with vocal anti-communists, and feeding disconcerting questions for communist officials to friendly journalists.

COINTELPRO succeeded almost too well. By 1959, factional bickering had all but destroyed the CPUSA. The collapse was so complete that the FBI chief told HCUA he smelled a rat. "The Communist Party of the United States," he commented, "is not out of business; it is not dead; it is not even dormant. It is, however, well on its way to achieving its current objective, which is to make you believe that it is shattered, ineffective, and dying." Hoover's anti-communist offensive also wrecked many lives along the way. For example, in one of over two thousand COINTELPRO operations, the FBI broke into the car of CPUSA National

Committee member William Albertson and planted a "snitch jacket" to make it appear that the long-time party member had turned bureau informant. CPUSA officials drummed Albertson out of the party as a traitor to communism, ostracizing him socially as well. His conviction under the Smith Act made employment impossible. Shortly after his house burned down, William Albertson died broke and bitter. In March 1960, with few communists left to persecute, Hoover expanded COINTELPRO to keep the CPUSA from infiltrating organizations such as the National Association For the Advancement of Colored People (NAACP) and the Boy Scouts of America. To cover himself and the bureau in the event of disclosure, Director Hoover gave Presidents Eisenhower and Kennedy briefings on COINTELPRO in the context of counterespionage activities, deliberately misleading his superiors as the bureau no longer considered CPUSA a real sabotage or espionage threat. He need not have worried: in the 1950s and early 1960s the invisible ideology of anti-communism made the FBI a sacrosanct state-within-a-state.

The Anti-Communist Consensus of the 1950s

The prolonged Red Scare after World War II made America as a whole more conservative and more willing to accept authoritarianism in the crusade against communism. Intellectuals were not immune from this trend. Writers who had toyed with communism, socialism, or the Progressive party of Henry Wallace took a long second look at democracy and capitalism in the 1950s. Clearly, they liked what they saw, especially the politics of compromise and the New Deal-style welfare state. While intellectuals such as Reinhold Niebuhr, Arthur Schlesinger, Jr., Daniel Bell, Seymour Martin Lipset, and Oscar Handlin still thought of themselves as social critics, their strictures were mild. They preferred to celebrate the new consensus with its complacent middle class, practical politics, economic prosperity, social conformity, and a labor movement dominated by leaders in the mold of Sam Gompers. The repressive Soviet system and boom times at home made it easy to forsake radicalism. Many agreed with Bell's "end of ideology" theory, the view that an objective base for following theories and practices in the service of radical political change no longer existed since the American system had already solved such basic problems as class conflict. Leftist dogmas were out; in came realism, capitalism, the welfare state, consensus, and the two-party system, all underpinned with the invisible ideology. Without realizing it, the intellectuals of the 1950s had not abandoned ideology so much as they had exchanged one set of ideas for another.

Some who had supported the old left through the first Red Scare, the 1920s, and the Great Depression—including Max Eastman, John Dos Passos, James Burnham, and Whittaker Chambers—not only abandoned Marxism, but became ultraconservative, anti-communist crusaders. For this group, which found a rallying point in William F. Buckley Jr.'s *National Review*, Senator McCarthy was to be deplored only because he gave anti-communism a bad name. While most intellectuals despised McCarthy, there was consensus that, because of its conspiratorial nature, communism had no legitimate part to play in the American marketplace of ideas.

The favorite politician among intellectuals was Adlai Stevenson. The Democratic nominee for president in 1952 and 1956 considered himself a liberal, but he was almost as conservative as Eisenhower. Stevenson defended the Truman/Acheson containment policy and the loyalty programs while skirting traditional liberal concerns such as poverty, black civil rights, and improving the lot of the working class. Ike came to the White House pledged to banish "the Left-Wingish, pinkish influence in our life," but in spite of some budget cutting the welfare state continued to grow unabated during his years in the White House because the public did not want to dismantle the New Deal. *Fortune* caught the political temper of the times when it noted that "Conventional political categories such as 'right' and 'left' are almost useless, both are scrambled together as an omelet." Eisenhower emerged as the most popular politician of the period because his policies reflected the consensus of the 1950s, a combination of political moderation, militant anti-communism, and defense of the status quo.

President Eisenhower's greatest accomplishments in foreign policy were negatives. Early on, he ended the Korean war and refused to bail out the French in Indochina. In 1956, the president avoided the temptation to give aid to Hungarians engaged in a revolt against the Soviets, understanding that short of total war, the U.S. lacked the means to carry out Republican promises of "liberation." That same year, he kept the United States out of the Suez crisis and forced Israel, Britain, and France to halt their military operations against Egypt. The president also helped to defuse crises with "red" China over the offshore islands of Quemoy and Matsu and with the Soviet Union over Berlin. Just before leaving office, he warned the nation that "the military-industrial complex" so necessary to safeguard the nation and the world from communism was undermining the economy, the political system, and higher education. In the end, the president had understood more than most the dangers behind the anti-communist crusade.

Anti-Communism on the New Frontier

"These have been the years of conformity and depression," Norman Mailer complained about the 1950s. "A stench of fear has come out of every pore of American life, and we suffer from a collective failure of nerve." John F. Kennedy offered the country a way out of the Eisenhower administration's seeming complacency, just as Ike's candidacy had held the implicit promise of an end to the Truman quagmire eight years earlier. "Superman Comes to the Supermarket" was how Mailer described Kennedy's appeal. A liberal in domestic matters, JFK had impeccable anti-communist credentials. As a senator, he had chided Eisenhower for failing to understand the role of nationalism in the postwar world, a misconception which hindered the fight against communism. In the campaign of 1960, Kennedy repeated the charges of columnist Joe Alsop, General James Gavin and others that a dangerous "missile gap" between the United States and the Soviets had developed under Eisenhower. He used this allegation (totally false, it turned out) as a way of using the invisible ideology of anti-communism against the Republicans without mentioning the popular Ike by name.

The highlight of the 1960 presidential campaign between Kennedy and Vice President Richard Nixon occurred in a series of debates, where the candidates argued over who would take on the communists with greater determination. Kennedy's very slim victory over Nixon created a mood of excitement in the country, David Halberstam wrote, a feeling "that America was going to change, that the government had been handed down from the tired, flabby chamber-of-commerce mentality of the Eisenhower years to the best and brightest of a generation." In his inaugural address, Kennedy promised that "we shall pay any price, bear any burden, meet any hardship, support any friend, oppose any foe to assure the survival and success of liberty." This bold and idealistic rhetoric concealed an arrogance unmatched since Wilson and an ignorance of global complexities. During his administration, some called Kennedy "young Truman," a sobriquet he did not mind. Townsend Hoopes, who served under both Truman and Eisenhower, found that "the fervent anti-Communist absolutes of John Foster Dulles were embedded in the very bone structure of John Fitzgerald Kennedy's inaugural address." Both comparisons were apt; for Kennedy and the intellectuals who came to Washington with him did not reevaluate the basic conceptual framework of their predecessors. Trapped by the invisible ideology, the exigencies of politics, and their own rhetoric, the liberal Democrats of the 1960s only modernized and upgraded the policies of Truman and Eisenhower. Results included continuing repression of the Left at home, nuclear brinksmanship, and a deepening obsession with Vietnam.

The Kennedy administration's new brand of activism proved contagious to a new generation of college students. The civil rights movement captured the imagination of those who went south during summer vacations. Many students became radicalized by the experience as did the young idealists sent overseas by the Peace Corps. For a time, dissent became more acceptable. President Kennedy rehabilitated several Red Scare victims with awards or appointments, including J. Robert Oppenheimer, "father" of the Atomic bomb denied a security clearance under Eisenhower, Philip Jessup, Henry Wallace, and Charles Bohlen. The president pardoned Julius Scales, a repentant ex-communist convicted under the Smith Act and suspended CPUSA prosecutions based on mere party membership. The Post Office allowed foreign communist literature to go through the mail.

Persecuting a New Generation

Like the domestic thaw of the middle 1950s, the relaxation of Cold War tensions at home in the early sixties was only partial. With support from Attorney General Robert Kennedy, the House passed a bill designed to negate the *Yates* decision against the Smith Act. Five states approved tough new anti-communist laws. The Kennedys prosecuted communists under the Taft-Hartley and McCarran Acts as well as students who defied a ban on travel to Cuba. At no time did the Kennedy administration question the loyalty apparatus built up under Truman and Eisenhower, the Attorney General's List, or the state-within-a-state authority of Hoover's FBI. By the time of Kennedy's presidency, Sanford J. Ungar has written, the bureau had become so powerful "that it had utterly lost the capability to recognize and examine its weaknesses." A 1962 Walt Disney film portraying "Federal security agents" in a humorous light caused J. Edgar Hoover to comment that "I am amazed Disney would do this: He probably has been infiltrated." After membership in the CPUSA dipped below ten thousand, Hoover decided that such statistics were "classified." The party had become too valuable as a paper tiger for the director to admit that it had virtually ceased to exist. COINTELPRO activities against CPUSA expanded during the Kennedy years. In 1961, Hoover launched parallel operations against the Socialist Workers Party, including a successful campaign to persuade the Boy Scouts of America not to renew the charter of a New Jersey troop whose scoutmaster was a suspected Trotskyite.

The FBI kept an eye on civil rights groups under the category of "racial matters," lest the Communists seek to exploit black unrest. From 1957 to 1962, the bureau monitored the Southern Christian Leadership Conference (SCLC) and its founder, Dr. Martin Luther King, Jr., since Hoover and other top bureau officials found King's use of mass demonstrations and extralegal nonviolent resistance to be a potentially subversive and a menace to national security. On 8 January 1962, an Atlanta-based civil rights group associated with the SCLC issued a report critical of the FBI for standing by while demonstrators were beaten in Albany, Georgia. That same day, Hoover wrote to Attorney General Kennedy to report that Stanley Levison, "a member of the Communist Party, USA...is allegedly a close advisor to the Reverend Martin Luther King, Jr." A white attorney, Levison had done financial work for CPUSA between 1952 and 1955. Convinced that King was "no good," Hoover upgraded the civil rights leader's status to "communist" and ordered up a COINTELPRO-style operation against him. The attorney general approved the tapping of Levison's telephone. Stories soon appeared in friendly newspapers based on bureau leaks charging SCLC staff member Jack O'Dell with Communist party affiliation. In June 1963, with the administration committed to passage of a comprehensive civil rights bill and Director Hoover threatening to destroy Martin Luther King, President Kennedy extracted a promise from the civil rights leader to disassociate himself from Levison and O'Dell.

Later that summer, on the eve of the March on Washington demonstration, the FBI's domestic intelligence prepared a lengthy report concluding that the miniscule CPUSA (down to 4,453 members) had failed to influence the civil rights movement. An enraged Hoover rejected this analysis and his obedient subordinates reversed themselves. After King delivered his "I Have a Dream" address at the March on Washington, Assistant Director William Sullivan wrote that "We must mark him [King] now, if we have not done so before, as the most dangerous Negro of the future in this Nation from the standpoint of communism, the Negro and national security." Worried that King had not broken contact with his former communist friends and believing that the FBI could not be wrong, the Kennedys gave the go ahead for intensive surveillance of the civil rights leader. The bureau would dog King's every step for the last five years of his life. He was not a communist and neither was the civil rights cause. "It was a Christian movement," one participant later remembered, "and Christians and Communists just don't mix." Anti-communism had blinded the FBI and the administration to the difference between dissent and communism.

Updating Anti-Communism

In the realm of foreign policy, the liberal intellectuals of the New Frontier were more aggressively anti-communist than the Eisenhower conservatives they replaced. Scorning the religious fervor of John Foster Dulles, their analysis seemed to reflect a more sophisticated understanding of the Cold War, a notion that the United States would have to present an activist alternative to communism if they were to best Khrushchev and Mao in the struggle for the "hearts and minds" of underdeveloped countries. The new administration set out to win the conflict against communism and restore order to the world. Just as Ike had won in 1952 by promising to go to Korea, so JFK won in 1960 by pledging, in effect, to embrace the military-industrial complex and close the missile gap. The president and Secretary of Defense Robert McNamara also sought to develop the capability of fighting two major wars and a minor conflict at one time. Ignoring Eisenhower's farewell caveat, the new team threw budgetary cautions to the wind, lengthening the American lead in nuclear weapons and delivery systems while developing counterinsurgency techniques to foster noncommunist political stability.

President Kennedy took a special interest in the creation of mobile strike forces to extinguish brushfire wars. Other techniques developed to fight communism in what was being called the "Third World" included training native police in riot control and interrogation techniques, tutoring bureaucrats, New Deal-style flood control and transportation projects, and community action programs. The ambitious Alliance for Progress envisioned social reform and economic growth in Latin America to blunt the appeal of the Cuban revolutionary example. Most of these programs had been tried before. The Peace Corps proved to be the most original contribution to the Kennedy offensive. Here too, as Garry Wills notes, "the implicit message, underneath the laudable desire to serve, was anti-Communist even when crude propagandizing was excluded. The message was: be like us."

When John Kennedy became president, there were eight hundred American advisers in South Vietnam; by the time of his assassination there were more than sixteen thousand, many of them advisers in name only. Ten years after the fact, Kennedy aide Kenneth O'Donnell claimed that the president had hinted in mid-1963 that he would pull out of Vietnam after the 1964 elections, saying "If I tried to pull out completely now from Vietnam we would have another Joe McCarthy red scare on our hands." If true, the comment reveals how much the invisible ideology ruled Washington politics in the 1960s. In a September 1963 interview, he reaffirmed his belief in the relevance of the domino theory, Ike's analogy that if one country fell to communism, others around it would tumble down too. "What I am concerned about," the president said, "is that Americans will get impatient and say, because they don't like events in Southeast Asia and they don't like the Government in Saigon, that we should withdraw. That only makes it easy for the Communists. I think we should stay." JFK made a dangerous situation he inherited from Eisenhower even more hazardous for Lyndon Johnson.

Far Right Anti-Communists

The Cold War policies of Eisenhower and Kennedy did not satisfy all Americans. The far right-wing of the Republican party and some Christian fundamentalists found contemporary political trends to be unacceptable. For these groups, the Soviet Union and China did not pose the greatest immediate threat to the American way of life. Rather, domestic communism, subversion from within, had undermined religion, the family, the schools, and business in the most diabolical conspiracy in history. "THIS IS NEITHER EXAGGERATION NOR FANTASY," wrote Robert Welch, founder of the John Birch Society. "The Communist conspiratorial apparatus is now closing in, with every conceivable pressure and deception, on all remaining resistance to the establishment of its police state over our own country." To people like Welch, the invisible ideology of anti-communism took on an all-consuming importance. The great danger of communism became a shorthand symbol for everything that was wrong with modern life, a feeling that, as radio personality Paul Harvey put it: "I am a displaced person, though I never left my homeland. I am a native-born American. I never left my country. It left me."

Fundamentalism

Fundamentalists preach the "old time" religious ideology of the Bible as literal truth. In the eternal struggle between God and Satan, they believe, the Antichrist conspires with evil men to demolish the true faith and all institutions associated with it, including capitalism. The rabid fears of communism engendered by the Cold War caused many fundamentalists to look to the political far right, which offered a conspiratorial explanation of history quite compatible with their religious millennialism. A defrocked Presbyterian minister, Dr. Carl McIntire, was one of the first to see the enormous potential in politicizing fundamentalism. In the early 1950s, McIntire latched on to the coat tails of Joe McCarthy, paralleling the senator's charges against the State Department with wild broadsides against communist infiltration of most Protestant sects. A decade later, hundreds of radio stations carried McIntire's "Twentieth Century Reformation Hour" and he received over a million dollars in annual contributions. By that time, though, Billy James Hargis had emerged as the most important preacher on the far right. Hargis first attracted attention during McCarthy's heyday, when McIntire put him in charge of a project to employ balloons to float thousands of Bibles behind the Iron Curtain. He built an empire based on a radio network, television programs, and American Christian College. Like so many on the radical right, Hargis did not seem concerned about the possibility of war with the Soviets; for, as he explained in *Communist America: Must It Be?*, "America reduced to rubble would be of no value to the Communists." Hargis saved his heaviest fire for what he called "the powerfully entrenched Liberal Establishment" which was under "a satanic influence" when it banned school prayers and reshaped America in the Soviet image with civil rights. "The antidote to every Communist intrigue," he wrote, "is to do the opposite, for all of Communism is based upon a lie."

Another McIntire discovery, Frederick Schwarz, an Australian physician, gained notoriety for "expert" testimony before HCUA on the communist blueprint for world conquest. Schwarz' *You Can Trust the Communists (To Be Communists)* sold over one million copies. His Christian Anti-Communism Crusade sponsored thousands of seminars on the communist conspiracy, which Schwarz predicted would take over the country by 1973. Explosions rocked the homes of ministers who dared to criticize the crusade in California. Tension mounted as Schwarz brought his crusade to Oakland in early 1962, boasting such faculty as Senator Thomas Dodd (chairman of SISS), Congressman Walter Judd, and other right-wing favorites. A team of political scientists who studied this crusade reported that two out of every three participants identified themselves as Republicans. While most all had voted for Richard Nixon in 1960, a majority said they preferred the more conservative Barry Goldwater for president. More than one third believed that their neighbors were communists. The great majority said that domestic communists posed a far graver threat than the Communist Bloc, an answer the political scientists expected. What surprised the academics was that less than one in five favored war with the Soviet Union, leading them to the conclusion "that isolationism, rather than aggressiveness, is the hallmark of many radical rightists' foreign-policy sentiments." In this respect, the adherents to the radical right differed markedly from those a decade earlier who identified themselves as followers of McCarthy. The Christian Crusade appealed to the middle class, also a departure from the pattern of McCarthyism, which drew its support from people with little formal education and menial, low income occupations. For the most part, the same characteristics applied to the largest organization of the far right, the John Birch Society.

The John Birch Society

Robert Welch was a successful businessman. With degrees from the University of North Carolina and Harvard Law School, he rose to the vice presidency of a large candy company and later held a similar position at the National Association of Manufacturers. He also dabbled in politics, losing a race for the Massachusetts lieutenant-governorship. Dwight Eisenhower's defeat of Robert Taft at the 1952 Republican convention disillusioned Welch. He later gave credence to the rumor that "the peculiar cancer of which Bob Taft died was induced by a radium tube planted in the upholstery of his Senate seat." In 1954, Welch wrote a book on the life of U.S. Army Captain John Birch, a Baptist missionary/soldier killed by Chinese communists in 1945 because he represented the only forces capable of resisting the Antichrist, America and Christianity. "With his death and in his death," Welch wrote, "the battle lines were drawn in a struggle from which either Communism or Christian-style civilization must emerge with one completely triumphant and the other completely destroyed." Having set up the apocalyptic framework, Welch founded the John Birch Society in 1958 because, as he put it, "I simply had to pick up and carry, to the utmost of my ability and energy, the torch of a humane righteousness which he [Birch] was carrying so well and so faithfully when the Communists struck him down." Welch organized local chapters to influence and keep watch on churches, schools, and the Parent-Teacher Association.

The John Birch Society combined the economic conservatism of the old Liberty League with the anti-communism of Joe McCarthy. Welch expended much of his energy developing a comprehensive conspiracy theory to explain how the United States came to be "60 to 80 per cent" under communist control. It all began with the Illuminati, an eighteenth century Masonic order founded by Adam Weishaupt in 1776 "to impose the brutal tyranny of their rule over the whole human race." The Illuminati, Welch contended in resurrecting old falsehoods, stirred up the French Revolution and employed Karl Marx to write the *Communist Manifesto*. In the twentieth century, it started both world wars, the Russian Revolution, and the United Nations. "History's most diabolical, long-range conspiracy...." he wrote, "now, has the world almost completely within its grasp" thanks to the work of traitors like Franklin D. Roosevelt (recognition of Russia and Pearl Harbor), George Marshall (a communist agent), and Harry Truman (a communist dupe). But communism made its greatest inroads under Dwight Eisenhower. In the first private edition of *The Politician*, Welch explained that Ike "is a dedicated, conscious agent of the Communist conspiracy...beyond any reasonable doubt." Other agents included the Dulles brothers and Milton Eisenhower, who supposedly headed the American communist party. Welch's charges against the popular Ike angered the far right enough that he later toned them down. His absurd conspiracy theories continued to attract followers to the John Birch Society and at the same time repelled conservative politicians such as Senators Barry Goldwater and John Tower, who denounced Welch. At first, William F. Buckley, Jr., a leading conservative celebrity, applauded the society but eventually excoriated the "paranoid and unpatriotic drivel" emanating from Welch's monthly *American Opinion* magazine. While he never abandoned his grand conspiracy theories, Welch launched a number of new campaigns in the middle 1960s which many conservatives could support such as the impeachment of Earl Warren, promotion of a "Liberty Amendment" to repeal income tax, saving the Panama Canal from Panama, getting the U.S. out of the U.N., exposing "the civil rights fraud," and a drive, by bumper sticker, to "support your local police."

The Extremist Network

Welch was not the only businessman interested in rescuing America from communism. The Coast Federal Savings and Loan Association of Los Angeles gave out over two million pieces of anti-communist literature. Joe Crail, the bank's president, explained that "anti-communism builds sales and raises employee performance." Many large corporations donated to the radical right. Texas oil man H. L. Hunt spent a million dollars a year battling communism through sponsorship of radio programs like "Life Line," which presented "freedom talks" every night on over 200 outlets. In the middle 1950s, General Electric hired a movie actor to host their weekly dramatic TV show and lecture audiences "concerning internal Communism and how it operated," an eight year experience which groomed Ronald Reagan to be the consummate anti-communist politician a few years later. Military men occasionally joined the crusade. Major General Edwin Walker circulated right-wing propaganda among his troops in Germany. After his forced retirement, the general led a rebellious group against his former comrades when the Kennedy administration desegregated the

University of Mississippi. Billy James Hargis soon signed Walker for the Christian Crusade Against Communism and he became a leading drawing card for his denunciations of recent presidents. Even among military people, General Curtis LeMay had been a war hawk. A former Air Force chief of staff, "Bombs Away" LeMay became a darling of the far right for his demand that North Vietnam be bombed "back to the Stone Age." When George Wallace tried to seize control of the radical right in 1968, he chose LeMay as his running mate.

Billy James Hargis brought the biggest names in extremism under one roof periodically for Christian Crusade conventions. Listeners could hear Hargis, General Walker, Robert Welch and a host of others explain over and over again that the reds had already taken control of the White House, Congress, the media, churches, and unions. In Houston and Los Angeles, where right-wing political revivalism burned brightest in the early 1960s, membership in the various crusades, caucuses, and societies frequently overlapped. The Houston Junior Chamber of Commerce, for example, sponsored Freedom-In-Action, a semisecret political society dedicated to stamping out "the poison of communism whether labeled as liberalism, socialism, welfare statism, or communism." Welch and Hargis, in turn, endorsed the political group to their followers.

The radical right also had its own grapevine which quickly spread rumors concerning creeping communism through letters, telegrams, phone calls, and petitions. In March 1963 the Army was to begin "Exercise Water Moccasin III," a field operation in Georgia designed to give American officers and soldiers from allied countries practical experience in counterinsurgency. A small band of drill instructors playing the role of communist guerillas would invade Claxton, Georgia, where the local citizenry considered cooperation to be part of their duty as anti-communist citizens. Before the exercise began, though, the Texas Voters for Enforcing the Constitution got wind of it and reported in a newsletter that "these foreign troops entering these United States in this huge Trojan Horse ruse will never leave our shores once they are permitted to make these illegal, unlawful landings upon our soil and 'occupy' our sovereign states." Another radical right group, the Keep America Committee, reprinted the alarming news, as did the Conservatives in their paper, where The Network of Patriotic Letter Writers of Pasadena, California picked it up and printed part of the rumor as a pamphlet. By the time word reached Defenders of the American Constitution, Inc., the Army's anti-communist exercise had become "the beginning of a crash program to disarm the U.S.A. and make us a province of the UN." California Congressman James B. Utt embellished the story with a lurid fantasy about African troops. Other groups printed up Utt's remarks, which sold for two cents a piece in John Birch Society American Opinion bookstores. The rumors spread in a thousand different directions from Welch's outlets: newspapers, religious bulletins, and even the *Congressional Record* reported the rumors as gospel. A mountain of mail arrived at Capitol Hill complaining about naked cannibals marching through Georgia and red Chinese pouring across the Canadian and Mexican borders. In March, the people of Claxton were disappointed to learn that Water Moccasin III had been curtailed drastically due to pressure from Congress. Ironically, officers who would have participated in the exercise were shipped out to Vietnam a little less prepared to deal with communism.

The civil rights movement and the Cold War created enough anxiety to foster a reincarnation of the Ku Klux Klan. This time, though, the so-called "Third Klan" consisted of a dozen distinct organizations, often competing with one another for membership and attention. In the late 1950s and early 1960s Southerners opposed to integration were more likely to turn to White Citizens Councils as a more respectable outlet for protest. Council literature portrayed the civil rights movement as communist dominated. Liberals and their welfare state were all part of the conspiracy. When integration proceeded unabated, many of the million or so council members dropped out, leaving rump organizations similar to the Klan in tactics and outlook which became part of the informal radical right network. The Louisiana White Citizens Council, for example, published a biweekly newspaper stridently anti-black in tone, but also reported statements and speeches by Robert Welch and Gerald L.K. Smith, who still ranted about "the twins of the antiChrist, Zionism and Communism."

The Movement in Decline

In the increasingly crowded field on the far right, not every organization was welcomed by the others with open arms. Two such groups received negative media attention out of all proportion to their numbers. In 1959, George Lincoln Rockwell formed the American Nazi party. With, at most, a dozen followers the Nazis divided their time between dressing up in uniforms and cranking out hate literature. Many rightists found the Nazi's homosexual role playing and open worship of Hitler to be revolting. Others disapproved of the activities of Robert De Pugh, who organized the Minutemen as a right-wing guerilla army. Building a fortune from the manufacture and sale of vitamins for dogs, De Pugh joined the John Birch Society, but the patriotic leaders he met disappointed him intellectually. De Pugh formed his armed resistance group in 1960 with headquarters at Independence, Missouri. The next year, he took out classified advertisements looking for recruits to join him in a weekend of anti-communist military training. Only twenty people showed up, but the Minutemen made national news. De Pugh's "On Target" newsletter caught the media's attention, especially an article warning congressmen who had voted against HCUA: "Traitors, beware! Even now the cross hairs are on the back of your necks." President Kennedy denounced "armed bands of civilian guerillas." Attorney General Robert Kennedy asked Walter and Victor Reuther, leaders of the United Auto Workers Union, for suggestions on how to deal with right-wing extremists. Four of the five recommendations dealt with generalities; the only specific was that "the Administration should take steps to end the Minutemen." Robert Welch did not like the Minutemen either. He expelled DePugh from the John Birch Society in 1963 for blatant anti-semitism. The Minutemen continued to operate, but in and out of trouble with the law—on charges raging from kidnapping to possession of rocket launchers to attempted murder—the bad boys of the far right.

Robert Welch's attempts to change the image of the John Birch Society by concentrating on more positive issues and purging the outlaws came too late. The radical right's strength had peaked in the mid-1960s. The movement was never as powerful as it seemed. The largest corporations, no matter how conservative, had not approved of Hargis, Welch, and their friends; their stake in the status quo was far too great. Bad publicity from liberal and conservative media sources also diminished interest. Perhaps most important, fear of the country falling behind the Russians in strategic arms faded away, thereby depriving extremists of the hysterical atmosphere of anti-communism on which they thrived.

Liberal Agony and Vietnam

The anti-communism of twentieth-century American liberalism and the Texas frontier merged in the presidency of Lyndon Johnson. To justify his foreign policy, Johnson quoted Woodrow Wilson as saying "that we created this nation, not to serve ourselves, but to serve mankind." Johnson's sense of mission led him to make a stand against communism in Vietnam. Believing that "our safest guide to what we do abroad is always what we do at home," LBJ launched a New Deal-style Great Society for Americans, while promising in regard to Vietnam that "we can turn the Mekong into a Tennessee Valley." If Johnson saw a New Deal for Vietnam in the future, the situation in late 1963 reminded him of an event out of Texas history. Told that the South Vietnamese government was on the verge of collapse, the new president replied: "Hell, Vietnam is just like the Alamo. Hell, it's just like if you were down at that gate and you were surrounded and you damn well needed somebody. Well by God, I'm going to go...." While the analogy made little sense, the war in Vietnam would be for Johnson and other liberal anti-communists a catastrophe a thousand times worse than the Alamo, and one with no redeeming Battle of San Jacinto, no final victory.

The 1964 Election

"I am not going to be the President who saw Southeast Asia go the way China went," Johnson told Ambassador Henry Cabot Lodge in November 1963, echoing the sentiments of Eisenhower and Kennedy. The president delayed large-scale involvement lest Vietnam interfere with passage of the Great Society program or imperil his chances for election in 1964. The Republican nominee, Senator Barry Goldwater of Arizona, turned out to be an easy mark for the wily Johnson. Chief spokesman for the Republican far right, the Arizona senator often sounded, as journalist Theodore H. White observed, like a man introduced to the world of books and ideas late in life. In his book, *Why Not Victory?*, Goldwater offered an alternative to the Cold War liberalism of Truman, Kennedy, and Johnson and to the cautious conservatism of Eisenhower. His agenda included putting an immediate end to Castro, refusing to negotiate with the Soviets on disarmament, discouraging European decolonization, cutting domestic programs and foreign aid drastically, and, above all, giving the military more power and more hardware. Taken together, Goldwater's ideas amounted to creation of a garrison state in place of the welfare state. "Extremism in the defense of liberty is no vice," he intoned, "moderation in the pursuit of justice is no virtue," a remark many interpreted to mean that virtuous intentions justified any act however rabid.

Johnson and Goldwater agreed to refrain from making Vietnam a campaign issue, thereby insuring that a consensus would be preserved for at least another two years. But the president was determined, as he told the National Security Council, to help South Vietnam "win their contest against the externally directed and supported Communist conspiracy." After the administration magnified two minor naval incidents into a major crisis, Congress hastily passed the Tonkin Gulf Resolution, granting the president the power to deal as he saw fit with the communist menace in Southeast Asia. According to a Louis Harris poll, LBJ's approval rating on Vietnam jumped from forty-two to seventy percent after the Gulf of Tonkin incidents. Three months later Johnson buried Goldwater in a landslide.

In 1965, President Johnson deliberately misled Congress, the media, and the public (to avoid "undue excitement," he said later) with regard to what the *Pentagon Papers* study of Vietnam called "a threshold-entrance into an Asian land war." Before the objective had been to deny the communists victory; now the enemy was to be beaten. Years later, Johnson insisted that to have done anything less would have meant another Munich, where Neville Chamberlain had rewarded Hitler's aggressive behavior. "[I]f we let Communist aggression succeed in taking over South Vietnam," he told Doris Kearns, "there would follow in this country an endless national debate—a mean and destructive debate—that would shatter my Presidency, kill my administration, and damage our democracy." Of course, Ho Chi Minh was not Hitler and Vietnam was not Czechoslovakia, but the "Munich syndrome" was readily recalled by administration leaders and older citizens who remembered the origins of World War II. Recognition long after the fact of a Sino-Soviet split in the communist world led to a new variation on the domino theory. Robert McNamara explained that an American failure in South Vietnam would lead to a "Red Asia" dominated by China. This analysis came at a time when the Chinese, suffering from costly foreign policy defeats in Cuba, Indonesia, Algeria, and other African nations were undergoing the chaos of the Cultural Revolution. The only major power to win in Vietnam, ironically, would be the Soviet Union, the original "Red Menace," a nation which reached nuclear parity with the United States while the Americans drained themselves fighting in the jungles of Asia.

Unintended Consequences

American troops arrived in Vietnam firmly believing in their mission to stop the communist conspiracy before it spread any further. Fitting a global strategy into the alien world of Asian villages and hamlets proved difficult. Soldiers quickly discovered the difficulty in distinguishing between communists and nationalists; Vietnam turned out to be a land of "gooks." As writer Frances Fitzgerald noted: "To say that one 'gook' was a communist whereas another was not was to make what seemed to be a purely metaphysical distinction which, if wrongly made, might cost you your life." In villages suspected of harboring communists, ground troops would surround the area and call in airstrikes, a strategy one officer described as "blow the hell out of him and police up." When villagers sided with the Saigon government, they were subject to Vietcong retribution. Under these conditions the Rural Development Program, designed to win popular support for the Saigon government and counter the appeal of communism, made little progress. The Central Intelligence Agency used Viet Cong terror tactics in the PHOENIX program of assassinations, kidnappings, and intimidation against suspected communist agents. Officials later claimed that some 50,000 Viet Cong had been "neutralized" in this manner. Tens of thousands of Vietnamese civilians died, many of them from high explosives and napalm.

For many Americans, the cost of this anti-communist crusade in terms of lives, suffering, and tax dollars had become too great. The war against underdeveloped North Vietnam by the world's richest nation bred dissent in a generation already moved by the struggle for black civil rights in the South. Opposition to the war manifested itself initially in the form of "teach-ins" on university campuses in 1965. Senator Thomas Dodd's Senate Internal Security Subcommittee investigation concluded that the burgeoning anti-war movement was in the control "of communist and extremist elements who are openly sympathetic to the Vietcong and openly hostile to the U.S." Old anti-communist tactics no longer worked though; the academic community simply disregarded SISS. The liberal Students for a Democratic Society (SDS) which had endorsed LBJ in 1964 became radicalized, moving from an anti-war position to a generalized, sometimes Marxist, critique of America. Scornful of both capitalism and the old Left of the 1930s, the "New Left" made short work of HCUA, using the committee as a forum for their views. There would be no more "naming names," no more exercises in degradation. new leftists proclaimed their communism proudly, even when they were not affiliated with SDS, the Progressive Labor Party (Maoist), Socialist Workers Party (Trotskyite), or the Du Bois Clubs (CPUSA). Some showed up at

HCUA hearings in costume; others spoke for so long that they had to escorted out forcibly. Deprived of its greatest weapon, fear, HCUA limped along until 1969, when Congress abolished it.

Many intellectuals broke with the administration over Vietnam. In the 1950s, they had rediscovered America and endorsed the Cold War. During Kennedy's tenure, liberal intellectuals had become more amenable to change, more cognizant of the country's flaws. Like the SDS, they supported LBJ's election in 1964 because he seemed more likely to seek peaceful solutions with the Soviet Union than Goldwater. Many liberals turned on the president because of the ROLLING THUNDER bombing campaigns and the escalating land war in South Vietnam. The emergence of polycentrism in the 1960s led them to conclude that administration foreign policy was based on obsolete assumptions about Moscow's domination of the Communist Bloc. To disaffected intellectuals and an increasing chorus of liberal politicians, including Senate Foreign Relations Committee Chairman J. William Fulbright and Senators Eugene McCarthy and Robert Kennedy, a negotiated settlement made more sense than an abrupt withdrawal. Liberals still believed in the nation's anti-communist crusade. "I do not see," Arthur Schlesinger, Jr. wrote, "that our original involvement in Vietnam was per se immoral. What was immoral was the employment of means of death out of all proportion to rational purposes." This argument made no sense to the New Left, which wanted out of the Cold War.

Red-baiting the Left

Government leaders redbaited the anti-war movement as the time-tested way of dismissing criticism by discrediting the source. Vice-President Hubert Humphrey denounced the "international communist movement" for masterminding public demonstrations against Vietnam. "The world-wide communist apparatus is working very hard" in the protest movement, Dean Rusk commented in 1967. Lyndon Johnson also saw the hand of Moscow behind the dissenters, although the president reserved his greatest fire for the liberal intellectuals and politicians who had turned against his Vietnam policy. In LBJ's mind, it all began with a few intellectuals spreading their doubts about America's global anti-communist mission. "Isn't it funny," Johnson said later, "that I always received a piece of advice from my top advisers right after each of them had been in contact with someone in the Communist world?" Unlike Robert Welch and his obsessional, delusional conspiracy theories, Johnson had the power to act on his—and FBI Director Hoover was pleased to oblige. The White House asked the bureau to report on congressmen, journalists and anyone else opposed to the war. Johnson had FBI agents watch Senator Fulbright's televised hearings on Vietnam to compare the statements of war critics with the Moscow, Peking, and Hanoi communist line. He also ordered Hoover to post agents around the Soviet Embassy in Washington to keep track of congressional critics entering the Russian compound. As losses mounted in Vietnam, the president became obsessed with the supposed domestic communist conspiracy against him.

Harassing the Left

Hoover carried out his mission against the New Left with a special vengeance as he sought to tie the moribund CPUSA to new generation of activists in order to revive flagging interest in combatting the internal communist menace. When longtime party boss Gus Hall boasted in a speech that SDS was an arm of CPUSA, Hoover had all the proof he needed. But the New Left, which distrusted the working class and most everyone over the age of thirty, had very few connections with the communist party, an organization whose average age was close to fifty. The FBI went after the New Left in much the same way they had the Old, using wiretaps, hidden-microphones, and infiltration. After the uprising on the campus of Columbia University in New York, Hoover ordered a series of COINTELPRO operations against the New Left. Disruption of the movement was necessary, one field supervisor explained, when "we couldn't find out their next move, because they didn't know it themselves." A twelve-point COINTELPRO campaign included stirring up personality conflicts, harassing new leftists on drug charges, anonymous mailings to legislatures, boards of regents, and the press concerning radical students and faculty, and miscellaneous "opportunities to confuse and disrupt New Left activities by misinformation." The bureau adapted to the new situation quickly. One memorandum gave advice on how to smear New Left leaders: "Attacking their morals, disrespect for the law, or patriotic disdain will not impress their followers, as it would normally to other groups, so it must be by attacking them through their own principles and beliefs. Accuse them of selling out to 'imperialistic monopoly capitalism.'" Under COINTELPRO—NEW LEFT, the FBI conducted some 290 disruptive operations.

The FBI remained very interested in the civil rights movement in general and the activities of Martin Luther King, Jr. in particular during the Johnson years. Intensive surveillance of King began in late 1963 in order, as one memo put it, to "expose King for the clerical fraud and Marxist he is at the first opportunity." Hoover allowed himself to be quoted in the press that "Communist influence does exist in the civil rights movement." Undaunted, King repeated his charges of the bureau's ineffectiveness when it came to protecting blacks in the South, a remark which prompted the director to spout that the civil rights leader was the "most notorious liar" in America and tied to the communists as well. When Hoover complained to one of his subordinates that the bureau had not been aggressive enough in harassing the civil rights leader, domestic intelligence chief William Sullivan mailed to King a composite tape of hidden-microphone recordings (of an apparently sexual nature) along with an unsigned note suggesting that he commit suicide. King's denunciations of the war in Vietnam and his plan to launch a "Poor People's Campaign" made him appear all the more threatening. In 1967, the FBI expanded COINTELPRO to include "black nationalist, hate-type organizations and groupings" in order to prevent the rise of a "black messiah" capable of uniting various groups under a communist/revolutionary banner. The bureau carried out almost three hundred separate operations under this program. Fending off charges of communist influence, black civil rights groups expended time and resources that would have better been spent on their own movement. Sources of donations dried up, friction between groups intensified, and men like King suffered immense anguish. The bureau knew well that King and other black leaders, be they Christians, Muslims or Panthers, were no more Soviet agents than was the New Left. But the FBI used the invisible ideology of anti-communism to police politics and cultures of which it did not approve.

During the Vietnam war, the Central Intelligence Agency became increasingly preoccupied with domestic affairs in violation of its charter. To obtain intelligence on groups with suspected communist connections the agency had launched Operations MERRIMAC and RESISTANCE. A complaint by President Johnson that the CIA was not doing enough to uncover "foreign money and foreign influence" in the anti-war movement led to Operation CHAOS. "The objective," an internal memorandum read, "is to discover the extent to which Soviets, Chi[nese] com[mmunist]s, Cubans, and other Communist countries are exploiting our domestic problem in terms of subversion and espionage." A special computer program (HYDRA) was developed to file, cross-reference, and analyze the mountains of material on a whole spectrum of peace and civil rights groups. Several years and billions of bytes later, the agency would conclude that "there is no evidence...that foreign governments, organizations, or intelligence services control New Left movements." Yet once again the government had engaged in massive lawbreaking in the name of a higher authority—the crusade against communism.

The Crusade Falters

Public approval for LBJ's handling of Vietnam declined from the middle of 1965 onward. By October 1967, almost half those polled said that American intervention had been a mistake. Many Americans felt whipsawed between administration-sponsored violence abroad and blacks rioting in the ghettos, dramatic increases in violent crime, and a growing anti-war movement. Opposition to the war increased dramatically in early 1968 when North Vietnam and the Vietcong launched the Tet Offensive, a coordinated military operation and guerrilla uprising on several fronts throughout the south. While American and South Vietnamese troops emerged victorious, the magnitude of Tet shocked Americans who had been told by the administration that the war was nearly won. After American soldiers had retaken a South Vietnamese village from the communists, the media quoted an officer as saying "We had to destroy the town in order to save it," a remark many found to be a telling summary of what conflict in Vietnam had become. Public approval of the president's handling of the war dropped to a new low. Senator Eugene McCarthy made a strong showing against Johnson in the New Hampshire primary. On 31 March 1968, an exhausted Johnson announced his decision not to run for reelection.

Like Truman before him, Johnson had foundered on the rocks of a foreign anti-communist crusade. But Vietnam was different from Korea. Johnson moved deeper and deeper into Southeast Asia because he did not want to be charged with "losing" Vietnam. He sought to manage the war because he did not want to "stir up undue excitement" on the Left or the Right. In a sense, the country ended up with both: a noisy and diverse New Left and an angry right-wing backlash. Johnson's failed crusade put the quintessential anti-communist cold warrior of the 1950s, Richard Nixon, into the White House. The "new" Nixon sought to ease tensions with the communist super power while reaffirming America's anti-communist resolve in Southeast Asia and at home. The old Nixon would not hesitate to use "McCarthyism without McCarthy" in service of the invisible ideology.

Legacies

The period 1954 to 1968 turned out to be an interlude between scares as McCarthyism faded and the Warren Court reviewed many of the anti-red laws and legal decisions. President Eisenhower ended the hot war in Korea and launched low-cost, low-risk clandestine operations on the peripheries of the Cold War. But he also opened talks with a new generation of Russian leaders. The obsession with communism continued, however, almost without interruption while the CIA snooped on Americans and the FBI fought a one-sided war against the aging, impotent CPUSA. The impatient Kennedy administration, trapped by its own rhetoric, betrayed Martin Luther King and stumbled toward disaster in Vietnam.

The political climate of those years was such that right-wing extremism flourished, much as during the red scares, but often stimulated by civil rights and other issues. Barry Goldwater, the darling of the far right, may have gone down to defeat in the presidential contest against Lyndon Johnson, but the liberal Texan's anti-communism led to a drastic escalation of the Vietnam war, a conflict which altered the American political landscape. Young people rebelled and the intelligensia became critical of the administration; in response, the government waged undeclared war on its own citizens. The anti-communist campaign in Vietnam splintered the consensus, creating legacies of anger, bitterness, alienation, and fear, many of the ingredients present in previous red scares.

Chapter 5

From an Abortive Red Scare to the New Right: America Since 1968

Throughout the Cold War years, the anti-communist consensus sustained the political center—at least until the protracted crisis over Vietnam. Richard Nixon's percentage of votes was the lowest for a winning candidate since Woodrow Wilson defeated Roosevelt and Taft in 1912. Nixon won because the Right, divided between Wallace and conservative Republicans, did less damage to his candidacy than the Left did to Humphrey. The center held for Nixon, a staunch anti-communist cold warrior with liberal views on many social issues. Although Nixon and a majority of the people had come to believe that the Vietnam war was a mistake, they were unprepared to accept either defeat or a continuance of the war. As one of the partisan chorus who denounced the State Department for practicing appeasement after the "fall" of China, Nixon could not abide the thought of losing Vietnam to the communists. But also, as he explained to the Soviet ambassador, his administration "[would] not hold still for being diddled to death in Vietnam." In spite of what was said on the campaign trail, Richard Nixon had no plan for ending the war, just a vague thought of nuclear saber-rattling—the way Ike had in Korea. "I call it the Madman Theory...," Nixon explained to an aide, "I want the North Vietnamese to believe that we've reached the point where I might do anything to stop the war. We'll just slip the word to them that, 'for God's sake, you know Nixon is obsessed about Communists. We can't restrain him when he's angry—and he has his hand on the nuclear button'—and Ho Chi Minh will be in Paris in two days begging for peace." His administration tried this approach on several occasions, from the secret air war launched against Cambodia in 1969 to the "Christmas bombing" campaign of 1972.

The "Madman Theory" represented only one way the president hoped to capitalize on his reputation as a hard-line anti-communist. Henry A. Kissinger, Nixon's top foreign policy adviser, wrote that his boss "shrewdly saw in East-West relations a long-term opportunity to build his new majority." Paradoxically, Nixon's reputation gave him a special flexibility in dealing with the communists since he could hardly be accused of being soft on them. By deemphasizing the threat of monolithic communism, the United States could have communist allies in the struggle against the Soviet Union. "Those on the right can do what those on the left only talk about," Nixon said to Mao Tse-tung during a trip to China which marked a stunning reversal in Sino-American relations. A foreign policy based primarily on geopolitics rather than ideology could allow the United States to cut back global commitments to realistic levels (the "Nixon Doctrine") while giving the administration more latitude in dealing with the Russians. Nixon, his successor Gerald Ford, and Henry Kissinger had only partial success with their grand design for relocating the focus of American anti-communism.

The Republicans wanted to bring the war to an end, but in such a way as to demonstrate America's continuing anti-communist resolve to the Soviet Union and China. In his first major speech on the war, Nixon announced that he had a plan for ending the war, but the arguments he made were for staying there and winning. "Our defeat and humiliation in South Vietnam," he said, "without question would promote recklessness in the councils of those great powers who have not yet abandoned their goals of world conquest." This notion of Vietnam as a test case of anti-communist will was a reaffirmation of the reasoning which had propelled the country into Vietnam under Kennedy and Johnson. Nixon concluded his speech with a warning to the anti-war movement. After asking for the support of "the great silent majority," the president declared: "North Vietnam cannot defeat or humiliate the United States. Only

Americans can do that." For the next several years, the war would be fought on two far-flung fronts, one in Southeast Asia, the other in the United States. Nixon tried to scale down the war and recast the anti-communist mission while cracking down on dissent at home.

In the late 1970s, following the fall of Nixon and Vietnam, the Right attacked two successive centrist presidents for weakness. Ronald Reagan brought to the White House an anti-communist rhetoric reminiscent of Truman, Dulles, and Kennedy. The president's hard line against the "evil empire" of the Soviet Union made him popular with the New Right. But as Reagan approached the end of his second term, America continued to drift, the people deeply divided over the nature of the anti-communist crusade.

The Return of Richard Nixon

Nineteen sixty-eight was a year which frightened many Americans. Like 1919 and 1947, the events of 1968 terrified enough people to have touched off another red scare. J. Edgar Hoover was certainly ready. Testifying before the National Commission on the Causes and Prevention of Violence, the director opined: "Communists are in the forefront of civil rights, anti-war, and student demonstrations, many of which ultimately become disorderly and erupt into violence." While the commission regarded Hoover's statement as simplistic at best, they considered it important because most Americans took the director's words as gospel.

Unlike other years when red scares took off, 1968 was a presidential election year. The three final presidential candidates vied with one another for control of the "law and order" issue, code words, many thought, implying repression of blacks and the anti-war movement. Democratic nominee Hubert Humphrey found himself trapped between taunting demonstrators ("Sieg heil!" and "Dump the Hump" they yelled) and Lyndon Johnson's insistence on total loyalty from his vice president. Humphrey defended Chicago Mayor Richard Daley, who had justified his police department's ferocious response to anti-war protesters during the Democratic Convention on the grounds that they were communists out to assassinate him. The vice president did not unstrap himself from LBJ's political cadaver until 30 September when he advocated "de-Americanization" of the Vietnam war. Garry Wills wrote of Humphrey that "there was something in the atmosphere that made it seem faintly obscene for a presidential candidate, in a country that admires 'happy warriors' and the banishing of fear, to use the phrase 'politics of joy.'" A Lyndon Johnson supporter four years earlier, New Leftist Tom Hayden evidently agreed, observing that he only wanted "to vomit on the politics of joy." The man largely responsible for sending Alger Hiss to prison during an earlier red scare seemed to better fit the temper of 1968.

The Republicans nominated Richard Nixon, long a practitioner of "McCarthyism without McCarthy," who two years earlier had argued that the Vietnam war had to be fought "to prevent World War III." This was an ambiguous "new Nixon" promising if elected to "end the war and win the peace." Master of what Wills called "a politics of resentment," Nixon hoped to forge "A New Alignment" of Republicans, disaffected liberals, blacks, and Southerners, as well as "the silent center, the millions of people in the middle of the American political spectrum, who do not demonstrate, who do not picket or protest loudly." Nixon left the mudslinging to running mate Spiro Agnew, just as Ike had chosen Nixon for that task sixteen years earlier. After Agnew redbaited Humphrey as "squishy soft on Communism" though, Nixon dispatched adviser Stephen Hess to keep his running mate from stirring the Democratic elite out of its lethargy. Hess convinced Agnew to shelve McCarthyite phrases like "Communists in our midst" and "lists of names" which impugned the patriotism of Democrats. Instead, the vice presidential candidate concentrated on linking leaders of the anti-war movement to Moscow and Hanoi, charging at one point that they "received instruction from active Communist leaders of the world."

Nixon chose Agnew for his running mate to blunt the appeal of George Wallace, a Southern demagogue liberal in economics riding a white racist backlash against the civil rights movement and the New Left. "I'm an Alabama Democrat, not a national Democrat," he boasted, "I'm not kin to those folks. The difference between an Alabama Democrat and a national Democrat is like the difference between a Communist and a non-Communist." In 1968, Wallace ran for president as an independent, forging a coalition of such right-wing groups as the Klan and the John Birch Society. While Barry Goldwater and William F. Buckley attacked Wallace as a New Deal populist, many on the Right found his anti-elitism and anti-intellectualism irresistible. Like Joseph McCarthy, he spoke of communism as a phenomenon of the wealthy. "I don't believe all this talk about poor folks turning Communist," he observed, "It's the damn rich who turn Communist. You ever seen a poor Communist?" Whereas McCarthy emphasized the theme of communist subversion, Wallace liked to compare Washington and Moscow as examples of the evil that follows power concentrated in central government. He presented simple and violent solutions to America's problems which seemed to indicate a rejection of the democratic process. To stop "trash" from demonstrating, Wallace said, "let the police run this country for a year or two and there wouldn't be any riots." Ghetto unrest would be dealt with in a similar fashion: "That's right, we gonna have a police state for folks who burn the cities down." Ironically, as election day drew nearer with Wallace trailing badly, he began to advocate street demonstrations against the government, just like the leftist "scum of the earth."

The New Left self-destructed in 1968-1969; barely eight years after a beginning which promised openness and independence, groups like SDS collapsed in orgies of factionalism, violence, and playing at revolution. In the year after the presidential election, the anti-war movement had been quiescent as the new administration worked to carry out Nixon's campaign promise to "bring the American people together." The president's speech impugning in advance those who would oppose his war policies and Vice-President Agnew's subsequent series of ferocious attacks on the liberal news media brought about a revival of protest. The administration hoped to create what Agnew called "positive polarization" between an isolated left and the rest of the country—the center-right—which would then gravitate toward a new majority Republican party. In this atmosphere, hundreds of thousands of protesters came to Washington to demonstrate. When a thousand radicals charged the Justice Department building only to be run off with tear gas, Attorney General John Mitchell commented that it "looked like a Russian Revolution going on." That was hardly the case, although the administration responded to protesters as if they were Bolsheviks. Opinion polls revealed that the public supported the president overwhelmingly.

A Near Red Scare

In addition to an unpopular war, Nixon inherited a powerful apparatus for political repression which Lyndon Johnson had used against the New Left and dissident liberals. Nixon not only exploited the precedents established by presidents from Wilson to LBJ against radicals, but expanded upon them in his search for a way to attain "peace with honor" in Vietnam. The president struggle against enemies at home and abroad spawned a near red scare. One year into Nixon's tenure, Supreme Court Justice William O. Douglas wrote that "a black silence of fear possesses the nation and is causing us to jettison some of our libertarian traditions." Historian Henry Steele Commager went even further, observing that "if repression is not as blatant or as flamboyant as it was during the McCarthy years, it is in many respects more pervasive and more formidable." Yet, this time the country did not dissolve into another period of fear. Vietnam proved to be too unpopular with key elites ("the establishment," as Nixon called them) and the population as a whole to sustain a domestic crusade against dissenters.

Hoover's Last Stand

"Dick," Lyndon Johnson had said to Nixon, "you will come to depend on [J.] Edgar [Hoover]. He is a pillar of strength in a city of weak men. You will rely on him time and time again to maintain security. He's the only one you can put your complete trust in." While the FBI continued to be the leading federal bulwark against domestic radicalism during the Nixon years, the aging director was slipping. In the past, the vigilant Hoover constantly urged presidents to move against the communist menace; now, the executive branch had to prod the bureau into expanding surveillance of suspected radicals. Like Hoover, his bureau saw anti-war protesters not as citizens expressing the right to political dissent but as a new generation of communists bent on subversion. A tiny minority of those radicalized by the war (and perhaps by the government's response to the protesters) did resort to violence. The Weather Underground, one of many SDS splinter groups, planted bombs, set fires, and welcomed confrontations with the law. But the FBI and other government agencies treated all those in the counterculture movement as potential mad bombers. Students belonging to anything smacking of the New Left, blacks who joined student union groups, people in communes, even high school kids protesting the poor quality of their lunches, were all put under bureau scrutiny. A blizzard of reports flooded FBI headquarters; Tom Hayden's file alone ran over eighteen thousand pages. As the self-appointed guardian of traditional values, Hoover took a special interest in linking the feminists or women's liberation with the communists. When the Chicago office suggested that an investigation of the Women's Liberation Movement (WLM) was not necessary, Hoover fired back that "it is absolutely essential that we conduct sufficient investigation to clearly establish subversive ramifications of the WLM and to determine the potential for violence...as well as any possible threat they may represent to the internal security of the United States." The bureau continued to compile a list of those to be arrested in the event of a national emergency—even after congressional repeal of the McCarran Act—rationalizing that Congress might repass the law in the future.

The FBI continued to carry out imaginative, vigilante-style COINTELPRO operations against radicals in the name of the invisible ideology. The Black Panther party, a militant organization numbering no more than eight hundred, became the primary target for destruction, according to a top secret report to the president, because it was communist, active, dangerous, and popular among black youths under twenty-one years of age. Anti-Panther activities included encouraging a feud with another black militant group (which resulted in several murders) and fomenting interparty bickering. The bureau helped Illinois authorities plan a raid on a "Panther Crib" during which state party chairman Fred Hampton was machine-gunned in his bed. Other groups suffered physical assaults, kidnappings, the theft of mail, and the destruction of property.

The bureau resorted to tactics of disruption against students in the movement because, as a field supervisor explained, "a normal investigation" was impossible on most campuses. With little idea of what the fragmented and disorganized New Leftists were up to next, frustrated agents sometimes helped dissidents to plan their moves as a means of neutralizing them. In Seattle, an agent provocateur provided a Vietnam veteran—who had turned against the war—with a bomb, money, and transportation to a real estate office, where waiting police shot him dead. Some of the most militant members of the Black Panthers and the Weather Underground turned out to be FBI informants. Ironically, the bureau's illegal operations against the Left halted officially (although some continued on an unofficial basis) in 1971 when members of a radical group raided an FBI office in Media, Pennsylvania, stealing tons of incriminating paperwork. Forty percent of the purloined Media documents dealt with surveillance of over two hundred left and liberal groups and two right-wing organizations—while a combined fifteen percent dealt with bank robberies, murder, rape, and theft, fourteen percent with military crimes, and one percent with organized crime. The captured papers showed that the FBI hoped to prove that foreign and domestic communists were behind the anti-war, civil rights, and feminist movements.

Other Government Operations

Many other government agencies engaged in covert oppression during this period of anxiety. At the behest of administration officials, the Internal Revenue Service engaged in COINTELPRO-style operations, targeting the tax returns of dissidents for special attention. The Central Intelligence Agency, responding to similar pressures, expanded Operation CHAOS to include the names of over 300,000 Americans, among them 75 members of Congress. The National Security Agency (NSA) drew up its own civil disturbance watch list, monitoring international communications closely for links to the communists. Active in domestic espionage since the first Red Scare, U.S. Army intelligence beefed up operations during the Nixon years. A 1969 Army directive warned of a "true insurgency, should external subversive forces develop successful control" of anti-war and civil rights groups. The military penetrated groups ranging from Milwaukee welfare mothers to the National Mobilization Committee, to gather information. In 1971, Captain Christopher Pyle, a disillusioned former intelligence officer, told the Ervin Subcommittee on Constitutional Rights that "the United States today possesses the intelligence buildup of a police state."

The Nixon Justice Department prosecuted most prominent leaders of the anti-war movement. The "Chicago 8" (reduced to seven when Black Panther Bobby Seale disrupted the proceedings repeatedly) were charged with crossing state lines to incite a riot at the Democratic National Convention under a 1968 statute. Although a jury found five of the defendants guilty and the judge sentenced them to long jail terms, a court of appeals overturned the verdicts. Another highly publicized political trial involved Philip Berrigan, a priest, and other Catholic activists indicted for smuggling letters out of prison, raiding draft boards, and plotting to blow up heating ducts in Washington and kidnap Henry Kissinger. All were acquitted, save Berrigan, who went to jail on the smuggling charge. A jury took just a few hours to acquit the "Gainesville 8" on charges of attempting to disrupt the 1972 Republican Convention after the government could only produce slingshots as evidence. The administration fared no better in other conspiracy cases, although it did succeed in tying the activists up in litigation and saddling them with legal bills. During Nixon's first term, the Justice Department launched extensive grand jury inquires into radical activities, a process whereby witnesses often had to testify in secret without the benefit of counsel, the threat of contempt charges hanging over them. Thirty activists went to jail for refusing to answer questions. The grand jury procedure also allowed the government to "launder" evidence obtained through illegal wiretaps and burglaries otherwise inadmissible in open court.

State and local officials provided the White House with plenty of help in the drive against dissidents. During this period, police departments in more than five hundred cities and towns had their own "red squads" to gather political intelligence and harass leftists. One of the oldest and most notorious of these police groups, the Chicago Red Squad waged an undeclared war against dissidents on orders from Mayor Daley after the 1968 Democratic convention until the mid-1970s. The U.S. Army 113th Military Intelligence Group gave money, tear gas, mace, and surveillance gear to the squad, which passed much of it along to the Legion of Justice, a right-wing terrorist group. In return, the Legion provided the Army with documents stolen from targeted groups. The New York Red Squad kept files on over one million people and thousands of groups. In some municipalities, surveillance was undertaken against any person or organization the red squad considered to be "controversial." The best available study on police during this time found that law enforcement officials tended to be poorly educated, from blue collar homes, and hostile to civil rights and civil liberties. These factors tended to make them susceptible to conspiracy theories and right-wing demagoguery. Most police had little or no sympathy with youthful protesters or much understanding of the issues which alienated them from society. Chief Edward Davis of the Los Angeles Police Department fought to convince the people of his city that "sophisticated Bolsheviks" stirred up black and Chicano unrest to further the communist conspiracy. Police magazines like *Law and Order* carried articles by Fred Schwarz and officials of the John Birch Society. To attract police to his group, Robert Welch launched a "Support Your Local Police" campaign.

The massive government campaign against the Left did not satisfy the White House. In 1970, Tom Charles Huston, coordinator of security affairs, found domestic intelligence information to be "fragmentary and unevaluated." The president remained confident that more digging would unearth connections between domestic radicals and foreign communists. Furthermore, Nixon was determined, as he put it in his *Memoirs,* "to discover the best means by which to deal with this new phenomenon of highly organized and highly skilled revolutionaries dedicated to the violent destruction of our democratic system." Apparently, the president meant the Black Panthers and the Weather Underground, groups the government had already put to flight. As a result of this concern, Nixon told Huston to bring domestic intelligence officials together to discuss ways of improving internal security. The resulting "Huston Plan" recommended broadened NSA communications coverage, a large increase in "electronic surveillance and penetrations" of groups threatening national security, massive mail openings, burglaries to obtain "vitally needed foreign cryptographic material," and expanded recruiting of college-age informants. While agencies like the FBI and the CIA had been doing these things for years without written permission from the executive branch, the president was now specifically ordering intelligence agencies to violate laws. Posing as a civil libertarian, J. Edgar Hoover succeeded in blocking the plan because he disliked competition from the other agencies and he resented focusing domestic intelligence inside the White House. In the end, the administration implemented most of the major recommendations in piecemeal fashion, but to little avail.

In Nixon's *Memoirs,* the president leaves the reader with the impression that "direct support for the Weathermen from both Cuba and North Vietnam" justified the largest government offensive against the Left in American history. A *New York Times* story based on a 1976 FBI report, Nixon's only proof for the international conspiracy argument, disclosed that Cuban and North Vietnamese officials met with an SDS delegation. Cuban military officers did give some students who had volunteered to cut sugar cane instruction in marksmanship and explosives. The Cubans also made travel arrangements to allow four members of the Weather Underground to get back into the United States. One American living in China received $5,000. Those were the only connections between American radicals and foreign communists which the government could come up with after twelve years and many millions of dollars worth of snooping. "The report," the *Times* concluded "appeared to be more significant for the paucity of support by Communist bloc nations than for the extent of it."

Government repression at home accompanied every major move Nixon made in the crusade against communism in Vietnam. When the *New York Times* discovered evidence of a secret air war against Cambodia in 1969, the White House called for illegal wiretaps to see who had leaked the story. The next year, after the ground invasion Cambodia, Nixon ordered up the ill-fated Huston plan. In 1971, with support for the president dwindling, the war at home eclipsed the conflict in Southeast Asia in importance—at least at the White House. On 3 May 1971, thousands of demonstrators blocked rush-hour traffic in Washington in a symbolic effort to paralyze the government. Police arrested over 7,200, the largest mass jailing since the Palmer raids. Many were detained including protesters, government employees trying to get to their jobs, and reporters in hastily erected outdoor stockades. Authorities tossed another six thousand suspected radicals into makeshift bullpens during the next days in what the deputy attorney general described as "'qualified' martial law." Subsequent court actions threw out almost all of the arrests on constitutional grounds.

The Pentagon Papers

Past Vietnam policies came home to roost that same spring when a former Pentagon analyst, Daniel Ellsberg, handed over to the *New York Times* a top secret Defense Department history of the Vietnam war from 1946 to 1968. The *Pentagon Papers* showed liberal Democrats (especially Lyndon Johnson) in an unflattering light, but contained nothing about Nixon's Vietnam policy. The president worried, however, that "critics of the war would use them to attack my goals and my policies." Attorney General John Mitchell suggested that Ellsberg was part of a communist conspiracy. To the president and his political advisors, the fifteen count indictment Ellsberg and a codefendant faced did not seem adequate for their purposes. Nixon and aide Charles Colson believed that the affair would either turn Ellsberg into a martyr or, as Colson put it, "it could be another Alger Hiss case, where the guy is exposed....We might be able to put this bastard into a hell of a situation and discredit the New Left." Since Hoover had scuttled the Huston Plan, the White House put together a secret unit nicknamed "the Plumbers" to destroy Daniel Ellsberg—and the Left along with him. The plumbers broke into the offices of Ellsberg's psychiatrist in search of derogatory information, a fatal mistake which forced a judge to dismiss the entire case.

The 1972 Election

Frustrated by the inability to make political hay out of the *Pentagon Papers,* the failure of the conspiracy prosecutions, and the lack of evidence linking domestic radicalism with international communism, Nixon moved into high gear for the 1972 election campaign. On the domestic front, the White House developed a plan of intelligence gathering and covert activities against the Democrats just as they had earlier against the Left. In foreign affairs, the president shocked and delighted the country in February 1972 by visiting the People's Republic of China, where he bantered with Chairman Mao and posed at the Great Wall.

Nixon used summits with China and the Soviet Union, the Strategic Arms Limitation Treaty (SALT I), and promises of a pending termination of the Vietnam conflict to seize the "peace issue." Democratic candidate George McGovern owed his nomination, in some small part, to the fact that White House dirty tricksters had sabotaged front runner Edmund Muskie's campaign with COINTELPRO-style operations. Other forays designed to divide the Democrats and gather intelligence also hurt McGovern. One such mission went awry when police caught a White House burglary squad inside Democratic party headquarters at the Watergate office building; but the day of reckoning was postponed until after the election. Seeking to justify the strategy of subverting the Democrats, Nixon later noted: "I thought it was critically important to the future of the country that his [McGovern's] radical ideas not prevail in November." They did not. On 21 October 1972, North Vietnam and the United States agreed to a peace settlement, but South Vietnamese President Nguyen Van Thieu balked at the deal, forcing Henry Kissinger to announce that "peace is at hand." Apparently reassured, voters reelected the president by a comfortable majority. A peace treaty was finally signed in January 1973 after the Air Force dropped forty thousand tons of explosives on the principal North Vietnamese cities in eleven days to convince the communists that the administration meant business.

White House lawbreaking against dissenters and the American Left, a well established practice by 1969, reached new heights during the Nixon years as the administration tried to prove American strength abroad. But there were more failures than successes for the government in this abortive red scare. The administration subverted the Black Panther party and the Weather Underground, two small, highly visible groups of militant Marxists. Government conspiracy trials tied up radical leaders in the courts. On the other hand, administration actions against the anti-war movement did not deter people from protesting; the anti-war movement continued to grow during the period when repression was most intense. By the time Nixon became president, the government itself suffered from a lack of credibility as a result of deceptions about Vietnam. The war had become unpopular with influential groups in American society, including intellectuals, middle-class youth, the media, and some members of Congress. When the White House tried to apply the same techniques of repression used for years against communists and other radicals on the margin of society to liberals and centrists, the public turned against Nixon. He could not create a red scare without a consensus. Instead, he presided over "a black silence of fear," but it was not the kind of gnawing dread produced by a Bolshevik Revolution or the early Cold War. Like the near Red Scare of 1939-1941, the repression of 1969-1973 ceased abruptly in the face of a national emergency. The Watergate scandals made everything commonly associated with Nixon (political spies, wiretaps, secret wars, the imperial presidency, and even détente) an anathema to the majority.

The Center Folds

Richard Nixon's political arrogance left the center in even worse shape than in 1968. Less than a year after the president's resignation, South Vietnam, on which the center had staked so much for so long, collapsed in defeat. Appointed to serve out the remainder of Nixon's second term, Republican Gerald Ford continued the policy of détente in the face of growing criticism from Left and Right. His successor, Democrat Jimmy Carter, also tried to build on the Nixon-Kissinger policies, finally abandoning the effort, only to lose his bid for reelection to Ronald Reagan. By 1980, the New Right, the neoconservatives, and other political groups well to the right of center had become powerful enough to elect Reagan, a man whom they hoped would roll back "creeping socialism" at home while aggressively confronting communism abroad.

By the time Ford replaced Nixon in August 1974, Congress was in the midst of a campaign to take back powers delegated over the years to the executive branch. The effort began in 1971 with the repeal of the the Gulf of Tonkin resolution. Two years later, the House cut off the money needed to continue the bombing of Cambodia, a prelude to another congressional amendment demanding the end of all military operations in Indochina. To prevent future Vietnams, the War Powers Act mandated that the president inform Congress fully of American military deployments within forty-eight hours and withdraw them within sixty days unless Congress approved the operation. Subsequent acts prohibited American troops from returning to Vietnam or entering a new hot spot, Africa, without explicit congressional permission. The breakdown of the Paris peace agreement led to the rapid deterioration of South Vietnam. When Secretary of State Henry Kissinger asked Congress to increase military aid to the South Vietnamese as a means of preserving American credibility, the argument fell on deaf ears for the first time in a quarter century. If the Saigon regime fell, Kissinger observed, "then we are likely to find a massive shift in the foreign policies of many countries and a fundamental threat over a period of time to the security of the United States." In April 1975, indigenous communist movements took over Cambodia and Vietnam.

Ironically the consequence of defeat feared most by successive presidents, a divisive domestic debate over "Who lost Indochina?", never happened. Aside from a few partisan volleys between the White House and Capitol Hill over the botched evacuation of Saigon, little was said about Vietnam, in part because of the painfulness of the loss and in part because both political parties shared the blame. Network television news operations quickly assembled documentaries and then ignored the legacies of the war. Americans went about their business, trying, as the historically-minded Kissinger suggested, to put Vietnam behind them with as little thought as possible. The lack of debate glossed over fundamental questions which might have been asked about the invisible ideology of anti-communism, which led America down the path to Vietnam. The unsuccessful crusade also eroded support for détente, the first coherent attempt to reduce Cold War tensions.

Vietnam, Watergate, congressional limits on presidential power, and Ford's limited leadership skills all made détente politically vulnerable. Liberals saw in it too much realism and not enough peace; conservatives charged that Nixon, Ford, and Kissinger had been too soft on the Russians. To reevaluate the Soviet threat, CIA chief George Bush brought in an outside group of conservatives ("Team B") headed by Paul Nitze, who was in the process of forming an anti-détente political action committee. Team B concluded that the CIA regulars had grossly underestimated Soviet strength. New evidence included a report revising estimates of Soviet military spending (upward from six to eight percent to eleven to twelve percent of the gross national product) and the discovery of a massive Soviet civil defense program. But the report on the Soviet budget had also concluded that the Russians were spending more because their costs had risen. The civil defense program, it turned out, consisted of plans for crude hole-in-the-ground shelters and the protection of equipment with shoveled earth. Nitze and Eugene Victor Debs Rostow went on to found the Committee on the Present Danger, a well-heeled organization of veteran cold warriors. Determined to bring American foreign policy back into line with the NSC-68 blueprint of 1950 (written principally by Nitze), the committee raised the old specter of "Red Fascism," observing in 1976 that the Soviet military build-up was "reminiscent of Nazi Germany's rearmament in the 1930's." A congressional study, however, concluded less dramatically that the Soviet Union's military expansion had been "surprisingly steady over time" in contrast to American cycles of increases and decreases. The committee quickly became influential among those who took it as an article of faith that détente reflected a failure of anti-communist resolve, including board member Ronald Reagan.

Challenging Ford for the 1976 Republican nomination, Reagan asked Americans "not to be satisfied with a foreign policy whose principal accomplishment seems to be our acquisition of the right to sell Pepsi-Cola in Siberia." Reagan charged that the moderate Republicans had made America number two in the world with a policy which fostered "collapse of the American will and the retreat of American power." While Ford did capture his party's nomination, he was compelled to stop using the word "détente" and to accept a platform plank which renounced much of his administration's foreign policy. Democratic nominee Jimmy Carter of Georgia repeated Reagan's criticisms, damning the president for giving up too much in arms control talks with the Soviets and in discussions with Panama on the status of the canal zone. Carter also hit hard at the administration for signing the 1975 Helsinki agreements, which traded Western recognition of Eastern European borders in return for communist pledges to respect human rights. During a debate on foreign policy, Ford tried to defend himself with the observation: "There is no Soviet domination of Eastern Europe. It just isn't true." This gaffe, along with Ford's pardon of Richard Nixon, helped to tilt the election to Carter.

Gerald Ford and Jimmy Carter helped the American people to recover from the traumas of Vietnam and Watergate. With the wings of the "Imperial Presidency" being clipped by what some feared was an "Imperial Congress," these two chief executives used communists to contain communists, negotiated for the reduction of nuclear armaments, and differentiated between vital and peripheral national interests. Ford, Carter, and Congress, as well as state and local officials, worked to halt domestic intelligence gathering activities long used to harass dissenters and leftists in the name of anti-communism. After the Watergate scandal, reporters used documents obtained under the 1966 Freedom of Information Act to expose the FBI's COINTELPRO operations and abuses by NSA and the IRS. Attorney General William Saxbe and his successor, Edward Levi, made additional revelations about the FBI, further tarnishing the late J. Edgar Hoover's once sacrosanct reputation. Red squads in Chicago, Houston, Los Angeles, and New York came under close scrutiny. In 1975, Congress appointed select committees, chaired by Senator Frank Church and Congressman Otis Pike to analyze the whole spectrum of spying activities, work which led to permanent congressional oversight committees. In response to new Justice Department guidelines, the FBI broke up the Domestic Intelligence Division. The leak of an internal CIA report on its illegal domestic operations ("the family jewels," as insiders called it) led President Ford to create the Rockefeller Commission. The president incorporated many of the commission's recommendations into Executive Order 11905, designed to get the agency out of the domestic spying business. The Tax Reform Act of 1976 made it more difficult for government officials to use the IRS for political purposes. The reform campaign climaxed in 1978 with Jimmy Carter's Executive Order 12036, putting further restrictions on the intelligence agencies and the Foreign Intelligence Surveillance Act, which narrowed the ground rules on eavesdropping.

The New Right

In the late 1970s, the confidence of the American people in their system and their leaders had eroded from a decade-long series of traumas including Vietnam, Watergate, Soviet nuclear equivalence, racial unrest, an energy crisis, and economic instability. To many, the centrism of Nixon, Ford, and Carter had failed as miserably as liberalism. This crisis of confidence produced the New Right, a loose-knit conservative coalition consisting of disillusioned young Republicans, fundamentalist Christians, disaffected liberal intellectuals ("neoconservatives"), the remnants of the George Wallace and Barry Goldwater movements, and old-line congressional Republicans. Well-organized and well-financed, New Right groups supported the presidential candidacy of Ronald Reagan, a highly skilled politician who shared much of their agenda. Like Reagan, the rightists yearned for a return to the world before government became too socialistic, and capitalism too fettered. The New Right developed not an ideology so much as a set of attitudes, often quite contradictory, conservative in outlook but also radical in objectives and methods. The inconsistencies and discrepancies of the movement produced tensions and confrontations which would hamper the new crusade against communism from within and without.

Political Organizers

The New Right began in the early 1970s as several energetic young conservatives grew disenchanted with what they saw as the moderation of Richard Nixon and the Republican party. William F. Buckley and Barry Goldwater were their heroes. At a time of "stagflation" (stagnation in production, inflation in prices) at home and frustration abroad, they wanted reduced government and taxes, defeat of the Equal Rights Amendment, constitutional amendments prohibiting abortion and mandating a balanced federal budget, public school prayers, an assortment of ideas to protect the traditional family, a military build-up, and an aggressive anti-communist foreign policy.

To unite right-wing political and religious forces into a comprehensive network, Paul Weyrich, a former journalist and political aide, founded the Committee for the Survival of a Free Congress. "We are different from previous generations of conservatives...," he explained, "We are radicals, working to overturn the present power structure of the country." Funds came from beer magnate Joseph Coors, a heavy contributor to far right causes, including the John Birch Society. Coors and Weyrich also created the first New Right "think tank," the Heritage Foundation. Designed initially to provide resources for right-of-center causes, within a few years such privately endowed foundations would constitute what one participant called a "second culture" with its own system of communications through newsletters, journals, academic organizations, and conferences. Vowing to wage "a war about our way of life" on the political front, Weyrich turned to computer specialist Richard A. Viguerie, a direct mail fund raiser. Millions of dollars began to pour into the Viguerie Company, most of it in small donations of ten to twenty dollars. With a computer bank containing 25 million names, the client list of organizations ranged from Gun Owners of America to the Panama Canal Truth Squad and conservative politicians like Senator Jesse Helms and a John Birch Society council member, Congressman Larry McDonald. Viguerie teamed up with another young conservative, Terry Dolan, to make the National Conservative Political Action Committee the largest right-wing PAC in the country. Relying heavily on research and polling, Dolan specialized in designing negative media blitzes against vulnerable liberal senators and congressmen. Another of these young Turks, Howard Phillips, launched the Conservative Caucus to concentrate on organizing the new right at the grass roots level. By 1978 their candidates were winning elections to Congress. Two years later they were ready to help elect a president.

The Religious Far Right

In their search for brethren, New Right pollsters found that fundamentalist Protestants (those believing in the Bible as "inerrant" and opposed to anything in society conflicting with the Good Book) constituted the largest group of unregistered voters in the country. Millions more considering themselves evangelicals (Christians identified with the more moderate Billy Graham brand of Protantism) were also seen as potential allies of the New Right. Furthermore, Jimmy Carter's candidacy in 1976 attracted between 5 and 7.5 million "born again" Christians, voters presumably disappointed with the president's centrism and ready to return to the right. Weyrich and Phillips concentrated on urging "electronic ministers" to become more active politically; men like Jerry Falwell, James Robison, and Pat Robertson, who, between them, were seen by at least twenty million people a week. While older radio-television preachers such as Carl McIntire and Billy James Hargis had based their crusades on denunciations of communism and supported only a vague rightist agenda, the new generation of fundamentalists urged their followers to register to vote, instructed them on specific issues, and targeted liberals for defeat.

Reacting against social developments of the 1960s and 1970s, the fundamentalists blamed welfare, abortion, busing, gun control, women's liberation, gay rights, pornography, and educational reforms, along with the traditional bogies of communism and labor unions, for the breakdown of morality, the family, and American world power. Reverend James Robison linked liberals and gays with the communist conspiracy, observing that he was "sick and tired hearing about all the radicals and the perverts and the liberals and leftists and the Communists coming out of the closet." Some fundamentalists concentrated heavy fire on what they felt was a new twist in the communist conspiracy: "secular humanism." A small movement with roots in nineteenth century Unitarian and Universalist theology, religious humanist faith emphasized ethics and human development rather than the worship of God. In the 1961 *Torcaso v. Watkins* decision, the Supreme Court ruled that nontheistic humanist beliefs (including "secular humanism" as Justice Black called it) were protected under the First Amendment. Fundamentalists contended that religious freedoms applied only to more traditional theological beliefs. If the government did not actively cultivate religion in public schools (with prayers and the teaching of the Biblical version of creation), the New Right charged, then secular humanism had become a de facto state religion. "Secular humanism," Jerry Falwell commented, "is nothing but communism waiting in the wings to be crowned with its political rights." Fundamentalists also saw conspiracy behind modern methods of education, specifically values clarification, which teaches students how to think more critically about moral questions. Writing in *Conquest*, a publication of the Kansas City Youth for Christ, Margaret Baldwin revealed: "Although it has many names and disguises...values clarification is the hedonistic grandchild of Communist brainwashing and the offspring of sensitivity training."

Jerry Falwell used fear of communism to build a religious empire, frightening his followers with sophisticated multimedia presentations climaxed by photographs of murderers, atomic explosions, homosexual lovers, and an aborted fetus as an announcer imitated the voice of CPUSA's Gus Hall. In *Listen, America!* Falwell endeavored to stir up his readers with quotations from newspapers in Thailand describing the various horrors of "godless communism" including the rape of an eight-year old girl by one hundred red pirates. By 1980, Falwell was receiving over one million dollars per week to pay for a staff of thirteen hundred, a sanatorium for alcoholics, a day school, a seminary, and a Baptist college with three thousand students. The previous year, he had established the Moral Majority (a name suggested by Paul Weyrich) to push the fundamentalists into front-line politics. When Falwell told his religious audiences that they could fight against wickedness in the voting booth and in the legislatures, millions took his lead. Many more found Moral Majority frightening; a poll revealed that while Reverend Falwell had become one of the most famous people in the country, he was also one of the most hated. Nevertheless, electronic preachers like Falwell and Pat Robertson made the New Right a political force to be reckoned with in the 1980s.

Neoconservatives

In the late 1970s, while Paul Weyrich and other secular activists were putting the New Right together, the neoconservatives emerged as the intelligensia of the movement. Leading lights included Daniel Bell, Seymour Martin Lipset, Irving Kristol, Daniel Moynihan, Nathan Glazer, Daniel Boorstin, Norman Podhoretz, and Sidney Hook. They represented the other side of the coin from 1960s radicalism. Many had been anti-Stalinist socialists in the 1930s and 1940s, drifting to Cold War liberalism in the 1950s. Some signed with the American Committee for Cultural Freedom, an organization of intellectuals covertly funded by the CIA to counteract communist propaganda and celebrate "cultural freedom." The New Left movement of the 1960s horrified them. Beseiged in his office by rioting students at Columbia University in 1968, Daniel Bell quipped: "Be careful what you wish when you are young; you may get it when you are old." "[R]adicalism is so beset with error and confusion," Nathan Glazer wrote, explaining his odyssey to neoconservatism, "that our main task, if we are ever to mount a successful assault on our problems, must be to argue with it and to strip it ultimately of the pretension that it understands the causes of our ills and how to set them right."

Long after despair and the government had devoured the New Left, the neoconservatives continued to counterattack in *Commentary* and *The Public Interest*. Soon, their polemics broadened to include liberalism. By 1971, Norman Podhoretz had branded almost every movement and individual left of center as "Stalinist" and "anti-American." While not racists or insensitive to the poor, neoconservatives heaped scorn on civil disobedience, affirmative action, busing, most anti-poverty programs, tax and campaign finance reforms, women's liberation and anything else viewed as a by-product of the counterculture. They accepted the welfare statism of the New Deal, but not the Great Society. Respect was reserved for the market place and the traditions of Western civilization—family, religion, and culture, all institutions threatened by instability. Like the fundamentalists, neoconservatives emphasized the deterioration of values and morals as primary reasons for America's decline in the 1970s. Although the New Right intellectuals concentrated at first on domestic affairs, the passing of the New Left and the embarrassments of Vietnam and Watergate led many of them to express equal anxiety over international affairs. As veteran anti-Stalinists and cold warriors, they felt particularly qualified to warn Americans about the increasing dangers from the Soviet Union and the virulent anti-Americanism rife in much of the Third World. To combat the external pressures, conservative theorists recommended massive rearmament and getting tough with the underdeveloped nations. In short, neoconservatives imagined America being again what it had been during the salad days of the Cold War. For a time, like millions of born-again Christians, they hoped that Jimmy Carter could start the country on the road back, especially after the president raided the predominantly neoconservative Trilateral Commission for many of his top appointments. Increasingly, they came to admire the tough-minded Committee on the Present Danger and its jeremiads about American weakness and Soviet strength. By 1980, the neoconservatives—and the rest of the New Right—were ready to gamble on Ronald Reagan.

Through the years, Ronald Wilson Reagan's political ideas covered almost the whole spectrum from left to right. As a Hollywood actor in the 1940s he was, as he later confessed, "a near-hopeless hemophiliac liberal" who cheerfully worked with communists in the Screen Actors Guild and served on the boards of two groups considered to be communist fronts. A wave of strikes disillusioned the handsome leading man, who denounced communism in 1946 and moved toward the political center. Elected president of the Screen Actors Guild, he testified before HCUA as a friendly witness, expressing the hope that "we are never prompted by fear of communism into compromising any of our democratic principles." Publicly, he refused to "name names"; privately, he provided them for the FBI. However, as a Cold War liberal, Reagan supported the naming names approach as a way of cleaning up Hollywood's tarnished image and the blacklist for communists who refused to repent. After Warner Brothers dropped his contract, Reagan went to work for General Electric in 1954, acting and making personal appearances. During the next eight years, he began to move to the right politically until he had become too controversial for the conservative GE. Reagan showed up at a Fred Schwarz Christian Anti-Communist Crusade rally. He helped to raise funds for the reelection to Congress of John Rousselot, an official of the John Birch Society. By the early 1960s, many of his opinions on domestic politics resembled those of Robert Welch. "I don't equate liberalism with socialism and communism," Reagan said in 1962, "but...they do have in common one characteristic—collectivism." He turned to selling soap and hosting a television western, but his dramatic appeal on behalf of Barry Goldwater's presidential campaign in 1964 raised millions of dollars and encouraged him to go into politics. He vaulted into the California governor's chair two years later in the wake of public anger over mounting disorder on university campuses. His two terms as governor disappointed his supporters on the far right. Taxes and government spending increased as he chose pragmatically to work with the liberal state legislature.

The 1980 Election

Reagan's unsuccessful run for the Republican presidential nomination in 1976 made him one of the best known and liked candidates in the country. Hoping to make another run in 1980, but out of political office, the former governor kept in touch with the voters through a series of syndicated radio commentaries which reestablished him as a darling of the Right. Once again, Reagan hit hard at the theme of liberals as communists, implying that the Soviets were duping proponents of nuclear disarmament in order to weaken American defenses. A 1979 broadcast on Joe McCarthy revealed how far the man who once told HCUA politely not to trample on democracy had come. "It's true," he said, "that the senator used a shotgun when a rifle was needed, injuring the innocent along with the guilty. Nevertheless, his broadsides should not be used today to infer that all who opposed Communist subversion were hysterical zealots." Reagan fired his rhetorical shotgun at McCarthy's favorite strawman, the Department of State, observing that it was time for a housecleaning of the appeasers who had carried out détente. Because the Kremlin had launched a campaign "to make anti-communism unfashionable," he said in another broadcast, "most people in public life are afraid to hint at a Communist conspiracy."

With the coalescing New Right firmly in his corner, Ronald Reagan set out to make anti-communism, with an anti-Soviet bent, fashionable again—even though it had never really been out of style. He had plenty of help from the Committee on the Present Danger, an organization, in the words of reporter Robert Scheer, which applied "a patina of intellectual respectability to what might otherwise have seemed to the voters no more than out-of-date and primitive anti-Communist ravings." The 1976 Team B report became the chief source for charges by Reagan and running mate George Bush that nuclear superiority, not détente, was the real Soviet aim. The committee also provided the Republican candidate with the "window of vulnerability" argument: in the mid-1980s the Soviet Union would have the capability to launch a successful nuclear first strike against the United States. "The Russians could just take us with a phone call," Reagan said many times on the campaign trail, meaning that the "window of vulnerability" would make America susceptible to Russian blackmail. Only a heavy arms buildup under their auspices, the Republicans said, could save the world from communism.

Challenger Reagan pressed his advantage, accusing President Jimmy Carter of "hypocrisy at its worst in cozying up to the Soviets." Asked if he thought the Soviet Union favored President Carter in the election, Reagan replied yes. His explanation revealed something of the Republican candidate's anti-communism. "You see," he began, "they [the Soviets] remember back, I guess [to] those union days when we had a domestic Communist problem. I was very definitely on the wrong side for them." Because he had grown to hate communism in the late 1940s, the feeling must have been mutual. "They" (Stalin? Khrushchev? Brezhnev?) had hated him all those years because he had helped to foil the red takeover of Hollywood. Reagan's heartfelt denunciations of the Soviet Union during the 1980 campaign and as president would have as much to do with an ancient union dispute as it did actual Soviet behavior. Ironically, the Kremlin hoped Reagan would win, reasoning (quite erroneously) that a Republican would return to the policy of détente.

During the fall campaign, Carter tried to make Reagan look like an irresponsible extremist, the way Lyndon Johnson's people had smeared Goldwater. Reagan would have none of it; with the Right already secured, he simply moved center, moderating his rhetoric. For the first time since the high 1920s, a genuine conservative had become president. Based on the new president's past anti-communist polemics, leftists saw a new red scare waiting in the wings. If that was what the New Right wanted, it would be disappointed.

Fighting "the Evil Empire"

In the 1980s, President Ronald Reagan sought to return the United States to a place in the world it occupied in the heady years between the end of World War II and the New Frontier, before Vietnam and Watergate destroyed the anti-communist consensus. The "Reagan Doctrine" of world-wide communist containment owed something to the policies of Truman and Eisenhower and much to the spirit of John F. Kennedy. At his inauguration, Kennedy said that "the torch has been passed to a new generation of Americans...unwilling to witness or permit the slow undoing of those human rights to which this nation has always been committed, and to which we are committed today at home and abroad." The generation JFK spoke for included Reagan, who was six years older than the president. "In one sense," Garry Wills has noted, "Reagan just came to fulfill that messianic view of America's place in the world." The Reagan policy of "peace through strength" led to great increases in military spending and concomitant red-bashing on the home front, just as it had during the previous era. But times had changed: economic woes and a multipolar world led to renewed frustration and insecurity. Even a president of immense personal popularity and great political savvy had trouble making the old formula work again.

For years liberals claimed that Reagan was merely lucky, a "teflon president" whose failings did not stick the way they did to other public officials. Journalist Leslie Gelb found Reagan unique among presidents "in possessing the mind of both an ideologue and a politician." His ideology rested on the bedrock of religious fundamentalism, laissez-faire capitalism, and anti-communism. Even when he made political concessions, the stern Reagan rhetoric, emanating from his sincere convictions, reinforced the image of absolute moral integrity. His pronouncements were the product of what his advisers referred to euphemistically as presidential "intellectual passivity." Reagan's knowledge of important subjects sometimes did not go further than the index cards staff members prepared for his perusal. For much of his first term, the president did not understand his administration's strategic and arms control programs. On several occasions, he criticized the Soviet Union for rejecting an American proposal of across the board cuts in land-based missiles. Later, he confessed to astonished members of Congress his ignorance of the fact that only twenty percent of American missiles fell into the land-based category compared to seventy percent for the Soviets. Just before a radio broadcast, Reagan chose to test his microphone with the lighthearted remark that "we have signed legislation today that would outlaw Russia forever. We begin bombing in five minutes." Few on either side of the Iron Curtain in Europe laughed. On another occasion he announced blithely that staunchly anti-communist South Africa's apartheid government had "eliminated the segregation that we once had in our own country." Reagan's talent for responding to complex questions with simple black and white, good and evil answers obviously pleased voters and seemed to have made up for his intellectual shortcomings.

People who had too many unpleasant surprises during the 1960s and 1970s liked Ronald Reagan because of his predictability. On communism in general and the Soviet Union especially, the president had been consistent. "The Soviet Union underlies all the unrest that is going on," he asserted during the 1980 campaign. "If they weren't engaged in this game of dominoes, there wouldn't be any hot spots in the world." The Cold War represented much more than traditional great power rivalry, he told Christian evangelists in 1983, for it meant "struggle between right and wrong, good and evil." The fight against the "evil empire," the Soviet Union, had to be carried to every corner of the globe, hence the "Reagan Doctrine" of world-wide containment. Two years later, with all the doctrinaire confidence of a Marxist, Reagan observed that "the tide of history is moving away from communism and into the warm sunlight of human freedom."

To support his rhetoric, Reagan stressed the modernization and expansion of U.S. strategic nuclear weaponry. He abhorred the strategy of deterrence, mutual assured destruction (MAD), because America was a hostage to Soviet nuclear missiles (as were the Soviets to US missiles). The "star wars" defensive system, if it would work, promised to change all this. Because he hoped to reestablish American nuclear superiority, Reagan showed little support, other than lip service, for arms control on the grounds that it only advanced Soviet interests. Some members of his administration spoke of winning the battle against communism with nuclear weapons. "It would be a terrible mess," said the head of the Federal Emergency Management Agency, "but it wouldn't be unmanageable." Thomas K. Jones, a deputy under secretary of defense, believed that the United States would recover from a full nuclear exchange in two to four years. "If there are enough shovels to go around," he told an interviewer, "everybody's going to make it." Since "the Russians could just take us with a phone call," once the "window of vulnerability" opened up, as Reagan warned in 1980, then the United States could do the same with nuclear supremacy. "Soviet leaders would have to choose between peacefully changing their Communist system," NSC staffer Richard Pipes fantasized, "...or going to war."

Preparing to battle communism on all fronts, Reagan fueled an arms race and an ideological war. That was half the battle. At home, the New Right worked to slash domestic spending for entitlement programs, prohibit abortion, mandate school prayers and balance the federal budget, all efforts at reversing the "communistic" trends toward big government and social permissiveness.

The New McCarthyism

The administration's fierce rhetoric and preparations for war, as well as the bellicose attitudes and actions of the Soviet Union, frightened people the world over. As the Cold War heated up, the Reagan administration engaged in McCarthyism against the anti-nuclear and environmentalist movements. When a broad-based peace movement represented by two million people marched in Western European capitals to protest against the new arms race in late 1981, Reagan told an interviewer: "Those are all sponsored by a thing called the World Peace Council, which is bought and paid for by the Soviet Union." The president smeared the American movement for a Soviet-American nuclear freeze with another "made in Moscow" line, commenting that the demonstrations were inspired "by some who want the weakening of America, and so are manipulating many honest and sincere people." Many objected to the president's remarks, including the *Washington Post*, which also chided the Peace Links freeze group (based on information provided by the Department of State) for associating with a Soviet front, Women's International League for Peace and Freedom. Shortly thereafter, the *Post* and the State Department backed off from the accusation. The president stuck to his charges as eight states and many cities and towns passed resolutions endorsing the freeze idea. A White House bibliography on red influence in the freeze movement included the now-discredited State Department report, a congressional hearing, and several magazine articles, including two from the leading neoconservative organs and three from the popular conservative monthly *Readers' Digest*—hardly an impressive reading list. While an FBI investigation subsequently concluded that the Soviets did not control or manipulate the American peace movement, opinion polls revealed that thirty-nine percent of those surveyed believed that communists had duped the freeze groups, just as the president had said.

Opposing the old Progressive idea of using government to safeguard the wilderness from business concerns, Interior Secretary James Watt called environmentalists "a left-wing cult" whose real motive was to weaken the country. Administration officials also implied that liberals served the communist cause when they opposed the president. "I never use the words Republicans and Democrats," Watt told a farmers' group, "It's liberals and Americans." "The opposition," Reagan charged in 1985, "often acts like a weaker America is a safer America."

Liberals, not surprisingly, disagreed. While remaining left of center on domestic social issues (welfare, civil rights, feminism, etc.) liberals quickly signed on for the renewed Cold War, just as they had chosen Truman over Henry Wallace in 1948 and supported consensus in the 1950s. The tactic of shifting blame to the Left, which liberals used to survive red scares in the past, became apparent as the news media showed fresh interest in the influence of communism in American life. The CBS news program "60 Minutes" attacked two church federations for supporting Marxism abroad. The *New York Times*, the *New Republic*, *Newsweek* and other liberal publications put distance between themselves and the tainted nuclear freeze movement. Liberal academics published books on the guilt of Alger Hiss and the Rosenbergs. Intellectuals picked up the old Sidney Hook-Arthur Schlesinger argument that communists, by their very nature, could not be part of the market place of ideas. The feisty Hook blasted professors attempting to organize opposition to Reagan's Strategic Defense Initiative, arguing "that commitment to academic freedom entails a moral obligation to support the defense of a free society threatened by a totalitarian enemy." "Communism is fascism," former leftist Susan Sontag announced. Explaining in the *Washington Post* "Why We Voted for Reagan," two former members of the New Left in the 1960s, Peter Collier and David Horowitz, noted: "[W]e agree with his vision of the world as a place increasingly inhospitable to democracy and increasingly dangerous for America." In early 1981, just a few months into Reagan's tenure, *The Progressive* (one of the last left-of-liberal magazines still publishing) predicted that a new red scare was just around the corner. It might have happened—if there had been something to be scared of on the domestic scene. With less than four thousand active members, the CPUSA frightened no one. Only briefly in the peace movement did American "radicals" find a rallying point.

Americans remained apprehensive over possible American intervention abroad, the implicit assumption behind the Reagan Doctrine of aiding Third World anti-communist revolutionaries. The Sandinista government of Nicaragua posed a special problem since American officials feared it had the makings of "another Cuba." The president put pressure on Congress to lift a ban on government funding of "contra" rebels, charging that those opposed to his policy suffered from "illusions about Communist regimes." Frustrated by the lack of public support for Reagan's policy and the congressional prohibitions, Lt. Colonel Oliver North secretly coordinated contra operations against Nicaragua in 1985-1986 under the supervision of successive national security advisers Robert C. McFarlane and John M. Poindexter. The administration and private supporters raised tens of millions of dollars (including profits from arms sales to Iran) for North's "Project Democracy," a paramilitary operation involving fleets of planes and ships, an airfield, and a secure communications system. Meanwhile, Congress voted to give the contra forces "non-lethal aid," a meaningless distinction since the rebels would have that much more money to buy guns and bullets from others sources. Several Democrats switched sides on the issue after a plea from a colleague to support the bill so that no one could accuse them of being "soft on communism" during the next election campaign. Eventually the president convinced Congress to vote the contras $100 million in aid, lethal and otherwise, to be channeled through the CIA. FBI Director William Webster revealed that he had received "specific taskings" from the National Security Council and the CIA to interview Americans who visited Nicaragua or took an active interest in the Sandinistas. Still, the public remained divided with many choosing to believe the president's assertion that the contras "are the moral equivalent of the Founding Fathers and the brave men and women of the French Resistance." Others, fearing "another Vietnam," put credence in the words of former contra leader Edgar Chamorro, who spoke of a "premeditated policy to terrorize civilian noncombatants....Hundreds of civilian murders, mutilations, tortures and rapes...which the contra leaders and their CIA superiors were well aware."

The New Right Chafes

The New Right became impatient with Ronald Reagan. Time and again, the president behaved more moderately than his rhetoric would have indicated. Arms talks with the Soviets continued during the murderous war in Afghanistan. Little was done when a military government declared martial law in Poland and the Soviets shot down a South Korean 747 passenger jet which strayed into Russian territory. Although his statement branding nations who support terrorism (Iran, Libya, North Korea, Cuba, and Nicaragua) as "outlaw states run by the strangest collection of misfits, looney tunes, and squalid criminals since the advent of the Third Reich" indicated a belief in terrorism as an adjunct of the communist conspiracy, Reagan's response to specific acts of political terror were relatively restrained. The president compromised with Congress over the Reagan Doctrine in Latin America and Africa and on the defense budget. Reagan even met with Soviet leader Mikhail Gorbachev in Geneva. But the sniping from the right began long before that. The New Right did not care for Reagan's first appointment to the Supreme Court, Sandra Day O'Connor (soft on abortion), Secretary of State Alexander Haig (soft on communism), and Attorney General William French Smith (soft on affirmative action). They resented the president's pursuit of closer relations with China, which they regarded as a "sell out" of Taiwan. Frustrated by the continuation of big government, New Right politicos embarrassed the White House at the 1984 Republican National Convention with a series of reactionary party platform planks calling for an end to the welfare state and the graduated income tax, and a return to the gold standard. Neoconservatives expressed displeasure with Reagan's restrained responses to terrorism which, in the words of Norman Podhoretz, "send the wrong signals to the Soviet Union." Republican conservatives, who dared not attack the popular Reagan personally, first assailed White House Chief of Staff James Baker III, and then Haig's replacement as secretary of state, George Shultz, for being soft on terrorism and communism. A faction on the GOP right, along with the Moral Majority, the Committee for the Survival of a Free Congress, the Conservative Caucus, and the Heritage Foundation all demanded the secretary of state's resignation.

An administration only slightly more conservative than Eisenhower and Dulles was not acceptable to those in the New Right who considered themselves radical activists. Reagan's veer toward moderate conservatism doubly vexed Jerry Falwell, Richard Viguerie, and some right-wing think tanks whose sources of funding diminished following Reagan's reelection in 1984. Once the wizard of direct-mail fundraising, Viguerie fell deeply into debt while bad publicity forced Falwell to scrap the Moral Majority in favor of the Liberty Federation, an organization concentrating on more lucrative, positive issues such as support for Reagan's "Star Wars" space defense plan and Israel. Senator Jesse Helms of North Carolina, the first politician elected by the New Right, won another term but invited ridicule with his futile scheme to purchase Columbia Broadcasting System so he could fire liberal newsman Dan Rather. Helms' penchant for wild charges such as the claim that the CIA had a "pro-Soviet bias" and that the Russians were manufacturing a deadly new flu from the genes of rattlesnakes further stretched his credibility. Accuracy in Academia, a New Right organization dedicated to secretly monitoring the lectures of college professors for communist propaganda, ran into widespread opposition from educators of all political stripes.

The leading right-wing ideologue of the Democratic party and self-proclaimed "greatest living economist," Lyndon LaRouche, Jr., organized a tightly-knit political cult which advertised itself aggressively. LaRouche also claimed that there existed a massive conspiracy to destroy the world which involved the Queen of England, *Playboy*, the Masons, the Jesuits, the Jews, the AFL-CIO, and, of course, the communists. Following two Democratic primary victories in Illinois in 1986, though, LaRouche received an avalanche of negative publicity for his strange theories and strong-arm fundraising methods. Old right extremists also fell on hard times in the mid-1980s. The John Birch Society went into decline after the death of founder Robert Welch with the once prosperous Houston branch reduced to sharing a dank office with an organization for hemophiliacs. The FBI broke up The Order, a splinter group associated with the Ku Klux Klan and the neo-Nazi Aryan Nations, following the robbery of an armored car.

For a time, others on the far right continued to prosper, especially those committed to an idea made fashionable by the Reagan Doctrine: "low intensity warfare" against communists in the Third World. Bankrolled by the governments of Taiwan, South Korea, Paraguay, and Saudi Arabia, the World Anti-Communist League (WACL) emerged as a leader in private aid to anti-communist insurgents. In 1985, wealthy Texans paid $500 a plate at a WACL fundraiser to share a meal with "freedom fighters" from Nicaragua and Afghanistan as well as aging emigres from China and the Soviet Union. The diners heard greetings from President Reagan and paid tribute to Ellen Garwood, who donated money to purchase a helicopter for the Nicaraguan contras. Former Major General John K. Singlaub (sacked by Carter for criticizing planned troop withdrawals from South Korea) steered the organization from the lunatic fringe of fascism and anti-semitism to a respectability which extended all the way to the Oval Office. With help from national security adviser Robert McFarlane, the WACL began shipping arms and supplies to Nicaraguan contras. The tax-exempt National Endowment for the Preservation of Liberty raised millions of dollars, some of which found its way into Swiss bank accounts used by Colonel Oliver North for "Project Democracy." Other groups jumped on the low intensity warfare bandwagon, including anti-ERA activist Phyllis Schafly's group Eagle Forum, which sent the contras "Freedom Fighter Friendship Kits" complete with toothbrushes, disposable razors, and breathe mints. The Omega Group, parent company to *Soldier of Fortune*, a magazine specializing in anti-communist adventure stories, also collected money for the Nicaraguan rebels. Private funds and foreign donations far outstripped government aid to anti-communists in Latin America, altogether appropriate considering the New Right's distaste for "big government," but potentially dangerous as well. "Contragate" revelations concerning North's secret war, the diversion to the contras of profits from the sale of weapons to Iran, and administration connivance with private anti-communist fundraisers led to an investigation by a special presidential commission and televised congressional hearings.

The Culture of Anti-Communism

Popular culture reflected the continuing popularity of the New Right's particular brand of anti-communism in the 1980s. Advertisers took advantage of heightened anti-Soviet feelings and a new American smugness to pitch their wares. A chain of appliance stores ran television commercials showing a Russian submarine crew stocking up on bargains only to discover that one of their number had yielded to the temptation of defecting to capitalism. To illustrate the joys of variety at their hamburger stands, "Wendy's" used a Russian fashion show where there were no choices—just baggy clothes modeled by sexless Soviet matrons. MCI telephone service set an ad in a Siberian fish market to show that evil flourished where there was no competition. Two major breweries sold beer on television with anti-communist jokes.

Movies also reflected the new mood epitomized by the Reagan Doctrine. After the fall of Saigon in 1975, Hollywood played out the pain, confusion, and guilt of the crusade in Southeast Asia in movies like *The Deer Hunter*, *Apocalypse Now*, and *Who'll Stop the Rain*. In 1981, Reagan's first year in office, actor Bill Murray bellowed in the comedy *Stripes*: "This is America! We're ten and one!" The one was Vietnam, but few could laugh it off. The New Right, especially the neoconservatives, decided that the war had been "a noble cause" (as Reagan said) which liberal and centrist politicians did not allow the military to win. Several films mirrored the notion that Americans still had unfinished business in Asia. In *Uncommon Valor* (1983), a group of troubled veterans shoots and dynamites their way into communist Laos to bring freedom to American prisoners of war. Sylvester Stallone's *Rambo: First Blood, Part II* (1985) effected a similar rescue in Vietnam, no thanks to an Army bureaucrat and a fat politician, who both sell him out.

The Russian commandant of the POW camp (speaking with a German accent) reminded the audience that Vietnam had indeed become part of the red monolith and that communists are really Nazis.

America took on the Kremlin more directly in other screen sagas such as *Rocky IV* (1985) which pits Stallone against a Russian giant in a boxing match Rocky describes as "Us against Them." Rocky trains the old-fashioned way; the handlers of the Russian Drago use scientists, computers, and steroids, metaphors for American fears of Russian technology and cheating. Only after the red giant has fallen does Rocky proclaim that "If you can change, and I can change, maybe we all can change." For the more cultured cold warrior, *White Nights* (1985) told the story of two ballet dancers, a black American living in Soviet exile and a Russian who fled to America only to have his plane crash in Siberia. Both decide America is a far better place and escape back to the West. Two anti-communist action films depict World War III in the United States. In *Red Dawn* (1984) Americans face a joint invasion by Nicaraguan, Cuban, and Russian soldiers, although the viewer soon learns that the Latins are but tender hearted dupes for the cold-as-steel Russians. *Invasion U.S.A.* (1985) plays out a similar scenario, with Arabs joining the Soviet-Latin communist attack fanning out from Miami. Cold War liberals had their favorites too, such as *The Killing Fields* (1984), a graphic portrait of the evils of communist Cambodia which followed American failure there and *Dangerous Moves* (1985), an anti-Soviet film about chess with a few good Russians in it. Unlike the essentially passive and defensive films of the 1950s, the 1980s movies exude aggression and a desire for revenge. Many end with a dramatic confrontation between the American hero and the communist bad guy in a symbolic showdown of ideologies. Experts disagree whether such entertainment fuels aggressive impulses or soothes them by providing an outlet for frustrations. Either way, most of these films reinforced caricatures and stereotypes which belie the complexities of East-West relations in a dangerous world.

Legacies

The United States was on the verge of another red scare in 1968. The faltering crusade in Vietnam brought the invisible ideology of anti-communism into question for the first time in a generation. Pledged to find a way out of the morass yet determined to retain American credibility in the world, Richard Nixon attempted to update the anti-communist mission. Results overseas included closer relations with the largest red nations and a widening of the war in Southeast Asia, while, in the United States, the administration expanded attacks on the dissident left. The government offensive yielded the largest mass dragnets since Palmer's Red Scare, political trials rivaling those of the Truman years, and rhetoric reminiscent of McCarthy and McCarran. But in the absence of anti-communist consensus, the attempt to make the country see red failed, netting only a few radical scalps and further political polarization. In desperation, Nixon's administration applied red scare tactics to liberals and moderates, coming to ruin after the failure of a frantic cover-up.

After Ford, Carter, and an imperial Congress cleaned up Nixon's attempted red scare, a new anti-communist movement gained momentum in the late 1970s. Mostly, the New Right offered an agenda that was old: a renewed commitment to fighting communism around the world and reversing the trend toward socialism in the United States. This coalition of ultraconservative activists, Christian fundamentalists, and soured liberals united behind Ronald Reagan, who had moved by degrees to the right himself over a period of more than thirty years. The New Right applauded Reagan the ideologue for denouncing "the evil empire," promising to oppose communist movements at all points on the globe, and red-baiting leftists. Reagan the pragmatist angered them with his talk of arms control and compromises with Congress over funding to anti-communist causes.

Ronald Reagan, George Bush, and their many allies proclaimed loud and often during their tenure of office that "America is back," as did liberal Democrats and a host of other elites. After the turbulent 1960s and the frustrating 1970s, that was what many

Americans wanted to hear. But opinion polls taken halfway through the second Reagan/Bush term indicated that people had no more faith in their government than they did during Vietnam and Watergate. Disunity prevailed rather than the harmony and consensus which dominated the 1950s. Ironically, the lack of unity forced Reagan toward the political center where his domestic conservatism came to resemble that of Dwight Eisenhower, much to the disappointment of the New Right. "Sometimes," Reagan said, only half in jest, "our right hand doesn't know what our far-right hand is doing." It would take more than slogans to put the anti-communist consensus back together again. The administration could rout the nuclear freeze movement yet polls showed that an overwhelming majority of Americans favored arms reduction rather than the president's "Star Wars" space defense system. Because the country could not be rallied to support intervention in Nicaragua, the administration turned to privately financed covert operations. The public seemed more interested in the moral issue of racial apartheid in South Africa than renewing the anti-communist crusade in the Third World. Perhaps the political leaders, Hollywood, and Madison Avenue did not give the voters enough credit; maybe they understood that there was no going back to the sunny 1950s when the United States had absolute nuclear superiority and the CIA managed containment in underdeveloped areas.

Concluding Thoughts

Throughout the twentieth century, anti-communism has played a significant, if intermittent, role in American life. The domestic and foreign targets of anti-communist wrath have changed with time and circumstance. During the Progressive Era, middle-class reformers attacked socialists, syndicalists, and anarchists for harboring "unAmerican" ideas. The Bolshevik Revolution of 1917 touched off a wave of fright leading to the Red Scare at home which turned into a xenophobic frenzy. The interwar period saw Americans isolating themselves from the Soviet contagion while keeping a wary eye on native and alien followers of Joseph Stalin. Hatred and anxiety deepened following the Nazi-Soviet Pact, swung rapidly the other way during a period of cooperation in the war against fascism, and plunged to new depths of dread during the Cold War era. The postwar consensus that communism constituted a mortal threat to national security led to a bigger federal government, an arms race, global containment, and periodic witch hunts for those deemed subversive, unpatriotic, or duped. The government launched military campaigns against communist governments in Korea, China, and Vietnam while undertaking clandestine wars against Marxists in Cuba, Latin America, Africa, Europe, and Asia. Meanwhile, the Soviet Union, mother country of communism, lurked always in the background as the ultimate threat.

While businessmen, politicians and self-appointed saviors have issued dire warnings for more than a century about the imminent triumph of communism in the United States, in reality no sizeable left or radical movement ever developed a significant number of followers. The Socialist Party of America, a nonrevolutionary organization, precipitated its decline and downfall by militantly opposing World War I, essentially a revolutionary stance. After the Bolshevik coup in Russia the party promptly divided into several weak factions. During the Great Depression and World War II the Communist Party briefly gained some popular support, much of it due to working with noncommunists. Wilson's New Freedom and FDR's New Deal, liberal Democratic programs institutionalizing a mixed economy, also helped to cut the legs out from under radicalism at critical junctures. The New Left of the 1960s seemed more interested in political culture than revolutionary politics and soon collapsed without ever having attracted the interest or support of American workers. In short, America has not provided fertile ground for leftists or radicals, a condition analysts since Marx have struggled to explain.

A good case can be made for "American exceptionalism," the idea that America evolved so differently from Marx's conception of European capitalist development, that a transition to socialism was improbable. It can also be argued that an American culture rooted in individualism rather than in any peculiar economic developments kept socialism from becoming a mass movement. Political traditions must be taken into consideration as well. The growth of two highly competitive, broad-based centrist political parties brought great stability to the American system at the expense of radicalism. Surely economics, politics, and culture all contributed to the formidable barriers facing the establishment of a politically viable Left. These factors, combined with the radicals' own blunders, make the Left's long record of failures understandable.

If conditions in America made life exceptionally difficult for the Left, that same environment has allowed anti-communism to thrive. Strident individualism, the most basic of American values, along with concomitant concerns for civil liberties and property rights shaped an anti-communist outlook grounded in tradition. As a nation of immigrants, Americans have a sense of nationalism which requires periodic reaffirmations of native ideals and loyalties. During times of crisis, critics (especially those left of center) are often perceived as disloyal to American values and frequently persecuted. Closely related to its intense nationalism is American xenophobia, a fear or hatred of things foreign. In colonial times

New Englanders feared that Catholics would thwart their divine mission to build a "city on the hill," the most perfect civilization in the world. Throughout most of the nineteenth century hatred of Britain simmered and sometimes boiled for the same reason. In the twentieth century, communism in general and the Soviet Union in particular have been the targets of this xenophobia. To those Americans who give credence to the conspiracy theory of history—the notion that a sinister force is planning secretly to subvert the American system—communism is the diabolical successor to the supposed conspiracies of Roman Catholicism, Mormonism, Judaism and the Masons. Protestant tradition, especially the religious heritage of fundamentalism, predisposes many to view the world only in terms of good and evil. Politics thus is reduced to Armageddon, a struggle of the chosen people against the red Satan.

These shared beliefs which shaped the American character all contributed to the rise of the invisible ideology of anti-communism. The Marxists emphasized collective rather than individual action and scorned the institution of private property. Communism was internationalist, a rival movement which denied the validity of America's mission. Foreign in origin, conspiratorial in nature, and explicitly atheistic, communism appeared to be the very antithesis of American civilization.

America's invisible ideology of anti-communism smacks more of dogma than doctrine. It is emotional, logically inconsistent, negative rather than positive, and prompted more by fear than a commitment to American values. The nation has been locked in this imbroglio for so long that many individuals use their anti-communism to define themselves as Americans. The struggle is thus reduced to a series of exact opposites: democracy v. despotism, atheists v. the godly, the peaceful v. the warlike, moderation v. extremism, and good v. evil. Ironically, anti-communists have used these misrepresentations of reality to justify becoming like the enemy; because, for example, "they" are immoral, then "we" must become immoral to defeat them. All communist actions become suspect. Warlike behavior demonstrates their evil; moderation, even gestures of friendship illustrate red deception.

Extreme anti-communism has distorted American ideals. Faced with the image of a wicked bogy, many people developed a low tolerance for legitimate dissent from government policies. In an atmosphere of unbearable tension, ambitious politicians and zealous followers spawn and then exploit periods of gnawing fear. Such red scares are not accidental aberrations, then, but the inevitable by-products of political extremism, demonstrations of the American ethic twisted into primitive and reactionary crusades. They endanger the civil liberties of all Americans and make it extremely difficult to function as an open society.

After World War II, a prolonged red scare helped to create a "military Keynesianism," which amounts to massive public subsidy of defense-related businesses engaged in defense work on an immense scale. It also put the American economy on a permanent wartime footing and forged a powerful alliance between the Pentagon and private defense industries. This military-industrial complex, so worrisome to Dwight Eisenhower that he warned the nation about it in his Farewell Address, has used the anti-communist consensus to protect American business interests abroad. On several occasions when Third World governments attempted to take control of their own domestic assets (oil in Iran, bananas in Guatemala, etc.) the United States saw nonaligned revolutionaries, religious nationalists, and proponents of democracy simply as "Reds." In the face of American coercion, targeted regimes sometimes turned to the Communist Bloc for assistance rather than capitulate, an option which served to justify further subversion or outright intervention by Washington. The invisible ideology also generated foreign military expeditions costly in blood and treasure.

Nothing enrages communists and anti-communists as much as the suggestion that the foreign policies of these ideological opponents have much in common. But history does suggest that they do. Ideologues on both sides use history to prove the righteousness of their cause. Communists invoke Marx's doctrine of "historical inevitability"; anti-communists point to the Declaration of Independence, the Constitution, the democratic heritage, a high standard of living based on "free enterprise," and the Bible. Both sides retain a fondness for comparing the other to Hitler and the

Nazis, stale analogies no more profound than bumper stickers. Still, a free inquiry into history unencumbered by either Marxist-Leninist dogmas or the invisible ideology can yield useful insights. American attitudes and actions toward communism seemed frozen in the days of Stalin, a tyrant whose reign the Soviets have tried to forget but who Americans constantly revive because his image satisfies the need for a villainous stereotype. A 1985 opinion poll asked Americans five elementary questions about recent Soviet communist history: whether they knew of the 1918 American invasion of Russia, which side the USSR was on during World War II, that the Soviets suffered more casualties than the U. S. in that war, and the identification of the KGB and the current Soviet leader. One in four respondents could not answer a single question while only fourteen percent knew four or five answers. The knowledgeable minority appeared more interested in reducing tensions with the communists than those who could not answer the questions. Other polls indicated that people knew even less about communism in the Third World. More education could allow Americans to deal with the reality of communism rather than just their fears. They would then be better able to examine each new crisis on the basis of reason rather than emotion.

While many American politicians have perpetuated anti-communism out of genuine concern for national security and some for less altruistic reasons such as getting re-elected, it is helpful to be aware of the dangers inherent in such negative crusades. In his Farewell Address, George Washington warned: "The nation which indulges towards another an habitual hatred or an habitual fondness is in some degree a slave. It is a slave to its animosity or to its affection....Antipathy in one nation against another disposes each more readily to offer insult and injury...." While the world has changed much since the time when Washington led a revolution to create a republic in a monarchist world, his wisdom is still apparent. Late in his life, the Protestant theologian Reinhold Niebuhr, who did so much to bring liberals into the anti-communist consensus, cautioned that "a frantic anti-communism can become so similar in its temper of hatefulness to communism itself." In the clash between two systems, each of which claims to be the greatest in human history, self-righteous hatred poses a threat as great as any ideology. Above all, negative crusades end up perpetuating wickedness, as Aldous Huxley understood. The author of the anti-communist classic *Brave New World* observed that "those who crusade, not for God in themselves, but against the devil in others, never succeed in making the world better, but leave it either as it was, or sometimes even perceptibly worse than it was, before the crusade began. By thinking primarily of evil we tend, however excellent our intentions, to create occasions for evil to manifest itself."

Communism poses threats to the United States on several fronts. As practiced thus far, Marxism challenges the heritage of liberal capitalism as do nations and movements espousing variations of communism. There also exists a menace from within, not so much from the "red" targets of Palmer, Truman, McCarthy, Nixon, Reagan and others as from the excesses of these zealous anti-communists. They would curtail civil liberties in order to protect them, warp American values to preserve them, destroy Third World peoples to save them, and gamble with nuclear weapons in the hope of victory. Americans must learn to be more responsible in their anti-communism, or their dreams and values as a people will continue to be distorted in periodic negative crusades and red scares rather than reflecting the positive yearnings of their heritage.

PART   II

Bibliography

References

There are thousands of books, pamphlets, and articles on communism and anti-communism. Items selected for this bibliography represent a cross section of works on topics and time periods discussed in Part I. For the student wishing to know more about a given subject area, they represent beginning points for research. Many of the books and articles cited contain extensive bibliographies. Footnotes and endnotes also provide sources of additional information, which may or may not be cited in bibliographies.

Bibliographies

No comprehensive bibliography of works on anti-communism has been published. In addition to works cited below, those seeking information on a special topic related to anti-communism should consult *Reviews in American History* as well as more specialized publications such as *Labor History* and *Wisconsin Magazine of History* for extended review essays on new works. Many scholarly journals print brief reviews of new monographs, although there can be a lapse of two to three years between the publication of a book and the review. The American Historical Associations's *Recently Published Articles* and "Recent Articles," a regular section in the *Journal of American History* are excellent sources for scholarly articles. The *Reader's Guide to Periodical Literature* covers popular magazines as well. The *New York Times*, self-proclaimed "newspaper of record," has an excellent index of its daily editions. Richard Dean Burns' Truman bibliography (entry 4) is the first in a series of compilations centering around presidential administrations.

The book edited by Walter Kolarz (entry 11) is an enlarged version of one by R.N. Hunt (entry 10).

1   American Historical Association. *Guide to Historical Literature*. New York: Macmillan, 1961--.

2   Basler, Roy P. et. al., eds. *A Guide to the Study of the United States of America*. Washington, D.C.: Library of Congress, 1960.

3   Burns, Richard Dean, ed. *Guide to American Foreign Relations Since 1700*. Santa Barbara, CA: ABC-Clio, 1983.

4   _____. *Harry S. Truman: A Bibliography of His Times and Presidency*. Wilmington, DE: Scholarly Resources, 1984.

5   Corker, Charles. *Bibliography on the Communist Problem in the United States*. New York: Fund For the Republic, 1955.

6   Davis, Lenwood G., and Sims-Wood, Janet L. *The Ku Klux Klan: A Bibliography*. Westport, CT: Greenwood, 1984.

7   Delaney, Robert Finley. *The Literature of Communism in America: A Selected Reference Guide*. Washington, D.C.: Catholic University Press, 1962.

8   Friedel, Frank, ed. *Harvard Guide to American History*. 2 vols. Cambridge, MA: Harvard University Press, 1974.

9   Haynes, John E. *Communism and Anti-Communism in the United States: An Annotated Guide to Historical Writings*. New York: Garland, 1987.

1 0   Hunt, R.N., ed. *Books on Communism: A Bibliography*. London: Ampersand, 1959.

1 1   Kolarz, Walter, ed. *Books on Communism: A Bibliography*. New York: Oxford University Press, 1964.

1 2   Orr, Oliver H., Jr. *A Guide to the Study of the United States of America: Supplement 1956-1965*. Washington, D.C.: Library of Congress, 1976.

1 3   Seidman, Joel, ed. *Communism in the United States—A Bibliography*. Ithaca, NY: Cornell University Press, 1969.

1 4   Shain, Russell E. "Cold War Films, 1948-1962: An Annotated Bibliography." *Journal of Popular Film* 3 (1974): 365-72.

1 5   U.S. Superintendent of Documents. *Monthly Catalog of United States Government Publications*. Washington, D.C.: G.P.O., 1895-.

General Works

Books by the American Friends Service Committe (entry 16), Sidney Lens (entry 33) and Michael Parenti (entry 37) are the only works which focus solely on the theme of anti-communism. The

Millibrand/Liebman article (entry 35) examines anti-communism from a socialist perspective. Robert J. Goldstein's encyclopedic account (entry 22) concentrates on repression of the Left. Curry/Brown (entry 17) and Davis (entry 18) present readings on the conspiracy minded, especially those obsessed with the communist conspiracy. Richard Hofstadter (entry 26) speculates on the American vulnerability to conspiracy theories. The Egbert/Persons volumes (entry 21) were the first academic studies of American leftists. The most important essay, Daniel Bell's "The Background and Development of Marxian Socialism in the United States," contains the now famous suggestion that socialists failed because they were "in but not of the world." After the appearance of these essays, the liberal Fund for the Republic sponsored a series of works on communism, the best of which are by Theodore Draper (entry 20) who emphasizes the American loss of innocence as the party bowed to the Kremlin's will in the 1920s and David Shannon (entry 38) who picks up the narrative after World War II. Other authors contributing volumes to this series include Clinton Rossier (entry 455) and Daniel Aaron (entry 141). Howe and Coser (entry 27) write critically of the Communist party from a socialist vantage point.

16   American Friends Service Committee. *Anatomy of Anti-Communism.* New York: Hill & Wang, 1969.

17   Curry, Richard O., and Brown, Thomas M., eds. *Conspiracy: The Fear of Subversion in American History.* New York: Holt, Rinehart & Winston, 1972.

18   Davis, David B., ed. *The Fear of Conspiracy: Images of Un-American Subversion from the Revolution to the Present.* Ithaca, NY: Cornell University Press, 1971.

19   Diggins, John P. *The American Left in the Twentieth Century.* New York: Harcourt, Brace, 1973.

20   Draper, Theodore. *The Roots of American Communism.* New York: Viking, 1957.

21   Egbert, Donald E., and Persons, Stow, eds. *Socialism and American Life.* 2 vols. Princeton, NJ: Princteon University Press, 1952.

22   Goldstein, Robert J. *Political Repression in Modern America: From 1870 to the Present.* Cambridge, MA: Schenkman, 1978.

23   Guttmann, Allen. *The Conservative Tradition in America.* New York: Oxford University Press, 1967.

24   Hamby, Alonzo. *Liberalism and Its Challengers, F.D.R. to Reagan.* New York: Oxford University Press, 1985.

25 Higham, John. *Strangers in the Land: Patterns of American Nativism, 1860-1925*. New York: Atheneum, 1963.

26 Hofstadter, Richard. *The Paranoid Style in American Politics*. Chicago: University of Chicago Press, 1979.

27 Howe, Irving, and Coser, Lewis. *The American Communist Party: A Critical History (1919-1957)*. Boston: Beacon, 1957.

28 Hyfler, Robert. *Prophets of the Left: American Socialist Thought in the Twentieth Century*. Westport, CT: Greenwood, 1984.

29 Jaffe, Philip J. *The Rise and Fall of American Communism*. New York: Horizon, 1975.

30 Kutler, Stanley I. *The American Inquisition: Justice and Injustice in the Cold War*. New York: Hill & Wang, 1982.

31 Lasch, Christopher. *The Agony of the American Left*. New York: Random House, 1969.

32 Laslett, John H. M., and Lipset, Seymour Martin, eds. *Failure of a Dream? Essays in the History of American Socialism*. Garden City, NY: Doubleday, 1974.

33 Lens, Sidney. *The Futile Crusade: Anti-Communism as American Credo*. Chicago: Quadrangle, 1964.

34 Levin, Murray. *Political Hysteria in America: The Democratic Capacity for Repression*. New York: Basic Books, 1971.

35 Millibrand, Ralph, and Liebman, Marcel. "Reflections on Anti-Communism." *Monthly Review* 37 (1985): 1-29.

36 Nelson, Harold, ed. *Freedom of the Press from Hamilton to the Warren Court*. Indianapolis: Bobbs-Merrill, 1967.

37 Parenti, Michael. *The Anti-Communist Impulse*. New York: Random House, 1969.

38 Shannon, David A. *The Decline of American Communism: A History of the Communist Party of the United States Since 1945*. New York: Harcourt, Brace, 1959.

39 _____. *The Socialist Party of America: A History*. New York: Macmillan, 1955.

40 Stouffer, Samuel A. *Communism, Conformity, and Civil Liberties*. Garden City, NY: Doubleday, 1955.

41 Wilson, Edmund. *To the Finland Station: A Study in the Writing and Acting of History*. Garden City, NY: Doubleday, 1953.

Nineteenth Century

With the exception of the Haymarket riot (items 42 and 50), historians have paid scant attention to anti-communism in the nineteenth century. Edward Bellamy's novel (entry 43) is included for its importance in introducing socialism to the American middle class. Goldstein (entry 22) provides a chapter on anti-communist repression from 1870 to 1900.

42   Avrich, Paul. *The Haymarket Tragedy.*   Princeton, NJ: Princeton University Press, 1984.

43   Bellamy, Edward. *Looking Backward: 2000-1887.* Boston: Ticknor, 1888.

44   Bruce, Robert V. *1877: Year of Violence.* Chicago: Quadrangle, 1970.

45   David, Henry. *The History of the Haymarket Affair.* New York: Collier, 1963.

46   Fogarty, Robert S. *Dictionary of American Communal and Utopian History.* Westport, CT: Greenwood, 1980.

47   Gutman, Herbert G. "Trouble on the Railroads in 1873-1874: Prelude to the 1877 Crisis?" In Daniel J. Leab, ed. *The Labor History Reader.* Urbana: University of Illinois Press, 1985, pp. 132-52.

48   Fried, Albert, ed. *Socialism in America: From the Shakers to the Third International.* Garden City, NY: Doubleday, 1970.

49   Harris, David J. *Socialist Origins in the United States: American Forerunners of Marx, 1817-1832.* Amsterdam: Van Gorcum, 1966.

50   Kebabian, John S. *The Haymarket Affair and the Trial of the Chicago Anarchists, 1886.* New York: H.P. Kraus, 1970.

51   Noyes, John Humphrey. *History of American Socialism.* New York: Hillary House, 1961.

52   Quint, Howard H. *The Forging of American Socialism: Origins of the Modern Movement.* Indianapolis: Bobbs-Merrill, 1964.

53   Webber, Everett. *Escape to Utopia: The Communal Movement in America.* New York: Hastings House, 1959.

Progressive Era

The Progressive Era was also the "golden age of socialism," a time when the Socialist party elected over one thousand candidates to office. Neil Basen (entry 55) covers the life and work of Kate Richards O'Hare, second only to Debs in popularity with the Socialist rank and file, while Buhle (entry 57) examines native-born and immigrant women in the movement. James R. Green (entry 64) provides superb coverage of socialism and anti-radicalism in Oklahoma, Texas, Louisiana, and Arkansas. Just as the IWW attracted much attention at the time, so historians have examined their "rough-and-tumble story" in more detail than other left-wing groups. Marxist Philip Foner (entry 61) concludes that Wobbly martyr Joe Hill was framed. James Weinstein (entry 72) points out that as a social force, the IWW was not nearly as important as the Socialist party. He also challenges Bell's assumption (entry 21) that Wilson's New Freedom cut the legs out from under the socialists. Writing at the time of the New Left's collapse, Bryan Strong (entry 69) chides consensus historians for distorting the history of American socialism.

54   Adams, Graham, Jr. *The Age of Industrial Violence, 1910-1915*. New York: Columbia University Press, 1966.

55   Basen, Neil K. "Kate Richards O'Hare: The 'First Lady' of American Socialism, 1901-1917." *Labor History* 21 (1980): 165-99.

56   Blum, John Morton. *The Republican Roosevelt*. New York: Atheneum, 1962.

57   Buhle, Mary Jo. *Women and American Socialism, 1870-1920*. Urbana: University of Illinois Press, 1981.

58   Cahn, Bill. *Mill Town*. New York: Cameron & Kahn, 1954.

59   Chaplain, Ralph. *Wobbly: The Rough-and-Tumble Story of an American Radical*. Chicago: University of Chicago Press, 1948.

60   Elliott, Russell R. "Labor Troubles in the Mining Camp at Goldfield, Nevada, 1906-1908." *Pacific Historical Review* 19 (950): 369-84.

61   Foner, Philip S. *The Case of Joe Hill*. New York: International Publishers, 1965.

62   Fox, Richard W. "The Paradox of 'Progressive' Socialism: The Case of Morris Hillquit, 1901-1914." *American Quarterly* 26 (1974): 127-40.

63   Golin, Steve. "Defeat Becomes Disaster: The Paterson Strike of 1913 and the Decline of the IWW." *Labor History* 24 (1983): 223-48.

64   Green, James R. *Grass-Roots Socialism: Radical Movements in the Southwest, 1895-1943*. Baton Rouge: Louisiana State University Press, 1978.

65   Kipnis, Ira. *The American Socialist Movement: 1897-1912*. New York: Columbia University Press, 1952.

66   Kolko, Gabriel. *The Triumph of Conservatism: A Reinterpretation of American History, 1900-1916*. Chicago: Quadrangle, 1963.

67   McWhiney, Grady. "Louisiana Socialists in the Early Twentieth Century: A Study of Rustic Radicalism." *Journal of Southern History* 20 (1954): 315-336.

68   Renshaw, Patrick. *The Wobblies: The Story of Syndicalism in the United States*. Garden City, NY: Doubleday, 1967.

69   Strong, Bryan. "Historians and American Socialism, 1900-1920." *Science and Society* 34 (1970): 387-97.

70   Tyler, Robert. *Rebels of the Woods: The IWW in the Pacific Northwest*. Eugene: University of Oregon Press, 1967.

71   Weinstein, James. *The Corporate Ideal in the Liberal State, 1900-1918*. Boston: Beacon, 1968.

72   _____. *The Decline of Socialism in America, 1912-1925*. New York: Vintage, 1969.

73   Winters, Donald E., Jr. *The Soul of the Wobblies: The I.W.W., Religion, and American Culture in the Progressive Era, 1905-1917*. Westport, CT: Greenwood, 1985.

World War I

The War at Home

Ferrell (entry 75) and Kennedy (entry 81) provide excellent overviews of the war years, including analysis of the growing intolerance toward dissenters. Peterson and Fite (entry 85) concentrate on the persecution of anarchists, the IWW, and the Socialist party. Scheiber (86) and Murphy (84) also have much to say about anti-radicalism. James Weinstein (entry 72) makes the point that although the federal government and local vigilantes disrupted Socialist activities, the party managed to increase its membership. Ficken (entry 76), Gambs (entry 77), Koppes (entry 82), and Taft (entry 87) trace the harassment and subsequent decline of the IWW, as do Renshaw (entry 68) and Tyler (entry 70). Joan Jensen (entry 80) examines the American Protective League's crusade against the Left.

74   Bailey, Thomas A. *Woodrow Wilson and the Great Betrayal*. New York: Macmillan, 1945.

75   Ferrell, Robert H. *Woodrow Wilson & World War I, 1917-1921*. New York: Harper & Row, 1985.

76 Ficken, Robert E. "The Wobblie Horrors: Pacific Northwest Lumbermen and the Industrial Workers of the World, 1917-1918." *Labor History* 24 (1983): 325-41.

77 Gambs, John S. *The Decline of the I.W.W.* New York: Columbia University Press, 1932.

78 Gutfeld, Arnon. "The Ves Hall Case, Judge Bourquin, and the Sedition Act of 1918." *Pacific Historical Review* 37 (1968): 163-78.

79 Hawley, Ellis W. *The Great War and the Search for Modern Order.* New York: St. Martin's, 1979.

80 Jensen, Joan. *The Price of Vigilance.* Chicago: Rand McNally, 1968.

81 Kennedy, David M. *Over Here: The First World War and American Society.* New York: Oxford University Press, 1980.

82 Koppes, Clayton R. "The Kansas Trial of the I.W.W., 1917-1918." *Labor History* 16 (1975): 338-58.

83 Mock, James R. *Censorship, 1917.* Princeton, NJ: Princeton University Press, 1941.

84 Murphy, Paul. *World War I and the Origins of Civil Liberties in the United States.* New York: Norton, 1979.

85 Peterson, H.C., and Fite, Gilbert C. *Opponents of War, 1917-1918.* Seattle: University of Washington Press, 1957.

86 Scheiber, Harry N. *The Wilson Administration and Civil Liberties, 1917-1921.* Ithaca, NY: Cornell University Press, 1960.

87 Taft, Philip. "The Federal Trials of the IWW." *Labor History* 3 (1962): 57-91.

America and the Russian Revolution

Filene (entry 88) contrasts the euphoria Americans felt following the overthrow of the Tsar in March 1917 with the hostile reaction to the rise of the Bolsheviks eight months later. Christopher Lasch (entry 92) examines how the revolution widened the rift between war liberals and liberals who considered themselves anti-imperialists. Why did Wilson join in the Allied intervention in the Russian civil war? The answer is far from clear since the president gave different people different explanations. Diplomat-scholar George Kennan (entry 90) and Lasch (entry 91) argue that Wilson did it for the sake of the war effort. Unterberger (97) makes a case for the intervention as a move to block Japanese expansionism while William A. Williams (entry 98) concludes that the president's motive was anti-Bolshevik. Levin (entry 93) manages to synthesize these interpretations convincingly.

8 8   Filene, Peter. *America and the Soviet Experiment, 1917-1933.* Cambridge, MA: Harvard University Press, 1967.

8 9   Graves, William S. *America's Siberian Adventure, 1918-1920.* New York: Jonathan Cape & Harrison Smith, 1931.

9 0   Kennan, George F. *Soviet-American Relations, 1917-1920.* 2 vols. Princeton, NJ: Princeton University Press, 1956-1958.

9 1   Lasch, Christopher. "American Intervention in Siberia: Reinterpretation." *Political Science Quarterly* 77 (1962): 205-23.

9 2   _____. *The American Liberals and the Russian Revolution.* New York: McGraw-Hill, 1972.

9 3   Levin, N. Gordon, Jr. *Woodrow Wilson and World Politics: America's Response to War and Revolution.* New York: Oxford University Press, 1968.

9 4   Pelzel, Sophia R. *American Intervention in Siberia, 1918-1920.* Philadelphia: University of Pennsylvania Press, 1946.

9 5   Strakhovsky, Leonid I. *The Origins of American Intervention in North Russia,1918.* Princeton, NJ: Princeton University Press, 1937.

9 6   Trani, Eugene P. "Woodrow Wilson and the Decision to Intervene in Russia: A Reconsideration." *Journal of Modern History* 48 (1976): 440-61.

9 7   Unterberger, Betty M. *America's Siberian Expedition, 1918-1920.* New York: Greenwood (1956), 1969.

9 8   Williams, William A. "The American Intervention in Russia, 1917-1920." *Studies on the Left* 3 (1963): 24-48.

The First Red Scare

General Accounts

More than thirty years after it was written, Robert K. Murray's account of the Red Scare (entry 104) remains the best single work on the subject. While their coverage is much broader than just 1919-1920, Zechariah Chaffee (entry 99) and Paul Murphy (entry 103) discuss the free speech issue during the Red Scare in some detail. William Preston (entry 106) also devotes significant attention to the federal government's role in the Red Scare as does Harry Scheiber (entry 86). Weinstein (entry 72) covers the disastrous effects of the scare on the Socialist party. Robert Tyler (entry 70) and Patrick Renshaw (entry 68) do the same for the IWW. Blair Coan's work (entry 100) is included as one of the few books which defends the Red Scare as necessary and proper. For a communist perspective, see Robert W. Dunn (entry 102).

99 Chaffee, Zechariah, Jr. *Free Speech in the United States.* Cambridge, MA: Harvard University Press, 1941.

100 Coan, Blair. *The Red Web.* Chicago: Northwest, 1925.

101 Coben, Stanley. "A Study in Nativism: The American Red Scare of 1919-1920." *Political Science Quarterly* 79 (1964): 52-75.

102 Dunn, Robert W. ed. *The Palmer Raids.* New York: International Publishers, 1948.

103 Murphy, Paul. *The Meaning of Freedom of Speech.* Westport, CT: Greenwood, 1972.

104 Murray, Robert K. *Red Scare: A Study in National Hysteria, 1919-1920.* Minneapolis: University of Minnesota Press, 1955.

105 Noggle, Burl. *Into the Twenties: The United States From Armistice to Normalcy.* Urbana: University of Illinois Press, 1974.

106 Preston, William, Jr. *Aliens and Dissenters: Federal Suppression of Radicals, 1903-1933.* Cambridge: Harvard University Press, 1963.

107 Warth, Robert D. "The Palmer Raids." *South Atlantic Quarterly* 48 (1949): 1-23.

Personalities

Biographers Ray Ginger (entry 112) and Nick Salvatore (entry 118) discuss the Red Scare's most famous victim, Eugene V. Debs, from different perspectives with Salvatore employing the "new labor history" which emphasizes the culture and collective life of ordinary workers. Emma Goldman (entry 113), who was deported to Soviet Russia during the Red Scare and "Big Bill" Haywood (entry 115) who fled to the Communist motherland rather than go to prison tell their own stories in moving autobiographies. Goldman's life has also been chronicled by Richard Drinnon (entry 111) and Alice Wexler (entry 120). For the biographies of two esteemed Harvard law professors accused of being "parlor reds," see Liva Baker (entry 108) on Felix Frankfurter and Peter Irons (entry 124) on Zechariah Chaffee. The autobiography of Oswald Garrison Villard (entry 119), a liberal critic of both communism and the Palmer raids, contains his observations on the Red Scare. Stanley Coben (entry 110) discusses the life of A. Mitchell Palmer, who hoped to ride the Red Scare into the White House but ended up as a laughing stock. Seattle Mayor Ole Hanson (entry 114) also hoped to profit from the fear, with similar results. By and large, Woodrow Wilson's biographers have glossed over his role in the scare.

108 Baker, Liva. *Felix Frankfurter.* New York: Coward-McCann, 1969.

109 Candeloro, Dominic. "Louis F. Post and the Red Scare of 1920."
     Prologue 11 (1979): 41-55.

110 Coben, Stanley. *A. Mitchell Palmer: Politician.* New York: Columbia
     University Press, 1963.

111 Drinnon, Richard. *Rebel in Paradise: A Biography of Emma Goldman.*
     Chicago: University of Chicago Press, 1961.

112 Ginger, Ray. *The Bending Cross.* New Brunswick, NJ: Rutgers
     University Press, 1949.

113 Goldman, Emma. *Living My Life.* 2 vols. New York: Knopf, 1934.

114 Hanson, Ole. *Americanism versus Bolshevism.* Garden City, NY:
     Doubleday, Page, 1920.

115 Haywood, William D. *Big Bill Haywood's Book: The Autobiography of
     William D. Haywood.* New York: International Publishers, 1929.

116 Hicks, Granville. *John Reed: The Making of a Revolutionary.* New York:
     Macmillan, 1936.

117 Hillquit, Morris. *Loose Leaves From a Busy Life.* New York:
     Macmillan, 1934.

118 Salvatore, Nick. *Eugene V. Debs: Citizen and Socialist.* Urbana:
     University of Illinois Press, 1982.

119 Villard, Oswald Garrison. *Fighting Years: Memoirs of a Liberal Editor.*
     New York: Harcourt, Brace, 1939.

120 Wexler, Alice. *Emma Goldman: An Intimate Life.* New York: Pantheon,
     1984.

121 Young, Art. *On My Way: Being the Book of Art Young in Text and
     Picture.* New York: Liveright, 1928.

State and Local Studies

More research is needed on the effects of the Red Scare at the state and local levels. Chamberlain (entry 122) and Jaffe (entry 125) focus on New York while Robert L. Morlan (entry 126) surveys the upper Midwest. Whitten (entry 129) touches on the Red Scare in his study of anti-syndicalism in California. The Seattle general strike, which helped to touch off the public hysteria, is analyzed by Robert Friedheim (entry 123).

122 Chamberlain, Lawrence. *Loyalty and Legislative Action: A Survey of
     Activity by the New York State Legislature, 1919-1949.* Ithaca, NY:
     Cornell University Press, 1951.

123 Friedheim, Robert. *The Seattle General Strike.* Seattle: University of
     Washington Press, 1964.

124   Irons, Peter.   "'Fighting Fair': Zechariah Chafee, Jr., the Department of Justice, and the 'Trial at the Harvard Club.'" *Harvard Law Review* 94 (1981): 1205-1236.

125   Jaffe, Julian F. *Crusade Against Radicalism:* New York During the Red Scare, 1914-1924. Port Washington, NY: Kennikat, 1972.

126   Morlan, Robert L. *Political Prairie Fire: The Non-Partisan League, 1915-1922.* Minneapolis: University of Minnesota Press, 1955.

127   Szajkowski, Zosa. *The Impact of the 1919-20 Red Scare on American Jewish Life.* New York: Ktav, 1974.

128   Walker, John T.   "Socialism in Dayton, Ohio, 1912-1925: Its Membership, Organization and Demise." *Labor History* 26 (1985): 384-404.

129   Whitten, Woodrow C. *Criminal Sydicalism and the Law in California, 1919-1927.* Philadelphia: American Philosophical Society, 1969.

The 1920s

Geoffrey Perrett (entry 136) presents a lively overview of a decade which saw little in the way of communist agitation. Paul Murphy (entry 135) discusses the 1920s as a time of sustained public intolerance toward radicals and other minorities. Previously cited works by Green (entry 64), Goldstein (entry 22), Preston (entry 106), and Weinstein (entry 72) contain chapters on anti-communist activities in this decade. Kenneth Jackson (entry 130) and David M. Chalmers (entry 537) cover the anti-radicalism of the Klan. For more information on this right-wing fringe group, see the bibliography by Davis and Sims-Wood (entry 6). Richard M. Whitney (entry 139), a member of the anti-radical American Defense Society, explains why he favored stringent laws prohibiting Communist activities. Douglas Little (entry 132) and Frederic Propas (entry 137) analyze the institutionalizing of anti-communism in the Department of State. Joughlin and Morgan (entry 131) is the best in a spate of books on Sacco and Vanzetti, who may or may not have committed murder and robbery but most certainly did not receive a fair trial because of their leftist beliefs.

130   Jackson, Kenneth T. *The Ku Klux Klan in the City, 1915-1930.* New York: Oxford University Press, 1967.

131   Joughlin, Louis, and Morgan, Edmund M.   *The Legacy of Sacco and Vanzetti.* Chicago: Quadrangle, 1964.

132 Little, Douglas. "AntiBolshevism and American Foreign Policy, 1919-1939: The Diplomacy of Self-Delusion." *American Quarterly* 35 (1983): 376-390.

133 McClurg, Donald J. "The Colorado Coal Strike of 1927." *Labor History* 4 (1963): 68-92.

134 Miller, Robert Moats. *American Protestantism and Social Issues, 1919-1939.* Chapel Hill: University of North Carolina Press, 1958.

135 Murphy, Paul L. "Sources and Nature of Intolerance in the 1920s." *Journal of American History* 51 (1964): 60-76.

136 Perrett, Geoffrey. *America in the Twenties.* New York: Simon & Schuster, 1982.

137 Propas, Frederic L. "Creating a Hard Line Toward Russia: The Training of State Department Experts, 1927-1937." *Diplomatic History* 8 (1984): 209-226.

138 Santos, Michael W. "Community and Communism: The 1928 New Bedford Textile Strike." *Labor History* 26 (Spring 1985): 230-249.

139 Whitney, Richard M. *The Reds in America.* New York: Beckwith, 1924.

140 Wilson, Joan Hoff. *Herbert Hoover, Forgotten Progressive.* Boston: Little, Brown, 1975.

"The Red Decade"

Just how "red" was the Depression decade of the 1930s? Eugene Lyons (entry 156) began this controversy in 1941 with the thesis that it was very red. Ex-communist Granville Hicks (entry 150) and Frank Warren (entry 161) argued that it was only pink. See also Earl Latham (entry 153) who wrote the last volume in the liberal anti-communist Fund For the Republic series. Harvey Klehr (entry 152) picks up where Theodore Draper left off from a similar liberal anti-communist perspective. Lowell Dyson (entry 147) examines Communist party activities among farmers. Mark Naison (entry 157) does the same for party agitation among Blacks. Richard Pells (entry 159) offers insights into Communist and anti-communist currents among intellectuals in his superb book. Allen Guttman (entry 149) analyzes the impact of the Spanish Civil War on Americans while David O'Brien (158) chronicles the response of American Catholics to the war in Spain and their "discovery" of the anti-communist issue.

While there have been many biographies of Franklin D. Roosevelt, the dominant anti-communist politician of the decade, James MacGregor Burns (entry 145) still offers an excellent starting point, as does William E. Leuchtenburg (entry 154). For FDR's relations with the Soviet Union, see Edward M. Bennett (entry 144). Harry Fleishman (entry 148) provides coverage of Roosevelt's unsuccessful rival on the Left, Norman Thomas. For FDR's enemies on the Right, see David Bennett (entry 143) on the abortive Union party and T. Harry Williams' biography of Huey Long (entry 162).

141 Aaron, Daniel. *Writers on the Left. New York:* Avon, 1965.

142 Alexander, Robert J. *The Right Opposition: The Lovestoneites and the International Communist Opposition of the 1930's.* Westport, CT: Greenwood, 1981.

143 Bennett, David H. *Demagogues in the Depression: American Radicals and the Union Party, 1932-1936.* New Brunswick, NJ: Rutgers University Press, 1969.

144 Bennett, Edward M. *Franklin D. Roosevelt and the Search for Security: American-Soviet Relations, 1933-1939.* Wilmington, DE: Scholarly Resources, 1985.

145 Burns, James MacGregor. *Roosevelt: The Lion and the Fox.* New York: Harcourt, Brace & World, 1956.

146 DeSantis, Hugh. *The Diplomacy of Silence: The American Foreign Service, the Soviet Union and the Cold War, 1933-1947.* Chicago: University of Chicago Press, 1980.

147 Dyson, Lowell K. *Red Harvest: The Communist Party and American Farmers.* Lincoln: University of Nebraska Press, 1982.

148 Fleischman, Harry. *Norman Thomas: A Biography, 1884-1968.* New York: Norton, 1964.

149 Guttman, Allen. *The Wound in the Heart: America and the Spanish Civil War.* New York: Free Press, 1962.

150 Hicks, Granville. "How Red was the Red Decade?" *Harpers' Magazine* 207 (July 1953), 53-61.

151 Kempton, Murray. *Part of Our Time: Some Ruins and Monuments of the Thirties.* New York: Simon & Schuster, 1955.

152 Klehr, Harvey. *The Heyday of American Communism: The Depression Decade.* New York: Basic Books, 1984.

153 Latham, Earl. *The Communist Controversy in Washington: From the New Deal to McCarthy.* New York: Atheneum, 1969.

154 Leuchtenburg, William E. *Franklin D. Roosevelt and the New Deal.* New York: Harper & Row, 1963.

155 Lisio, Donald J. *The President and Protest: Hoover, Conspiracy and the Bonus Riot.* Columbia: University of Missouri Press, 1974.

156 Lyons, Eugene. *The Red Decade: The Stalinist Penetration of America.* New York: Bobbs-Merrill, 1941.

157 Naison, Mark. *Communists in Harlem During the Great Depression.* Urbana: University of Illinois Press, 1983.

158 O'Brien, David J. *American Catholics and Social Reform: The New Deal Years.* New York: Oxford, 1968.

159 Pells, Richard H. *Radical Visions and American Dreams: Culture and Social Thought in the Depression Years.* New York: Harper & Row, 1973.

160 Smith, Geoffrey S. *To Save a Nation: American Countersubversives, the New Deal and the Coming of World War II.* New York: Basic Books, 1973.

161 Warren, Frank A., III. *Liberals and Communism: The "Red Decade" Revisited.* Bloomington: Indiana University Press, 1966.

162 Williams, T. Harry. *Huey Long.* New York: Knopf, 1969.

163 Wilson, Edmund. *The American Jitters: A Year of the Slump.* New York: Scribner, 1932.

Labor and Anti-Communism

Labor historians have produced a number of excellent works on anti-communism in American unions. For an overview, begin with Bert Cochran (entry 168). The creation of the CIO in 1936 gave the Communist party a new chance to organize American workers and they made the most of the opportunity—at least for a time. See the remembrance by Max M. Kampelman (entry 174) and the monograph by Harvey Levenstein (entry 179). On the struggle against communism in the United Auto Workers Union, consult John W. Barnard (entry 165), Irving Howe and B.J. Widick (entry 173), Roger Keeran (entry 175), Harvey Klehr (entry 177), and UAW leader Victor Reuther's memoir (entry 185). Ronald Radosh (entry 184) examines how American labor came to join the anti-communist consensus in American foreign policy.

Harry Bridges, the most prominent communist labor leader, is the subject of a biography by Charles Larrowe (entry 178). "Red Mike" Quill's life is covered by L.H. Whittemore (entry 188). Fred Beal, who turned against communism after fleeing to the Stalinist workers' paradise, wrote an autobiography (entry 166) as did another former communist, Steve Nelson (entry 182). For the lives of other anti-communist labor leaders, there are Dubovsky and Van Tine's biography of John L. Lewis (entry 170), Joseph C.

Goulden's profile of George Meany (entry 172), and Harold
Livesay's portrait of Samuel Gompers (entry 180).

164   Andrew, William D. "Factionalism and Anti-Communism: Ford Local
      600." *Labor History* 20 (1979): 227-55.

165   Barnard, John W. *Walter Reuther and the Rise of the Auto Workers.*
      Boston: Little, Brown, 1983.

166   Beal, Fred E. *Proletarian Journey: New England, Gastonia, Moscow.* New
      York: Hillman-Curl, 1937.

167   Brody, David. *Steelworkers in America.* New York: Harper & Row,
      1969.

168   Cochran, Bert. *Labor and Communism: The Conflict that Shaped
      American Unions.* Princeton, NJ: Princeton University Press, 1977.

169   Dowell, Elbridge F. *A History of Criminal Syndicalist Legislation in the
      United States.* Johns Hopkins University Studies in Historical and
      Political Science. Series 56. Baltimore, MD: Johns Hopkins
      University Press, 1939.

170   Dubovsky, Melvyn, and Van Tine, Warren. *John L. Lewis: A Biography.*
      New York: New York Times Book Co., 1977.

171   Freeman, Josh. "Delivering the Goods: Industrial Unionism During World
      War II." *Labor History* 19 (1978): 570-593.

172   Goulden, Joseph C. *Meany.* New York: Atheneum, 1972.

173   Howe, Irving, and Widick, B.J. *The UAW and Walter Reuther.* New
      York: Random House, 1949.

174   Kampelman, Max M. *The Communist Party Vs. the CIO: A Study in
      Power Politics.* New York: Praeger, 1957.

175   Keeran, Roger. *The Communist Party and the United Auto Workers.*
      Bloomington: Indiana State University Press, 1980.

176   Leab, Daniel J., ed. *The Labor History Reader.* Urbana: University of
      Illinois Press, 1985.

177   Klehr, Harvey. "American Communism and the United Auto Workers:
      New Evidence on an Old Controversy." *Labor History* 24 (1983): 404-
      13.

178   Larrowe, Charles P. *Harry Bridges: The Rise and Fall of Radical Labor in
      the United States.* New York: Lawrence Hill, 1972.

179   Levenstein, Harvey. *Communism, Anticommunism, and the CIO.*
      Westport, CT: Greenwood, 1981.

180   Livesay, Harold C. *Samuel Gompers and Organized Labor in America.*
      Boston: Little, Brown, 1978.

181 Meier, August, and Rudwick, Elliot. "Communist Unions and the Black Community: The Transport Workers Union, 1934-1944." *Labor History* 23 (1982): 165-97.

182 Nelson, Steve, Barrett, James R., and Ruck, Rob. *Steve Nelson, American Radical.* Pittsburgh: University of Pittsburgh Press, 1981.

183 Oshinsky, David M. *Senator Joseph McCarthy and the American Labor Movement.* Columbia: University of Missouri Press, 1976.

184 Radosh, Ronald. *American Labor and United States Foreign Policy.* New York: Random House, 1969.

185 Reuther, Victor. *The Brothers Reuther and the Story of the U.A.W.: A Memoir.* Boston: Houghton Mifflin, 1976.

186 Sims, Robert C. "Idaho's Criminal Syndicalism Act." *Labor History* 15 (Fall 1974): 511-27.

187 Waldman, Louis. *Labor Lawyer.* New York: Dutton, 1944.

188 Whittemore, L.H. *The Man Who Ran the Subways: The Story of Mike Quill.* New York: Holt, Rinehart & Winston, 1968.

189 Zieger, Robert H. *American Workers, American Unions, 1920-1985.* Baltimore: Johns Hopkins University Press, 1986.

World War II

John Morton Blum (entry 191) gives an excellent overview of America during World War II, a time when the United States and the Soviets joined together to fight Hitler. Maurice Isserman (entry 195) argues that the CPUSA was not merely a creature of Moscow during the war years, but a Soviet-American party. For the attitudes and actions of leading government figures toward communism, see Attorney General Francis Biddle's autobiography (entry 190), Burns's second volume on FDR (entry 193), and the diary of Vice President Henry Wallace (entry 191). The most controversial episode of the war, Roosevelt's performance at Yalta, has been the subject of a number of books, including Clemens (entry 194), Snell (entry 197), and Theoharis (entry 198).

190 Biddle, Francis. *In Brief Authority.* Garden City, NY: Doubleday, 1962.

191 Blum, John Morton, ed. *The Price of Vision: The Diary of Henry A. Wallace, 1942-1946.* Boston: Houghton Mifflin, 1973.

192 _____. *V Was For Victory: Politics and American Culture During World War II.* New York: Harcourt Brace Jovanovich, 1976.

193 Burns, James MacGregor. *Roosevelt: The Soldier of Freedom. 1940-1945.* New York: Harcourt Brace Jovanovich, 1970.

194 Clemens, Diane Shaver. *Yalta*. New York: Oxford University Press, 1970.

195 Isserman, Maurice. *Which Side Were You On? The American Communist Party During the Second World War*. Middleton, CT: Wesleyan University Press, 1982.

196 Johnson, Claudius O. "The Status of Freedom of Expression Under the Smith Act." *Western Political Quarterly* 11 (1958): 469-80.

197 Snell, John L., ed. *The Meaning of Yalta: Big Three Diplomacy and the New Balance of Power*. Baton Rouge: Louisiana State University Press, 1956.

198 Theoharis, Athan G. *The Yalta Myths: An Issue in U.S. Politics, 1945-1955*. Columbia: University of Missouri Press, 1970.

The Second Red Scare—"Trumanism"

General Accounts

As used in this study, "Trumanism" refers to anti-communism as practiced by the Truman administration and its allies in the years after World War II, a new kind of liberalism born under stress as Mary S. McAuliffe (entry 213) observes in her monograph on Cold War politics. By no stretch of the imagination can Trumanism be equated with the political excesses of the 1950s commonly known as McCarthyism, but the two isms together made up the second Red Scare. Trumanism was the precursor of McCarthyism, just as the hysteria of World War I contributed to the first Red Scare. Athan Theoharis (entry 221) argues that Truman and McCarthy "differ not so much over ends as over means and emphasis." David Caute (entry 203) views the two isms as one "Great Fear" in his encyclopedic account. See also a group of essays edited by Barton Bernstein (entry 202). Robert Griffith and Athan Theoharis present essays on right-wing groups which helped to spawn McCarthyism including the Catholic Church (entry 204), the Chamber of Commerce (entry 210), and conservative intellectuals (entry 212) as well as Cold War liberals (entries 215 and 220).

William O'Neill (entry 216) roasts leftists who refused to renounce Stalinism during the Cold War. One who did, Joseph Starobin (entry 218), explains how and why the Communist party fell apart. Penn Kimball (entry 211), relates how the government and important liberal Democrats decided he was a communist and thus began amassing "The File" on him. For analysis of the connections between Truman's foreign policy and McCarthyism, see Freeland (entry 206) and Purifoy (entry 217). Adler and

Paterson (entry 199) explain how Americans came to blend Hitler and Stalin into the false but useful image of "red fascism."

199 Adler, Leslie K., and Paterson, Thomas G. "Red Fascism: The Merger of Nazi Germany and Soviet Russia in the American Image of Totalitarianism, 1930's—1950's." *American Historical Review* 75 (1970): 1046-64.

200 Bailey, Percival R. "The Case of the National Lawyers Guild, 1939-1958." In Athan G. Theoharis, ed. *Beyond the Hiss Case: The FBI, Congress, and the Cold War.* Philadelphia: Temple University Press, 1982, pp. 129-75.

201 Belknap, Michael R. *Cold War Political Justice: The Smith Act, the Communist Party, and American Civil Liberties.* Westport, CT: Greenwood, 1977.

202 Bernstein, Barton J., ed. *Politics and Policies of the Truman Administration.* Chicago: Quadrangle, 1970.

203 Caute, David. *The Great Fear: The Anti-Communist Purge Under Truman and Eisenhower.* New York: Simon & Schuster, 1978.

204 Crosby, Donald F. "The Politics of Religion: American Catholics and the Anti-Communist Impulse." In Robert Griffith and Athan Theoharis, eds. *The Specter: Original Essays on the Cold War and the Origins of McCarthyism.* New York: New Viewpoints, 1974, pp. 18-38.

205 Divine, Robert A. "The Cold War and the Election of 1948." *Journal of Modern History* 59 (1972): 90-110.

206 Freeland, Richard M. *The Truman Doctrine and the Origins of McCarthyism: Foreign Policy, Domestic Politics, and Internal Security, 1946-1948.* New York: Knopf, 1972.

207 Goulden, Joseph C. *The Best Years, 1945-1950.* New York: Atheneum, 1976.

208 Griffith, Robert. "Truman and the Historians: The Reconstruction of Postwar American History." *Wisconsin Magazine of History* 54 (1971): 299-308.

209 Hamby, Alonzo. *Beyond the New Deal: Harry S. Truman and American Liberalism.* New York: Columbia University Press, 1973.

210 Irons, Peter H. "American Business and the Origins of McCarthyism: The Cold War Crusade of the United States Chamber of Commerce." In Robert Griffith and Athan Theoharis, eds. *The Specter: Original Essays on the Cold War and the Origins of McCarthyism.* New York: New Viewpoints, 1974, pp. 72-89.

211 Kimball, Penn. *The File.* New York: Harcourt Brace Jovanovich, 1983.

212 Lora, Ronald. "A View From the Right: Conservative Intellectuals, the Cold War, and McCarthy." In Robert Griffith and Athan Theoharis, eds.

The Specter: Original Essays on the Cold War and the Origins of McCarthyism. New York: New Viewpoints, 1974, pp. 40-70.

213   McAuliffe, Mary S. *Crisis on the Left: Cold War Politics and American Liberals, 1947-1954.* Amherst: University of Massachusetts Press, 1978.

214   McWilliams, Carey. *Witch Hunt: The Revival of Heresy.* Boston: Little, Brown, 1950.

215   Markowitz, Norman. "A View From the Left: From the Popular Front to Cold War Liberalism." In Robert Griffith and Athan Theoharis, eds. *The Specter: Original Essays on the Cold War and the Origins of McCarthyism.* New York: New Viewpoints, 1974, pp. 90-115.

216   O'Neill, William L. *A Better World: The Great Schism: Stalinism and the Anmerican Intellectuals.* New York: Simon & Schuster, 1982.

217   Purifoy, Lewis M. *Harry Truman's China Policy: McCarthyism and the Diplomacy of Hysteria, 1947-1951.* New York: New Viewpoints, 1976.

218   Starobin, Joseph. *American Communism in Crisis, 1943-1957.* Cambridge: Harvard University Press, 1972.

219   Stone, Isadore F. *The Truman Era.* New York: Monthly Review Press, 1953.

220   Theoharis, Athan. "The Politics of Scholarship: Liberals, Anti-Communism, and McCarthyism." In Robert Griffith and Athan Theoharis, eds., *The Specter: Original Essays on the Cold War and the Origins of McCarthyism."* New York: New Viewpoints, 1974, pp. 262-280.

221   _____. *Seeds of Repression: Harry S. Truman and the Origins of McCarthyism.* New York: Quadrangle, 1977.

222   _____, ed. *The Truman Presidency: The Origins of the Imperial Presidency and the National Security State.* Stanfordville, NY: Earl M. Coleman, 1979.

The Loyalty Issue

In March 1947, for reasons of politics and state, Truman issued an executive order to investigate the loyalty of government employees. For general background on the loyalty issue, see Roger S. Abbott (entry 223) and Harold Hyman (entry 226). Liberal anti-communist James Wechsler (entry 229) offers a contemporary defense of Truman's loyalty program. Alan D. Harper (entry 225) finds that the president largely succeeded in balancing liberty against national security during a time of peril. Truman's intentions may have been good, argues revisionist Athan Theoharis (entry 227), but civil liberties were sacrificed to the Cold War. Freeland (entry 206) and Caute (entry 203) agree in large part. Francis H. Thompson (entry 228) offers a careful assessment of the revisionist critique.

223 Abbott, Roger S. "The Federal Loyalty Program: Background and Problems." *American Political Science Review* 42 (1948): 486-99.

224 Brown, Ralph S., Jr. *Loyalty and Security: Employment Tests in the United States.* New Haven: Yale University Press, 1958.

225 Harper, Alan D. *The Politics of Loyalty: The White House and the Communist Issue, 1946-1952.* Westport, CT: Greenwood, 1969.

226 Hyman, Harold M. *To Try Men's Souls: Loyalty Tests in American History.* Berkeley and Los Angeles: University of California Press, 1959.

227 Theoharis, Athan. "The Escalation of the Loyalty Program." In Barton J. Bernstein, ed. *Politics and Policies of the Truman Administration.* Chicago: Quadrangle, 1970, pp. 242-68.

228 Thompson, Francis H. *The Frustration of Politics: Truman, Congress, and the Loyalty Issue, 1945-1953.* Rutherford, NJ: Fairleigh Dickinson University Press, 1979.

229 Wechsler, James. "How to Rid the Government of Communists." *Harper's Magazine* 195 (1947): pp. 438-43.

Personalities

The place to begin any serious examination of the Truman years is with the president himself. Truman's two volumes of memoirs (entry 246) are almost as feisty as the man, although just as self-serving as other presidential autobiographies. Ferrell's "autobiography" (entry 235) consists of Truman's recollections as written over a number of years. The same author's biography of Truman (entry 236) which is quite favorable to the president. On the Truman presidency, see the two volumes by Robert J. Donovan (entries 233 and 234) and one by Alonzo Hamby (entry 209). Two of Truman's secretaries of state, Dean Acheson (entry 230) and James F. Byrnes (entry 232) left behind memoirs as did George F. Kennan (entry 237), the "father of containment," who was anything but happy with the implementation of his ideas. For the origins of liberal anti-communism see Reinhold Niebuhr ("the father of us all," as Kennan said) (entry 240). For Truman's conservative political rivals, there are biographies of Robert Taft by James T. Patterson (entry 241) and William S. White (entry 250) and Richard Smith's study of Thomas Dewey (entry 245). Henry Wallace, who broke with Truman over the Cold War and ran for president as a Progressive in 1948 has been the subject of a number of books, including those by Dwight MacDonald (entry 238), Norman D. Markowitz (entry 239), Karl M. Schmidt (entry 244), J. Samuel Walker (entry 248), and Richard J. Walton (entry 249). William O'Neill (216) includes a chapter on the Wallace campaign. F. Ross Peterson (entry 242) has written a biography of Wallace running mate Glen Taylor.

230 Acheson, Dean G. *Present at Creation: My Years in the State Department.* New York: Norton, 1969.

231 Buhite, Russell D. *Patrick J. Hurley and American Foreign Policy.* Ithaca, NY: Cornell University Press, 1973.

232 Byrnes, James F. *Speaking Frankly.* New York: Harper, 1947.

233 Donovan, Robert J. *Conflict and Crisis: The Presidency of Harry S. Truman, 1945-1948.* New York: Norton, 1977.

234 _____. *Tumultuous Years: The Presidency of Harry S. Truman, 1949-1953.* New York: Norton, 1982.

235 Ferrell, Robert H., ed. *The Autobiography of Harry S. Truman.* Boulder: Colorado Associated University Press, 1980.

236 _____. *Harry S. Truman and the Modern Presidency.* Boston: Little, Brown, 1983.

237 Kennan, George F. *Memoirs, 1925-1963.* 2 vols. Boston: Little, Brown, 1967, 1972.

238 MacDonald, Dwight. *Henry Wallace: The Man and the Myth.* New York: Vanguard, 1948.

239 Markowitz, Norman D. *The Rise and Fall of the People's Century: Henry A. Wallace and American Liberalism, 1941-1948.* New York: Free Press, 1973.

240 Niebuhr, Reinhold. *The Irony of American History.* New York: Charles Scribner, 1952.

241 Patterson, James T. *Mr. Republican: A Biography of Robert A. Taft.* Boston: Houghton Mifflin, 1972.

242 Peterson, F. Ross. *Prophet Without Honor: Glen Taylor and the Fight for American Liberalism.* Lexington: University of Kentucky Press, 1974.

243 Rees, David. *Harry Dexter White: A Study in Paradox.* New York: Coward, McCann & Geoghegan, 1973.

244 Schmidt, Karl M. *Henry A. Wallace: Quixotic Crusade, 1948.* Syracuse, NY: Syracuse University Press, 1960.

245 Smith, Richard N. *Thomas E. Dewey and His Times.* New York: Simon & Schuster, 1982.

246 Truman, Harry S. *Memoirs.* 2 vols. Garden City, NY: Doubleday, 1955-56.

247 Vandenberg, Arthur H., Jr., ed. *The Private Papers of Senator Vandenberg*. Boston: Houghton Mifflin, 1952.

248 Walker, J. Samuel. *Henry A. Wallace and American Foreign Policy*. Westport, CT: Greenwood, 1976.

249 Walton, Richard J. *Henry A. Wallace, Harry Truman, and the Cold War*. New York: Viking, 1976.

250 White, William S. *The Taft Story*. New York: Harper, 1954.

Regional Studies

The lack of state and local accounts of anti-communism in the Truman era is just as apparent as for the first Red Scare. David Caute (203) surveys "The Great Fear" in several states. Edward Barrett (entry 251) examines California's little HCUA in this dated account. James Selcraig (entry 254) scans the Midwest for anti-communist activities in the Truman-McCarthy period. Melvin Rader (entry 252) explains what it was like to be hauled before Washington state's HCUA while Jane Sanders (entry 253) devotes a portion of her book to the purge on the campus of the University of Washington. Chamberlain (entry 122) closes his account of anti-communism in the New York legislature with a look at the Truman years.

251 Barrett, Edward L., Jr. *The Tenney Committee: Legislative Investigation of Subversive Activities in California*. Ithaca, NY: Cornell University Press, 1951.

252 Rader, Melvin. *False Witness*. Seattle: University of Washington Press, 1969.

253 Sanders, Jane. *Cold War on the Campus: Academic Freedom at the University of Washington, 1946-64*. Seattle: University of Washington Press, 1979.

254 Selcraig, James Truett. *The Red Scare in the Midwest, 1945-1955: A State and Local Study*. Ann Arbor, MI: UMI Research, 1982.

255 Yarnell, Allen. "Pension Politics in Washington State, 1948." *Pacific Northwest Quarterly* 61 (1970): 147-55.

The Cold War

Rapidly deteriorating relations with the Soviet Union after World War II brought about a foreign policy based on anti-communism. There has been great disagreement among historians in regard to the origins of the Cold War. Liberals like George Kennan (entry 269) and Arthur Schlesinger, Jr. (entry 276) blamed the Russians for the Cold War while criticizing Americans for their excessive moralism. This "orthodox" position evolved into a realist interpretation, represented by Herbert Feis (entry 260) and Louis J. Halle (entry 266), who were critical of American policymakers for not paying enough attention to balance of power considerations without challenging the basic premise that the Soviets had to be contained to prevent a Communist world. In the 1960s, revisionist or New Left historians like D.F. Fleming (entry 262), Walter LaFeber (entry 271), Thomas G. Paterson (entries 274 and 275) and William Appleman Williams (entry 277) began to split the blame for the Cold War between the Soviets and the United States, emphasizing, to varying degrees, the need for the capitalist system to expand economically and politically. More recently, a postrevisionist hybrid has arisen headed by John Lewis Gaddis (entries 263-65) which attempts to synthesize bits and pieces of the New Left into the realist mainstream, "orthodoxy plus archives," as one skeptical historian has observed.

Other works also contain insights into the effect the "invisible ideology" has had on foreign affairs. Robert Dallek (entry 258) examines the American need for unifying external enemies like communism. On Vietnam, start with Frances Fitzgerald (entry 261), George C. Herring (entry 267), and Stanley Karnow (entry 268). For the 1970s, see an article by Melvyn P. Leffler (entry 272) comparing and contrasting the Truman and Carter Doctrines as well as monographs by Destler, Gelb, and Lake (entry 259) and Alan Wolfe (entry 278).

256 Bohlen, Charles E. *Witness to History, 1929-1969*. New York: Norton, 1973.

257 Cohen, Warren I. "Harry Truman, China, and the Cold War in Asia." *Reviews in American History* 6 (1978): 146-154.

258 Dallek, Robert. *The American Style of Foreign Policy: Cultural Politics and Foreign Affairs*. New York: New American Library, 1983.

259 Destler, I.M., Gelb, Leslie H., and Lake, Anthony. *Our Own Worst Enemy: The Unmaking of American Foreign Policy*. New York: Simon & Schuster, 1984.

260 Feis, Herbert. *From Trust to Terror: The Onset of the Cold War, 1945-1950*. New York: Norton, 1970.

261 Fitzgerald, Frances. *Fire in the Lake: The Vietnamese and the Americans in Vietnam*. Boston: Little, Brown, 1972.

262 Fleming, D.F. *The Cold War and Its Origins, 1917-1960.* 2 vols. Garden City, NY: Doubleday, 1961.

263 Gaddis, John Lewis. "The Emerging Post-Revisionist Synthesis on the Origins of the Cold War." *Diplomatic History* 7 (1983): 171-90.

264 _____. *Strategies of Containment: A Critical Appraisal of Postwar American National Security Policy.* New York: Oxford University Press, 1982.

265 _____. *The United States and the Origins of the Cold War, 1941-1947.* New York: Columbia University Press, 1972.

266 Halle, Louis J. *The Cold War as History.* New York: Harper & Row, 1968.

267 Herring, George C. *America's Longest War: The United States and Vietnam, 1950-1975.* New York: John Wiley, 1979.

268 Karnow, Stanley. *Vietnam: A History.* New York: Viking, 1983.

269 Kennan, George F. *American Diplomacy, 1900-1950.* New York: New American Library, 1952.

270 Koen, Ross Y. *The China Lobby in American Politics.* New York: Harper & Row, 1974.

271 LaFeber, Walter. *America, Russia and the Cold War, 1945-1984.* 5th ed. New York: Knopf, 1985.

272 Leffler, Melvyn P. "From the Truman Doctrine to the Carter Doctrine: Lessons and Dilemmas of the Cold War." *Diplomatic History* 7 (1983): 245-66.

273 Messer, Robert L. *The End of an Alliance: James F. Byrnes, Roosevelt, Truman and the Origins of the Cold War.* Chapel Hill: University of North Carolina Press, 1982.

274 Paterson, Thomas G. *On Every Front: The Making of the Cold War.* New York: Norton, 1979.

275 _____. *Soviet-American Confrontation: Postwar Reconstruction and the Origins of the Cold War.* Baltimore: Johns Hopkins University Press, 1973.

276 Schlesinger, Arthur M., Jr. "Origins of the Cold War." *Foreign Affairs* 46 (1967): 22-52.

277 Williams, William Appleman. *The Tragedy of American Diplomacy.* 2nd ed. New York: Dell, 1972.

278 Wolfe, Alan. *The Rise and Fall of the "Soviet Threat": Domestic Sources of the Cold War Consensus.* Washington, D.C.: Institute for Policy Studies, 1979.

279 Yergin, Daniel. *Shattered Peace: The Origins of the Cold War and the National Security State.* Boston: Houghton Mifflin, 1977.

House Committee on Un-American Activities (HCUA)

HCUA in Washington

History has not been kind to HCUA, just as it has not been very good to Senator McCarthy. Only a book of essays edited by conservative iconoclast William F. Buckley, Jr. (entry 286) seeks to defend the committee. Contemporary accounts considered critical of HCUA include Bert Andrews (entry 280), two by Alan Barth (entries 281 and 82), Carl Beck (entry 283), Robert Carr (entry 287), John Caughey (entry 288), and Telford Taylor (entry 296). Writing during World War II, August Ogden (entry 293) also finds fault. Committee critics in government include Attorney General Biddle (entry 285) and Harlem Congressman Vito Marcantonio, whose life story is told by Salvatore LaGumina (entry 292). Liberal journalist Walter Goodman (entry 291) has produced the best volume on the committee, although it has many flaws. To get the flavor of HCUA hearings, see Eric Bentley's compilation of edited transcripts (entry 284). Martin Dies warns America about the Trojan Horse of communism (entry 289). His biographer, William Gellerman (entry 290), compares him to Hitler. Charles Potter (entry 294) was a former member of HCUA, who turned against his political ally Joseph McCarthy in 1954. The chief investigator for HCUA for ten years, Robert E. Stripling (entry 295) details his findings in a 1949 memoir.

280   Andrews, Bert. *Washington Witch Hunt*. New York: Random House, 1948.

281   Barth, Alan. *Government by Investigation*. New York: Viking, 1955.

282   _____. *The Loyalty of Free Men*. New York: Viking, 1951.

283   Beck, Carl. *Contempt of Congress: A Study of the Prosecutions Initiated by the Committee on Un-American Activities, 1945-1957*. New Orleans: Hauser, 1959.

284   Bentley, Eric, ed. *Thirty Years of Treason: Excerpts From Hearings Before the House Committee on Un-American Activities, 1938-1968*. New York: Viking, 1971.

285   Biddle, Francis. *The Fear of Freedom*. Garden City, NY: Doubleday, 1952.

286   Buckley, William F., Jr., ed. *The Committee and Its Critics: A Calm Review of the House Committee on Un-American Activities*. New York: Putnam, 1962.

287   Carr, Robert K. *The House Committee on Un-American Activities, 1945-1950*. Ithaca, NY: Cornell University Press, 1952.

288 Caughey, John. *In Clear and Present Danger: The Crucial State of Our Freedoms.* Chicago: University of Chicago Press, 1958.

289 Dies, Martin. *The Trojan Horse in America.* New York: Dodd, Mead, 1940.

290 Gellerman, William. *Martin Dies.* New York: John Day, 1944.

291 Goodman, Walter. *The Committee: The Extraordinary Career of the House Committee on Un-American Activities.* New York: Farrar, Straus & Giroux, 1968.

292 LaGumina, Salvatore J. *Vito Marcantonio: The People's Politician.* Dubuque, IA: Kendall/Hunt, 1969.

293 Ogden, August Raymond. *The Dies Committee.* Washington, D.C: Catholic University Press, 1944.

294 Potter, Charles E. *Days of Shame.* New York: Coward-McCann, 1965.

295 Stripling, Robert E. *The Red Plot Against America.* Drexel Hill, PA: Bell, 1949.

296 Taylor, Telford. *Grand Inquest: The Story of Congressional Investigations.* New York: Simon & Schuster, 1955.

HCUA and Hollywood

The committee's Hollywood expeditions have been the subject of a number of books and articles, in part because of the glamor of "tinsel town" and in part because the purge in the movie capital, as Les Adler notes (entry 297) paralleled anti-communist developments elsewhere. It seems more important than ever to understand what went on with HCUA in Hollywood because of the vital part it played in the life of actor/union leader Ronald Reagan. For background, see Nancy Lynn Schwartz (entry 307), which covers events up to 1946. Eric Bentley (entry 298), Ceplair and Englund (entry 301), and Robert Vaughn (entry 311) provide overviews. Victor Navasky (entry 306), outspoken editor of *The Nation*, examines the "naming names" ritual in great detail. Merle Miller (entry 305) provides a contemporary account. For Reagan's own reminiscences, see his autobiography (entry 611).

Screenwriter Lillian Hellman (entry 304) looks back on her brush with HCUA in a book which includes a controversial introduction by Garry Wills. Gordon Kahn (entry 303) wrote about the Hollywood 10 with their cooperation immediately after the indictments. Two of the ten, Alvah Bessie (entry 299) and Dalton Trumbo (entry 310) present their versions of what happened.

297 Adler, Les K. "The Politics of Culture: Hollywood and the Cold War." In Robert Griffith and Athan Theoharis, eds. *The Specter: Original Essays on the Cold War and the Origins of McCarthyism.* New York: New Viewpoints, 1974, pp. 240-60.

298 Bentley, Eric. *Are You Now or Have You Ever Been? The Investigation of Show Business by the Un-American Activities Committee, 1947-1958.* New York: Harper & Row, 1972.

299 Bessie, Alvah. *Inquisition in Eden.* New York: Macmillan, 1965.

300 Biberman, Herbert. *Salt of the Earth: The Story of a Film.* Boston: Beacon, 1965.

301 Ceplair, Larry, and Englund, Steven. *The Inquisition in Hollywood: Politics in the Film Community, 1930-1960.* Garden City, NY: Doubleday, 1980.

302 Cook, Bruce. *Dalton Trumbo.* New York: Scribner's, 1977.

303 Kahn, Gordon. *Hollywood on Trial: The Story of the 10 Who Were Indicted.* New York: Boni & Gaer, 1948.

304 Hellman, Lillian. *Scoundrel Time.* Boston: Little, Brown, 1976.

305 Miller, Merle. *The Judges and the Judged.* Garden City, NY: Doubleday, 1952.

306 Navasky, Victor. *Naming Names.* New York: Viking, 1980.

307 Schwartz, Nancy Lynn. *The Hollywood Writers War.* New York: Knopf, 1982.

308 Sigal, Clancy. "Hollywood During the Great Fear." *Present Tense* 9 (1982): 45-48.

309 Suber, Howard. "Politics and Popular Culture: Hollywood at Bay, 1933-1953." *American Jewish History* 68 (1979): 517-34.

310 Trumbo, Dalton. *The Time of the Toad: A Study of Inquisition in America and Two Related Pamphlets.* New York: Harper & Row, 1972.

311 Vaughn, Robert. *Only Victims: A Study of Show Business Blacklisting.* New York: Putnam's, 1972.

The Alger Hiss Case

There are no simple answers in the Hiss case—and more questions than answers. Most leftists presumed him innocent or hoped he was, while most rightists felt just the opposite. The case, as Kenneth O'Reilly (entry 324) observes, became a litmus test for liberals torn between concern for national security and concern for civil liberties. Who was lying, Hiss or his accuser, Whittaker Chambers? The principals each tell their side with Hiss (entry 319) defending himself ably and Chambers (entries 313-15) making an eloquent case for his side. Richard Nixon (entries 479 and 563) details his crucial role in the case. Fawn M. Brodie (entry 558) and Garry Wills (entry 569) analyze Nixon analyzing Hiss. Bert and Peter Andrews (entry 312) and Alistair Cooke (entry 317) provide still useful contemporary accounts as do Murray Kempton (entry 151) and Rebecca West (entry 330). Hede Massing (entry 322) was an ex-Communist who testified at Hiss' trial. Ralph DeToledano and Victor Lasky (entry 318), two prolific right-wing journalists, come down on the side of Chambers. Those favoring Hiss include Fred Cook (entry 316), Ronald Seth (entry 325), John C. Smith (entry 326), and Athan Theoharis (entries 327 and 328). In a recent scholarly treatment of the Hiss case, Allen Weinstein (entry 329) created a major controversy with his conclusion that Hiss was indeed guilty of perjury. For a rebuttal of Weinstein, see Navasky's essay (entry 323).

312 Andrews, Bert, and Andrews, Peter. *A Tragedy of History: A Journalist's Confidential Role in the Hiss-Chambers Case.* Washington, D.C.: Luce, 1962.

313 Buckley, William F., Jr., ed. *Odyssey of a Friend: Whittaker Chambers's Letters to William F. Buckley, Jr., 1954-1961.* New York: Putnam's, 1969.

314 Chambers, Whittaker. *Cold Friday.* Duncan Norton-Taylor, ed. New York: Random House, 1964.

315 _____. *Witness.* Random House, 1952.

316 Cook, Fred J. *The Unfinished Story of Alger Hiss.* New York: William Morrow, 1958.

317 Cooke, Alistair. *A Generation on Trial: U.S.A. v. Alger Hiss.* New York: Knopf, 1950.

318 DeToledano, Ralph, and Lasky, Victor. *Seeds of Treason: The True Story of the Hiss-Chambers Tragedy.* New York: Funk & Wagnalls, 1950.

319 Hiss, Alger. *In the Court of Public Opinion.* New York: Knopf, 1957.

320 Jowitt, William Allen [Earl Jowitt]. *The Strange Case of Alger Hiss.* Garden City, NY: Doubleday, 1953.

321 Levitt, Morton, and Levitt, Michael. *A Tissue of Lies: Nixon Vs. Hiss.* New York: McGraw-Hill, 1979.

322 Massing, Hede. *This Deception.* New York: Duell, Sloan & Pearce, 1951.

323 Navasky, Victor. "Weinstein, Hiss and the Transformation of Historical Ambiguity into Cold War Verity." In Athan G. Theoharis, ed. *Beyond*

the Hiss Case: The FBI, Congress, and the Cold War. Philadelphia: Temple University Press, 1982, pp. 215-45.

324 O'Reilly, Kenneth. "Liberal Values, the Cold War, and American Intellectuals: The Trauma of the Alger Hiss Case, 1950-1978." In Athan G. Theoharis, ed. *Beyond the Hiss Case: The FBI, Congress, and the Cold War.* Philadelphia: Temple University Press, 1982, pp. 309-340.

325 Seth, Ronald. *The Sleeping Truth: The Hiss-Chambers Affair Reappraised.* New York: Hart, 1968.

326 Smith, John C. *Alger Hiss: The True Story.* New York: Holt, Rinehart & Winston, 1976.

327 Theoharis, Athan, ed. *Beyond the Hiss Case: The FBI, Congress, and the Cold War.* Philadelphia: Temple University Press, 1982.

328 _____. "Unanswered Questions: Chambers, Nixon, the FBI, and the Hiss Case." In Athan G. Theoharis, ed. *Beyond the Hiss Case: The FBI, Congress, and the Cold War.* Philadelphia: Temple University Press, 1982, pp. 246-308.

329 Weinstein, Allen. *Perjury: The Hiss-Chambers Case.* New York: Knopf, 1978.

330 West, Rebecca. "Whittaker Chambers." *Atlantic Monthly* 189 (1952), pp. 33-39.

331 Zeligs, Meyer A. *Friendships and Fratricide.* New York: Viking, 1967.

McCarthyism

McCarthy—The Man

Joe McCarthy, Thomas C. Reeves has commented, "is our King John," which is to say that few writers have had much good to say about him. The earliest biographies by Anderson and May (entry 332) and Richard Rovere (entry 338) reflect the biases of liberal journalists and contain many inaccuracies. Fred J. Cook (entry 333) tries to put McCarthy into perspective as a product of his times. Recently, two scholars, David M. Oshinsky (entry 336) and Thomas C. Reeves (entry 337) have produced excellent, balanced works on a driven, haunting man who was much more complex than most people imagined.

332 Anderson, Jack, and May, Ronald W. *McCarthy: The Man, the Senator, the Ism.* Boston: Beacon, 1952.

333 Cook, Fred J. *The Nightmare Decade: The Life and Times of Senator Joe McCarthy.* New York: Random House, 1971.

334 Ingalls, Robert P. *Point of Order: A Profile of Senator Joe McCarthy.* New York: Putnam, 1981.

335 Matusow, Allen, ed. *Joseph R. McCarthy.* Englewood Cliffs, NJ: Prentice-Hall, 1970.

336 Oshinsky, David M. *A Conspiracy So Immense: The World of Joe McCarthy.* New York: Free Press, 1983.

337 Reeves, Thomas C. *The Life and Times of Joe McCarthy.* Briarcliff Manor, NY: Stein and Day, 1982.

338 Rovere, Richard. *Senator Joe McCarthy.* New York: Harcourt, Brace, 1959.

"McCarthyism"

An excellent place to begin the study of McCarthyism is with an essay by Thomas C. Reeves (entry 353) discussing interpretations since Richard Hofstadter's influential musings (entry 26) published in the 1950s. Richard Fried (entry 346) and Robert Griffith (entry 349) have also written perceptive review essays. In other books and articles, Fried (entry 345) and Griffith (entries 347, 348, and 350) argue that fear of communism produced by the Cold War and partisan politics combined to produce McCarthyism, a phenomenon which went far beyond the junior senator from Wisconsin. The prolific Athan Theoharis (entry 357) contends that McCarthyism really began in the executive branch of government under Truman, an argument he has made in several books and articles (entries 221, 222, and 227). These revisionist interpretations were greatly influenced by two books published in the 1960s. Earl Latham (entry 153) saw McCarthyism as a conventional political movement, the product of a revolt of the Republican right against the party's center. Michael Paul Rogin (entry 354) further undercut the old interpretation of McCarthyism as a mass movement created by status anxiety with his brilliant study of McCarthy's base of support.

For the role of the Catholic Church in McCarthyism, see Donald Crosby (entry 342) and Vincent DeSantis (entry 343). Eisenhower's role in the politics of McCarthyism is assessed by William Bragg Ewald, Jr. (entry 344) and Allen Yarnell (entry 359). Michael Straight (entry 356) offers a contemporary analysis of the Army-McCarthy hearings. Army counsel John Adams (entry 339) provides an inside perspective. Arthur Watkins (entry 358), chairman of the Senate committee which censured McCarthy, explains how the senator destroyed himself.

339 Adams, John G. *Without Precedent: The Story of the Death of McCarthyism.* New York: Norton, 1983.

340 Beth, Loren P. "McCarthyism." *South Atlantic Quarterly* 55 (1956): 135-52.

341 Caridi, Ronald J. "The G.O.P. and the Korean War." *Pacific Historical Review* 37 (1968): 423-43.

342 Crosby, Donald F. *God, Church, and Flag: Senator Joseph R. McCarthy and the Catholic Church, 1950-1957.* Chapel Hill: University of North Carolina Press, 1978.

343 DeSantis, Vincent P. "American Catholics and McCarthyism." *Catholic Historical Review* 51 (1965): 1-20.

344 Ewald, William Bragg, Jr. *Who Killed Joe McCarthy?* New York: Simon & Schuster, 1984.

345 Fried, Richard M. "Electoral Politics and McCarthyism: The 1950 Campaign." In Robert Griffith and Athan Theoharis, eds. *The Specter: Original Essays on the Cold War and the Origins of McCarthyism.* New York: New Viewpoints, 1974, pp. 190-222.

346 _____. "McCarthyism Without Tears: A Review Essay." *Wisconsin Magazine of History* 66 (1982-83): 143-6.

347 Griffith, Robert. "American Politics and the Origins of 'McCarthyism.'" In Robert Griffith and Athan Theoharis, eds. *The Specter: Original Essays on the Cold War and the Origins of McCarthyism.* New York: New Viewpoints, 1974, pp. 2-17.

348 _____. "The Political Context of McCarthyism." *Review of Politics* 33 (1971): pp. 24-35.

349 _____. "The Politics of Anti-Communism: A Review Article." *Wisconsin Magazine of History* 54 (1971): 299-308.

350 _____. *The Politics of Fear.* Lexington: University of Kentucky Press, 1970.

351 Niebuhr, Reinhold. "The Cause and Cure of the American Psychosis." *American Scholar* 25 (1955-56):11-20.

352 Reeves, Thomas C. *Freedom and the Foundation: The Fund for the Republic in the Era of McCarthyism.* New York: Knopf, 1969.

353 _____. "McCarthyism: Interpretations Since Hofstadter." *Wisconsin Magazine of History* 60 (1976): 42-54.

354 Rogin, Michael Paul. *The Intellectuals and McCarthy: The Radical Specter.* Cambridge, MA: MIT Press, 1967.

355 Rorty, James, and Decter, Moshe. *McCarthy and the Communists.* Boston: Beacon, 1954.

356 Straight, Michael. *Trial by Television.* Boston: Beacon, 1954.

357 Theoharis, Athan. "McCarthyism: A Broader Perspective." *Maryland History* 12 (1981): 1-7.

358 Watkins, Arthur V. *Enough Rope*. Englewood Cliffs, NJ: Prentice Hall and University of Utah Press, 1969.

359 Yarnell, Allen. "Eisenhower and McCarthy: An Appraisal of Presidential Strategy." *Presidential Studies Quarterly* 10 (1980): 90-98.

"McCarranism"

"McCarranism" has been used in this book to mean McCarthyism of the Democratic party. Indeed, available evidence indicates that as chairman of the Senate Internal Security Subcommittee, Pat McCarran did more than McCarthy to fan the flames of second Red Scare. On McCarran the man, see Jerome Edwards' fine biography (entry 363) which makes the point that McCarran's anti-communist crusade did not do him much good back home in Nevada. A book on Nevada by Gilman Ostrander (entry 367) also contains material on McCarran the political boss. Zechariah Chaffee, Jr. (entries 360 and 361) and Walter Gelhorn (364) examine the McCarran Act with a critical eye. Cotter and Smith (entry 362) and Richard Longaker (entry 366) examine the act's chilling emergency detention provisions. Tanner and Griffith (entry 368) observe that while the McCarran Act has been associated with McCarthy, the junior senator had nothing to do with it. R. Alton Lee (entry 365) looks at Karl Mundt's role in the bipartisan anti-communist legislation.

360 Chaffee, Zechariah, Jr. "Investigations of Radicalism and Laws Against Subversion." In Henry Steele Commager, ed,. *Civil Liberties Under Attack*. Philadelphia: University of Pennsylvania Press, pp. 46-84.

361 _____. *The Blessings of Liberty*. Philadelphia and New York: Lippincott, 1956.

362 Cotter, Cornelius P., and Smith, Malcolm. "An American Paradox: The Emergency Detention Act of 1950." *Journal of Politics* 19 (1957): 20-33.

363 Edwards, Jerome E. *Pat McCarran: Political Boss of Nevada*. Reno: University of Nevada Press, 1982.

364 Gelhorn, Walter. *American Rights: The Constitution in Action*. New York: Macmillan, 1963.

365 Lee, R. Alton. "'New Dealers, Fair Dealers, Misdealers, and Hiss Dealers': Karl Mundt and the Internal Security Act of 1950." *South Dakota History* 10 (1980): 277-290.

366 Longaker, Richard. "Emergency Detention: The Generation Gap, 1950-1971." *Western Political Quarterly* 27 (1974): 395-408.

367 Ostrander, Gilman M. *Nevada: The Great Rotten Borough, 1859-1964.* New York: Knopf, 1966.

368 Tanner, William R., and Griffith, Robert. "Legislative Politics and 'McCarthyism': The Internal Security Act of 1950." In Robert Griffith and Athan Theoharis, eds., *The Specter: Original Essays on the Cold War and the Origins of McCarthyism.* New York: New Viewpoints, 1974, pp. 172-89.

McCarthy's Defenders

In this short list, William, F. Buckley and L. Brent Bozell (entry 370) praise the senator for opposing the nefarious schemes of communists and liberals. James Burnham (entry 371) defends McCarthyism as necessary since Communists have penetrated government, schools, and churches. Yet another Buckley protege, Frank S. Meyer (entry 372), offers a similar argument.

369 Bruhn, Alfred W. *Stop Communism Now.* Chicago: Midwest Publishers, 1952.

370 Buckley, William F., Jr., and Bozell, L. Brent. *McCarthy and His Enemies: The Record and Its Meaning.* Chicago: Regnery, 1954.

371 Burnham, James. *The Web of Subversion.* New York: John Day, 1954.

372 Meyer, Frank S. "Principles and Heresies: The Meaning of McCarthyism." *National Review*, 14 June 1958.

McCarthy's Critics

Richard M. Fried (entry 375) examines how McCarthy's Republican colleagues used him for partisan purposes against the Democrats until he outlived his usefulness and why the Democrats behaved as they did. Several of McCarthy's political opponents have been the subjects of biographies: Sidney Hyman (entry 376) on William Benton, who crossed McCarthy early; Donald J. Kemper (entry 377) on Thomas Hennings, Jr., whose committee examined the senator's finances; Allan Nevins (entry 378) on New York liberal Herbert Lehman; and A. Robert Smith (entry 379) on Oregon maverick Wayne Morse. Congressman Emanuel Celler of Brooklyn (entry 373) was an outspoken opponent of McCarthy in the House. See the autobiographies of Paul H. Douglas (entry 374) and Margaret Chase Smith (entry 380) for the lives of two of McCarthy's more eloquent political enemies.

373   Celler, Emanuel. *You Never Leave Brooklyn.* New York: John Day, 1953.

374   Douglas, Paul H. *In the Fullness of Time: The Memoirs of Paul H. Douglas.* New York: Harcourt Brace Jovanovich, 1971.

375   Fried, Richard M. *Men Against McCarthy.* New York: Columbia University Press, 1976.

376   Hyman, Sidney. *The Lives of William Benton.* Chicago: University of Chicago Press, 1969.

377   Kemper, Donald J. *Decade of Fear: Senator Hennings and Civil Liberties.* Columbia: University of Missouri Press, 1965.

378   Nevins, Allan. *Herbert H. Lehman and His Era.* New York: Scribner, 1963.

379   Smith, A. Robert. *Tiger in the Senate: The Biography of Wayne Morse.* Garden City, NY: Doubleday, 1962.

380   Smith, Margaret Chase. *Declaration of Conscience.* Garden City, NY: Doubleday, 1972.

Victims

Cedric Belfrage (entry 381), a procommunist radical deported during the second Red Scare, examines the victims of the country's growing obsession with communism after World War II. E.J. Kahn, Jr. (entry 386) looks at what happened to State Department experts accused by McCarthy, McCarran, and others of "selling out" China to communism. China experts O. Edmund Clubb (entry 382), John K. Fairbank (entry 384), and Owen Lattimore (entry 387) have written their own accounts as victims of of the Red Scare. An art teacher's fight for re-instatement in California is told by Frank Rowe (entry 388). Phillip M. Stern (entry 389) and Charles P. Curtis (entry 383) present sympathetic portraits of J. Robert Oppenheimer, "father of the atomic bomb" who fell victim to the Red Scare. Texas humorist and radio personality John Henry Faulk (entry 385) explains how he fought back against being blacklisted.

381   Belfrage, Cedric. The American Inquisition, 1945-1960. Indianapolis: Bobbs-Merrill, 1973.

382   Clubb, O. Edmund. *The Witness and I.* New York: Columbia University Press, 1974.

383   Curtis, Charles P. *The Oppenheimer Case: The Trial of a Security System.* New York: Simon and Schuster, 1955.

384   Fairbank, John K. *Chinabound: A Fifty-Year Memoir.* New York: Harper & Row, 1982.

385 Faulk, John Henry. *Fear on Trial.* New York: Simon and Schuster, 1964.

386 Kahn, E.J., Jr. *The China Hands: America's Foreign Service Officers and What Befell Them.* New York: Viking, 1975.

387 Lattimore, Owen. *Ordeal by Slander.* Boston: Little, Brown, 1950.

388 Rowe, Frank. *The Enemy Among Us: A Story of Witch-Hunting in the McCarthy Era.* Sacramento: Cougar Books, 1980.

389 Stern, Phillip M. *The Oppenheimer Case.* New York: Harper & Row, 1969.

The Media and the Second Red Scare.

Fred J. Cook (entry 392) and Elmer H. Davis (entry 393) were outspoken opponents of McCarthy in the media. Alexander Kendrick's biography of Edward R. Murrow (entry 395) details that broadcaster's role in turning the public against McCarthy. Edwin R. Bayley (entry 390) details the symbiotic relationship between McCarthy and the newspapers, the latter judged guilty of "timid neutrality," a subject David Halberstam (entry 394) also examines in passing.

390 Bayley, Edwin R. *Joe McCarthy and the Press.* Madison: University of Wisconsin Press, 1981.

391 Cade, Dozier C. "Witch Hunting, 1952: The Role of the Press." *Journalism Quarterly* 29 (1952): 396-407.

392 Cook, Fred J. *Maverick: 50 Years of Investigative Reporting.* New York: GP Putnam's Sons, 1985.

393 Davis, Elmer H. *But We Were Born Free.* New York: Bobbs-Merill, 1954.

394 Halberstam, David. *The Powers That Be.* New York: Knopf, 1980.

395 Kendrick, Alexander. *Prime Time: The Life of Edward R. Murrow.* New York: Avon, 1970.

Regional Studies

Walter Gelhorn (entry 397) presents essays critical of Red Scare activities in the states of California, Illinois, Maryland, Michigan, New York, and Washington. David Caute (entry 203) also surveys "The Great Fear" at the state and local levels. Don E. Carleton (entry 396) writes extensively about Texas during the Red Scare, especially Houston where the power elite redbaited to keep Communists, blacks, and labor unions in their places. Michael

O'Brien (entry 399) explains McCarthy's potency in terms of the emerging conservative/liberal anti-communist consensus.

396 Carleton, Don E. *Red Scare! Right-Wing Hysteria, Fifties Fanaticism, and Their Legacy in Texas*. Austin: Texas Monthly Press, 1985.

397 Gelhorn, Walter, ed. *The States and Subversion*. Ithaca, NY: Cornell University Press, 1952.

398 Green, George N. "McCarthyism in Texas: the 1954 Campaign." *Southern Quarterly* 16 (1978): 255-76.

399 O'Brien, Michael. *McCarthy and McCarthyism in Wisconsin*. Columbia: University of Missouri Press, 1980.

The Rosenbergs

The Rosenbergs, Allen Weinstein has noted, are "icons of the Cold War." As such, their lives and their fate have stirred controversy for more than thirty years, especially on the Left, where the couple's innocence was taken as a matter of faith. Morton Sobell (entry 412), co-defendant with the Rosenbergs, tells his story. The Rosenbergs' prison letters (entry 410) inspired essays by literary critics Robert Warshow (entry 414) and Leslie Fiedler (entry 402) which damned them as tragic Stalinist dupes. Early on, leftist William A. Reuben (entry 408) found the Rosenbergs innocent. Jonathan Root (entry 409) took another look at the case in 1964 and pronounced them guilty. The next year, Walter and Miriam Schneir (entry 411) published their enormously influential book which attacked the government's evidence and conduct. Alvin Goldstein (entry 403) whose film documentary leaned on the Schneir's account, found enough interest in the case to publish the script. E. L. Doctorow (entry 618) wrote a novel based on the Rosenberg family which avoids taking sides, but still expressed skepticism over the government's case. In the 1970s, the Rosenberg children (entry 404) surfaced to begin a new crusade to exonerate their parents, obtaining hundreds of thousands of government documents through the Freedom of Information Act.

A book by former New Left historian Ronald Radosh and Joyce Milton (entry 407) and a revised edition of the Schneirs' book reignited the controversy in 1983. The Schneirs debated Radosh and Milton before a packed house at New York Town Hall, on local radio and national television. Radosh and Milton make a strong case for the guilt of Julius Rosenberg and the innocence of Ethel. They also castigate the government (especially the FBI) and the

Communist party for exploiting the case. The controversy will undoubtedly continue as more evidence turns up.

400 Anders, Roger M. "The Rosenberg Case Revisited: The Greenglass Testimony and the Protection of Atomic Secrets." *American Historical Review* 83 (1978): 388-400.

401 Beier, Norman S., and Sand, Leonard B. "The Rosenberg Case: History and Hysteria." *American Bar Association Journal* 40 (1954): 1046-50.

402 Fiedler, Leslie A. *An End to Innocence.* Boston: Beacon, 1955.

403 Goldstein, Alvin H. *The Unquiet Death of Julius and Ethel Rosenberg.* New York: Lawrence Hill, 1975.

404 Meeropol, Robert, and Meeropol, Michael. *We Are Your Sons: The Legacy of Julius and Ethel Rosenberg.* Boston: Houghton Mifflin, 1975.

405 Nizer, Louis. *The Implosion Conspiracy.* Garden City, NY: Doubleday, 1973.

406 Parrish, Michael E. "Cold War Justice: The Supreme Court and the Rosenbergs." *American Historical Review* 82 (1977): 805-42.

407 Radosh, Ronald, and Milton, Joyce. *The Rosenberg File: A Search for the Truth.* New York: Holt, Rinehart & Winston, 1983.

408 Reuben, William A. *The Atom Spy Hoax.* New York: Action Books, 1954.

409 Root, Jonathan. *The Betrayers: The Rosenbergs—A Reappraisal of an American Crisis.* New York: Coward-McCann, 1964.

410 Rosenberg, Ethel G., and Rosenberg, Julius. *Death House Letters.* New York: Jero Publishing, 1953.

411 Schneir, Walter, and Schneir, Miriam. *Invitation to an Inquest: A New Look at the Rosenberg-Sobell Case.* New York: Doubleday, 1983.

412 Sobell, Morton. *On Doing Time.* New York: Scribner's, 1974.

413 Strout, Cushing. "Reconsidering the Rosenbergs: History, Novel, Film." *Reviews in American History* 12 (1984): 309-21.

414 Warshow, Robert. *The Immediate Experience.* Garden City, NY: Doubleday, 1962.

Anti-Communist Culture

Anti-Communism has been so pervasive in American society since World War II that it has become an integral part of our culture. Kenneth Davis (entry 416) includes a discussion of anti-communist pulp fiction in his survey of the rise of paperback books. Charles Glicksberg (entry 417) surveys the effects of the second Red Scare on popular fiction while George Lipsitz (entry 420) provides a general survey of the postwar scene. Anti-communism in films in the 1940s and 1950s is covered in books by Peter Biskind (entry 415) and Nora Sayre (entry 424) and articles by Les Adler (entry 297) Daniel J. Leab (entries 418 and 419), Frank McConnell (entry 422), Russell Shain (entry 425), and James M. Skinner (entry 426). Shain (entry 14) has written an excellent bibliographic essay on Cold War movies. See also entries under HCUA and Hollywood. Marcia Pally (entry 418) looks at the Rambo-style anti-red movies of the 1980s. J. Fred MacDonald (entry 421) finds that television fed viewers a powerful new menu of anti-communist propaganda which led to the Vietnam war.

415 Biskind, Peter. *Seeing is Believing: How Hollywood Taught Us to Stop Worrying and Love the Fifties*. New York: Pantheon, 1983.

416 Davis, Kenneth C. *Two-Bit Culture: The Paperbacking of America*. Boston: Houghton Mifflin, 1984.

417 Glicksberg, Charles I. "Anti-Communism in Fiction." *South Atlantic Quarterly* 53 (1954): 485-96.

418 Leab, Daniel J. "The Hollywood Feature Film as Cold Warrior." Organization of American Historians *Newsletter* 13 (1985): 13-15.

419 _____. "How Red Was My Valley: Hollywood, the Cold War Film, and I Married a Communist" *Journal of Contemporary History* 19 (1984): 59-88.

420 Lipsitz, George. *Class and Culture in Cold War America*. New York: Praeger, 1981.

421 MacDonald, J. Fred. *Television and the Red Menace: The Video Road to Vietnam*. New York: Praeger, 1985.

422 McConnell, Frank D. "Pickup on South Street and the Metamorphosis of the Thriller." *Film Heritage* 8 (1973): 9-18.

423 Pally, Marcia. "Red Faces." *Film Comment* 22 (1986): 32-37.

424 Sayre, Nora. *Running Time: Films of the Cold War*. New York: Dial, 1982.

425 Shain, Russell E. "Hollywood's Cold War." *Journal of Popular Film* 3 (1974): 334-50.

426 Skinner, James M. "Cliche and Convention in Hollywood's Cold War Anti-Communist Films." *North Dakota Quarterly* 46 (1978): 35-40.

Ex-Communists

Hannah Arendt (entry 427) compares and contrasts former communists, that is, those who dropped away from the party while retaining some leftist sympathies and ex-communists, who crossed the political spectrum to the Right, actively exposing the conspiracy along the way.   Some ex-communists became professional witnesses, offering expert testimony in committee hearings and political trials, sometimes for pay. Their autobiographies played an important role in creating the anti-communist consensus. Benjamin Gitlow (entry 437) was the first to publish a confessional. Next came Louis Budenz (entries 429 and 430) who made a living from anti-communism for many years, excoriating liberalism as well as Marxism. Another HCUA favorite, Elizabeth Bentley (entry 428) detailed her life as a red spy. Freda Utley (entry 443) became the darling of the China Lobby and the McCarthyites, although never felt completely comfortable with either. The best of the ex-communists books are by Granville Hicks (entry 438) and the colorful Max Eastman (entries 433-35). See also George Charney (entry 431), John Gates (entry 436), and Sandor Voros (entry 444). Richard Crossman (entry 432) has edited a book of essays by ex-Communists explaining why Stalinism appealed to them. On this point, see William O'Neill (entry 216) whose treatment of ex-communists is sympathetic. Harvey Matusow (entry 440) makes a different sort of confession: he details how testimony was systematically fabricated.   The most famous professional ex-communist was, of course, Whittaker Chambers (entries 313-15). Herbert L. Packer (entry 441) examines the tesitimony of Chambers, Budenz, Bentley, and John Lautner. Harold Josephson (entry 439) believes that more attention should be paid to the ex-communists themselves, who were used by liberals and conservatives alike for partisan purposes. See Al Richmond (entry 442) for an example of the recent trend of ex-communists to be critical of the Left without the handwringing.

427 Arendt, Hannah. "The Ex-Communists." *Commonweal* 20 March 1953, 595-99.

428 Bentley, Elizabeth. *Out of Bondage: The Story of Elizabeth Bentley.* New York: Devin-Adair, 1951.

429 Budenz, Louis F. *Men Without Faces: The Communist Conspiracy in the U.S.A.* New York: Harper, 1950.

430 _____. *This is My Story.* New York: McGraw-Hill, 1947.

431 Charney, George. *A Long Journey.* Chicago: Quadrangle, 1968.

432 Crossman, Richard, ed. *The God That Failed.* New York: Harper, 1949.

433 Eastman, Max. *Enjoyment of Living.* New York: Harper, 1948.

434 _____. *Love and Revolution: My Journey Through an Epoch.* New York: Random House, 1964.

435 _____. *Marxism: Is It Science?* New York: Norton, 1940.

436 Gates, John. *The Story of an American Communist.* New York: Nelson, 1958.

437 Gitlow, Benjamin. *I Confess: The Truth About American Communism.* New York: Dutton, 1940.

438 Hicks, Granville. *Part of the Truth.* New York: Harcourt, Brace & World, 1965.

439 Josephson, Harold. "Ex-Communists in Crossfire: A Cold War Debate." *Historian* 44 (1981): 69-84.

440 Matusow, Harvey M. *False Witness.* New York: Cameron & Kahn, 1955.

441 Packer, Herbert L. *Ex-Communist Witnesses: Four Studies in Fact Finding.* Stanford, CA: Stanford University Press, 1962.

442 Richmond, Al. *A Long Look From the Left.* Boston: Houghton Mifflin, 1973.

443 Utley, Freda. *The China Story.* Chicago: Regnery, 1951.

444 Voros, Sandor. *American Commissar.* Philadelphia and New York: Chilton, 1961.

445 Wright, Richard. "I Tried to Be a Communist." Atlantic Monthly 174 (Aug.-Sept. 1944): 61(Aug.); 48(Sept.).

The Eisenhower Years

Liberal and Leftist Anti-Communists

For an excellent overview of liberalism in this period, see Richard Pells (entry 454). Arthur Schlesinger, Jr. (entry 456) jetisons the Popular Front and pushes liberalism to the political right in order to reach the "Vital Center." Carroll Engelhardt (entry 446) and James Nuechterlein (entry 453) analyze Schlesinger's liberal anti-communism. Clifton Rossiter (entry 455) reaffirms that communism and liberalism are anything but bedfellows. Richard W. Fox (entry 447) and Paul Merkley (entry 452) tackle the life of theologian Reinhold Niebuhr, whose political philosophy profoundly influenced a generation of liberals. Niebuhr's calls to arms against communism (entry 240) and Senator McCarthy (entry 351) have been cited previously. Nathan Liebowitz (entry 449) examines the liberal thought of Daniel Bell. Ronald Steel (entry

457) has written a superb biography of liberal journalist Walter Lippmann. John Bartlow Martin (entry 451) contributes a biography on the liberals' favorite politician, Adlai Stevenson. Chief Justice Earl Warren (entry 459) whose unexpected liberalism irritated Dwight Eisenhower left behind a disappointingly thin memoir. Socialist leader Norman Thomas (entry 458) warns of the Communist menace. Stephen J. Whitfield (entry 460) scrutinizes the politics of iconoclast Dwight MacDonald.

446 Engelhardt, Carroll. "Man in the Middle: Arthur M. Schlesinger, Jr. and Postwar American Liberalism." *South Atlantic Quarterly* 80 (1981): 119-38.

447 Fox, Richard Wightman. *Reinhold Niebuhr*. New York: Pantheon, 1985.

448 Hook, Sidney. *Heresy, Yes—Conspiracy, No*. New York: John Day, 1953.

449 Liebowitz, Nathan. *Daniel Bell and the Agony of Modern Liberalism*. Westport, CT: Greenwood, 1985.

450 McAuliffe, Mary S. "Liberals and the Communist Control Act of 1954." *Journal of American History* 63 (1976):351-67.

451 Martin, John Bartlow. *Adlai Stevenson of Illinois*. Garden City, NY: Doubleday, 1977.

452 Merkley, Paul. *Reinhold Niebuhr: A Political Account*. Montreal: McGill-Queen's University Press, 1975.

453 Nuechterlein, James A. "Arthur M. Schlesinger, Jr. and the Discontents of Postwar American Liberalism." *Review of Politics* 39 (1977): 3-40.

454 Pells, Richard H. *The Liberal Mind in a Conservative Age: American Intellectuals in the 1940s & 1950s*. New York: Harper & Row, 1985.

455 Rossiter, Clinton. Marxism: The View From America. New York: Harcourt, Brace, 1960.

456 Schlesinger, Arthur M., Jr. *The Vital Center: The Politics of Freedom*. Boston: Houghton Mifflin, 1949.

457 Steel, Ronald. *Walter Lippmann and the American Century*. Boston: Little, Brown, 1980.

458 Thomas, Norman. *The Test of Freedom*. New York: Norton, 1954.

459 Warren, Earl. *The Memoirs of Earl Warren*. Garden City, NY: Doubleday, 1977.

460 Whitfield, Stephen J. *A Critical American: The Politics of Dwight MacDonald*. Hamden: Archon, 1984.

Conservative Anti-Communists

To examine the conservatism of the 1950s, begin with George Nash's survey of the intellectual scene (entry 465) and David W. Reinhard's overview of the political Right (entry 467). Peter Viereck (entry 472) argues that liberal intellectuals are communist sympathizers. John P. Diggins (entry 461) examines the conservative ideology of four former Communists who came to work for William F. Buckley's *National Review*: Max Eastman, John Dos Passos, Will Herberg, and James Burnham. Turning to politics, Ronald Radosh (entry 466) sketches the ideas of right-wing isolationists, who, in the wake of Vietnam and Watergate, seemed refreshing to some. For biographies of conservative politicians, see David Loth (entry 462) on the staunchly anti-communist Frances Bolton, Neil MacNeil (entry 463) on McCarthy ally Everett Dirksen, Henry Z. Scheele (entry 463) on House Republican leader Charlie Hallack, Stephen C. Shadegg (entry 468) on the acid-tongued Clare Booth Luce, and Alfred Steinberg (entry 470) on Democrat Sam Rayburn. Long time House Republican leader Joe Martin (entry 464) tells his own anti-communist story.

461 Diggins, John P. *Up From Communism: Conservative Odysseys in American Intellectual History.* New York: Harper & Row, 1975.

462 Loth, David. *A Long Way Forward: The Biography of Congresswoman Frances P. Bolton.* New York: Longmans, Green, 1957.

463 MacNeil, Neil. *Dirksen, Portrait of a Public Man.* New York: World, 1970.

464 Martin, Joe. *My Fifty Years in Politics As Told to Robert J. Donovan.* New York: McGraw-Hill, 1960.

465 Nash, George. *The Conservative Intellectual Movement in America Since 1945.* New York: Basic Books, 1976.

466 Radosh, Ronald. *Prophets on the Right: Profiles of Conservative Critics of American Globalism.* New York: Simon & Schuster, 1975.

467 Reinhard, David W. *The Republican Right Since 1945.* Lexington: University of Kentucky Press, 1983.

468 Scheele, Henry Z. *Charlie Hallack: A Political Biography.* New York: Exposition, 1966.

469 Shadegg, Stephen C. *Clare Boothe Luce.* New York: Simon & Schuster, 1970.

470 Steinberg, Alfred. *Sam Rayburn.* New York: Hawthorn, 1975.

471 Toy, Eckard. "Spiritual Mobilization: The Failure of an Ultraconservative Ideal in the 1950's." *Pacific Northwest Quarterly* 61 (1970): 77-86.

472 Viereck, Peter. *Shame and Glory of the Intellectuals: Babbitt Jr. vs. the Rediscovery of Values.* Boston: Beacon, 1953.

The Eisenhower Administration

Ezra Taft Benson (entry 473), Eisenhower's secretary of agriculture, warns of the dangers of "creeping socialism." The best book on Ike's secretary of state, John Foster Dulles, is by Townsend Hoopes (entry 478). Vice President Richard Nixon (entry 479) wrote an episodic memoir while plotting his political comeback in 1962 and a more systematic autobiography (entry 563) following his resignation. On Eisenhower, see his two volumes of memoirs (entry 476) and a disappointing diary (entry 477). Herbert Parmet (entry 480) is the president's leading biographer. Robert Divine (entry 475) reviews the Eisenhower foreign policy favorably. Blanche Wiesen Cook (entry 474) takes a close look at Guatemala as a model for anti-communist operations.

473 Benson, Ezra Taft. *The Red Carpet.* Salt Lake City: Bookcraft, 1962.

474 Cook, Blanche Wiesen. *The Declassified Eisenhower.* Garden City, NY: Doubleday, 1981.

475 Divine, Robert. *Eisenhower and the Cold War.* New York: Oxford University Press. 1981.

476 Eisenhower, Dwight D. *The White House Years.* 2 vols. Garden City, NY: Doubleday, 1963-1965.

477 Ferrell, Robert H., ed. *The Eisenhower Diaries.* New York: Norton, 1981.

478 Hoopes, Townsend. *The Devil and John Foster Dulles.* Boston: Beacon, 1973.

479 Nixon, Richard M. *Six Crises.* Garden City, NY: Doubleday, 1962.

480 Parmet, Herbert S. *Eisenhower and the American Crusades.* New York: Macmillan, 1972.

The 1960s

Anti-Communist Politics

William L. O'Neill (entry 494) is a good place to begin studying the 1960s. Allen J. Matusow (entry 492) examines how the collapse of liberal politics almost tore the country apart. There have been many books written about the Kennedy years, many of them falling just short of hagiography. For those exposed to this genre,

Garry Wills (498) offers an antidote of uniformly negative analysis. David Burner and Thomas R. West (entry 481) probe the Kennedy brothers' liberal anti-communism. Two former New Leftists, Peter Collier and David Horowitz (entry 482) labored to produce an interesting portrait of the Kennedy clan. David Halberstam (entry 488) is still unmatched for his study of Kennedy's advisers. There is much good material on politics to be found in Bruce Miroff (entry 493) and Herbert Parmet (entry 495). Richard Walton (entry 497) casts a critical eye on Kennedy's plans for countering Third World Communists.

Robert Divine (entry 483) has edited a book of insightful essays on the Johnson years. Although Ronnie Dugger's biography of Lyndon Johnson (entry 484) stops short of his presidency, readers will find it useful in understanding the expansive Texan's anti-communism. See Johnson's own memoir (entry 490) which is self-serving even by the standards of presidential reminiscences. LBJ "sings mammy" (as Garry Wills put it) to former aid Doris Kearns (entry 491). For other leading politicians of this period, see biographies of Hubert Humphrey by Carl Solberg (entry 496) and Winthrop Griffith (entry 487). Haynes Johnson and Bernard Gwertzmann (entry 489) discuss the career of LBJ nemesis J. William Fulbright (entry 485), who discusses the state of liberal empire in his own book of essays. Barry Goldwater (entry 486) offers no apologies for his brand of conservative anti-communism in his memoir.

481   Burner, David, and West, Thomas R. *The Torch is Passed: The Kennedy Brothers and American Liberalism.* New York: Atheneum, 1984.

482   Collier, Peter, and Horowitz, David. *The Kennedys: An American Drama.* New York: Summit, 1984.

483   Divine, Robert A., ed. *Exploring the Johnson Years.* Austin: University of Texas Press, 1981.

484   Dugger, Ronnie. *The Politician: The Life and Times of Lyndon Johnson.* New York: Norton, 1982.

485   Fulbright, J. William. *The Arrogance of Power.* New York: Random House, 1966.

486   Goldwater, Barry. *With No Apologies.* New York: William Morrow, 1979.

487   Griffith, Winthrop. *Humphrey: A Candid Biography.* New York: William Morrow, 1965.

488   Halberstam, David. *The Best and the Brightest.* New York: Random House, 1972.

489 Johnson, Haynes, and Gwertzmann, Bernard M. *Fulbright: The Dissenter.* Garden City, NY: Doubleday, 1968.

490 Johnson, Lyndon B. *The Vantage Point: Perspectives on the Presidency, 1963-1969.* New York: Holt, Rinehart & Winston, 1971.

491 Kearns, Doris. *Lyndon Johnson and the American Dream.* New York: Harper & Row, 1976.

492 Matusow, Allen J. *The Unraveling of America: A History of Liberalism in the 1960s.* New York: Harper & Row, 1984.

493 Miroff, Bruce. *Pragmatic Illusions: The Presidential Politics of John F. Kennedy.* New York: David McKay, 1976.

494 O'Neill, William L. *Coming Apart: An Informal History of America in the 1960's.* Chicago: Quadrangle, 1971.

495 Parmet, Herbert S. *JFK: The Presidency of John F. Kennedy.* New York: Dial, 1983.

496 Solberg, Carl. *Hubert Humphrey: A Biography.* New York: Norton, 1984.

497 Walton, Richard. *Cold War and Counterrevolution.* New York: Viking, 1972.

498 Wills, Garry. *The Kennedy Imprisonment.* Boston: Little, Brown, 1982.

The New Left

Little has been written about the New Left and much of that is unsatisfactory. William O'Neill (entry 494) offers many insights into the movement as does Jerome Skolnick (entry 502). Kirkpatrick Sale (entry 501) discusses the rise and fall of Students for a Democratic Society. Edward J. Bacciocco, Jr. (entry 499) presents a conservative view of the New Left while Phillip Abbott Luce (entry 500) writes from the extreme Right.

499 Bacciocco, Edward J., Jr. *The New Left in America: Reform to Revolution, 1956 to 1970.* Stanford, CA: Hoover Institution Press, 1974.

500 Luce, Phillip Abbott. *The New Left.* New York: McKay, 1966.

501 Sale, Kirkpatrick. *SDS.* New York: Vintage, 1974.

502 Skolnick, Jerome H. *The Politics of Protest.* New York: Ballantine, 1969.

Anti-Communism and the Intelligence Agencies

General Studies

Before the middle 1970s, when the Watergate scandal led to revelations about the activities of American intelligence agencies, little was known about covert government campaigns against communism at home and abroad, only an occasional book like that by Jacob Spolansky (entry 508) broke through the secrecy. The best general account of clandestine activities against the Left is by Athan Theoharis (entry 509).   Books edited by Berman and Halperin (entry 503) and Borosage and Marks (entry 504) contain useful material as do monographs by Frank Donner (entry 505), Morton Halperin, et. al. (506), and David Wise (entry 510), although there is a certain breathlessness about these works competing to reveal the abuses of power.   Richard Morgan (entry 507) includes a discussion on reforming the agencies.

503   Berman, Jerry J., and Halperin, Morton H., eds. *The Abuses of the Intelligence Agencies.* Washington, D.C.: Center for National Security Studies, 1975.

504   Borosage, Robert L., and Marks, John, eds. *The CIA File.* New York: Grossman, 1976.

505   Donner, Frank J. *The Age of Surveillance: The Aims and Methods of America's Political Intelligence System.* New York: Knopf, 1980.

506   Halperin, Morton, et. al. *The Lawless State: The Crimes of the United States Intelligence Agencies.* New York: Penguin, 1976.

507   Morgan, Richard E. *Domestic Intelligence: Monitoring Dissent in America.* Austin: University of Texas Press, 1980.

508   Spolansky, Jacob. *The Communist Trail in America.* New York: Macmillan, 1951.

509   Theoharis, Athan G. *Spying on Americans: Political Surveillance From Hoover to the Houston Plan.* Philadelphia: Temple University Press, 1978.

510   Wise, David. *The American Police State: The Government Against the People.* New York: Random House, 1976.

The FBI

Perhaps because J. Edgar Hoover had been on a pedastal for so long, revelations about the FBI's covert activities created a special sense of outrage on the part of the public.   Before the 1960s Max Lowenthal (entry 517) wrote the only account which dared to be critical of the bureau.   Hoover's agency is lionized by Don

Whitehead (entry 528). Richard Gil Powers has written a balanced account of Hoover's life (entry 523) as well as a thoughtful analysis of the FBI in popular culture (entry 522). J. Edgar Hoover (entries 515 and 516) made a fortune in royalties from these and other ghost written denunciations of the Red Menace. Angela Calomiris (entry 511) and Herbert Philbrick (entry 521) explain how they spied on the Communist party for the bureau in bestsellers from the early 1950s.

The best overall account of the FBI is by journalist Sanford J. Ungar (entry 525). Former agent William Turner (entry 524) roasts Hoover in an account which is none the less useful. Pat Watters and Stephen Gillers (entry 527) present the proceedings of a 1971 Princeton conference on bureau abuses of power. Kenneth O'Reilly (entry 518) has written an excellent monograph on the powerful alliance Hoover forged with HCUA which did much to create the second Red Scare. Sigmund Diamund (entry 512) surveys FBI snooping at Harvard while Kenneth Waltzer (entry 526) does the same for the American Labor Party. A lawsuit filed on behalf of the Socialist Workers Party led to the publication of bureau documents detailing COINTELPRO operations edited by Cathy Perkus (entry 520). David J. Garrow (entry 514) details Hoover's special vendetta against Martin Luther King, Jr. For a look at burerau reforms in the post-Hoover era, see John T. Eliff (entry 513).

511 Calomiris, Angela. *Red Masquerade: Undercover for the F.B.I.* New York: Lippincott, 1950.

512 Diamund, Sigmund. "The Arrangement: The FBI and Harvard University in the McCarthy Period." In Athan G. Theoharis, ed. *Beyond the Hiss Case: The FBI, Congress, and the Cold War.* Philadelphia: Temple University Press, 1982, pp. 341-71.

513 Elliff, John T. *The Reform of FBI Intelligence Operations.* Princeton, NJ: Princeton University Press, 1979.

514 Garrow, David J. *The FBI and Martin Luther King, Jr.* New York: Penguin, 1983.

515 Hoover, J. Edgar. *Masters of Deceipt: The Story of Communism in America and How to Fight It.* New York: Holt, 1958.

516 _____. *A Study of Communism.* New York: Holt, Rinehart and Winston, 1962.

517 Lowenthal, Max. *The Federal Bureau of Investigation.* New York: Sloane, 1950.

518 O'Reilly, Kenneth. *Hoover and the Un-Americans: The FBI, HUAC and the Red Menace.* Philadelphia: Temple University Press, 1983.

519 Overstreet, Harry, and Overstreet, Bonaro. *The FBI in Our Open Society.* New York: Norton, 1969.

520 Perkus, Cathy, ed. *COINTELPRO: The FBI's Secret War on Political Freedom.* New York: Monad, 1975.

521 Philbrick, Herbert A. *I Led Three Lives: Citizen, Communist, Counterspy.* New York: McGraw-Hill, 1952.

522 Powers, Richard Gid. *G-Men: Hoover's FBI in American Popular Culture.* Carbondale: Southern Illinois University Press, 1983.

523 _____. *Secrecy and Power: The Life of J. Edgar Hoover.* New York: Macmillan, 1987.

524 Turner, William W. *Hoover's FBI.* New York: Dell, 1971.

525 Ungar, Sanford. *FBI.* Boston: Little, Brown, 1975.

526 Waltzer, Kenneth. "The FBI, Congressman Vito Marcantonio, and the American Labor Party." In Athan G. Theoharis, ed. *Beyond the Hiss Case: The FBI, Congress, and the Cold War.* Philadelphia: Temple University Press, 1982, pp. 176-214.

527 Watters, Pat, and Gillers, Stephen, eds. *Investigating the FBI.* New York: Ballantine, 1974.

528 Whitehead, Don. *The F.B.I. Story: A Report to the People.* New York: Random House, 1956.

529 Williams, David. "The Bureau of Investigation and Its Critics, 1919-1921: The Origins of Federal Political Surveillance." *Journal of American History* 68 (1981): 560-79.

Radical Right Anti-Communsim

General Accounts

In 1955 a book of essays edited by Daniel Bell (entry 532) was published on the new American Right, including Richard Hofstadter's influential piece theorizing about "status anxiety." Hofstadter contended that the radical right or ultraconservatives consisted of a few "soured patricians," the new rich, middle class ethnic groups (especially Irish and Germans) and ex-communists. In a revised version of his essay, he expanded the list to include some in the old middle class, business executives, and military men. Yet another essay in the Bell volume by Seymour Martin Lipset surveyed earlier movements from the Know-Nothings to the KKK as a way of accounting for contemporary political intolerance. From this beginning, Lipset and Earl Raab (entry 544) produced a survey of extremism from the beginning of the republic through the George Wallace movement. Ellsworth and Harris (entry 538) and Jonathan

Kolkey (entry 543) look at extremism in the 1960s, while journalist Phillip Finch (entry 539) describes his journey underground in search of contemporary extremists. Robert Rosenstone (entry 545) and Robert A. Schoenberger (entry 546) have edited readers full of good material.

Extreme right wingers, as these historians and sociologists remind us, are prone to belief in conspiracy theories, especially by the Communist party, which account for every ill known to man. Outstanding examples of this genre include Gary Allen (entry 530), Anthony Bouscarn (entry 533), Ralph DeToledano (entries 535 and 536), Dan Jacobs (entry 541), William R. Kintner (entry 542), and John A. Stormer (entry 547). Roscoe Baker (entry 531) looks at the influence of the American Legion on foreign policy. For the Ku Klux Klan, see David Chalmers (entry 537) and Robert A. Goldberg (entry 540).

530 Allen, Gary. *None Dare Call It Conspiracy.* Rossmoor, CA: Concord, 1973.

531 Baker, Roscoe. *The American Legion and American Foreign Policy.* New York: Bookman, 1954.

532 Bell, Daniel, ed. *The Radical Right.* Revised ed. Garden City, NY: Doubleday, 1964.

533 Bouscaren, Anthony T. *America Faces World Communism.* New York: Vantage, 1953.

534 Conquest, Robert, and White, Jon Manchip. *What to Do When the Russians Come: A Survivor's Guide.* New York: Stein and Day, 1984.

535 DeToledano, Ralph. *The Greatest Plot in History.* New York: Duell, Sloan, & Pearce, 1963.

536 _____. *Spies, Dupes, and Diplomats.* New York: Duell, Sloan, & Pearce, 1952.

537 Chalmers, David M. *Hooded Americanism: The History of the Ku Klux Klan.* New York: Franklin Watts, 1981.

538 Ellsworth, R.E., and Harris, S.M. *The American Right Wing.* Washington: Public Affairs Press, 1962.

539 Finch, Phillip. *God, Guns, and Guts: A Close Look at the Radical Right.* New York: Seaview/Putnam, 1983.

540 Goldberg, Robert A. *Hooded Empire: The Ku Klux Klan in Colorado.* Urbana: University of Illinois Press, 1981.

541 Jacobs, Dan N. *The Masks of Communism.* Evanston, IL: Harper & Row, 1963.

542 Kintner, William R. *The Front is Everywhere: Militant Communism in Action.* Norman: University of Oklahoma Press, 1950.

543 Kolkey, Jonathan Martin. *The New Right, 1960-1968, With Epilogue, 1969-1980.* Washington, D.C.: University Press of America, 1983.

544 Lipset, Seymour Martin, and Raab, Earl. *The Politics of Unreason: Right-Wing Extremism in America, 1790-1970.* New York: Harper & Row, 1970.

545 Rosenstone, Robert A., ed. *Protest From the Right.* Beverly Hills, CA: Glencoe, 1968.

546 Schoenberger, Robert A., ed. *The American Right Wing: Readings in Political Behavior.* New York: Holt, Rinehart & Winston, 1969.

547 Stormer, John A. *None Dare Call It Treason.* Florissant, MO: Liberty Bell, 1964.

The John Birch Society

The John Birch Society received much attention from alarmed liberal academics and journalists in the 1960s, among them, J. Allen Broyles (entry 548) and Arnold Forster and Benjamin Epstein (entries 549-51). Scott McNall (entry 552) details life as a Bircher in Portland, Oregon, while Gerald Schomp (entry 553) offers an unflattering portrait of founder Robert Welch. A great believer in conspiracies, Welch wrote several books (entries 554-56) outlining his theories.

548 Broyles, J. Allen. *The John Birch Society: Anatomy of a Protest.* Boston: Beacon, 1964.

549 Forster, Arnold, and Epstein, Benjamin. *Danger on the Right.* New York: Random House, 1964.

550 _____. *The Radical Right.* New York: Random House, 1967.

551 _____. *Report on the John Birch Society, 1966.* New York: Random House, 1966.

552 McNall, Scott G. *Career of a Radical Rightist: A Study in Failure.* Port Washington, NY: Kennikat, 1975.

553 Schomp, Gerald. *Birchism was My Business.* New York: Macmillan, 1970.

554 Welch, Robert. *The Blue Book of the John Birch Society.* n.p., 1961.

555 _____. *The Life of John Birch.* Boston: Western Islands, 1960.

556 _____. *The Politician.* Belmont, MA: Belmont Publishing, 1963.

A Near Red Scare, 1968-1974

Three British journalists, Chester, Hodgson, and Page (entry 559) teamed up to write a perceptive account of the 1968 election which featured three-way redbaiting. For contemporary accounts of the repression of the Left and the anti-war movement, see Becker and Murray (entry 557), Wasserstein and Green (entry 567), and Alan Wolfe (570). Geoffrey Rips (entry 564) looks at how government stifled counterculture newspapers. Phillip A. Luce (entry 561) and Alice Widener (entry 568) represent the far right's reaction to the dissenters. Paul Chevigny (entry 560) and Rodney Stark (entry 566) examine anti-communist attitudes among law enforcement officials.

More information on the campaigns against the Left by various government agencies, including the FBI, CIA, NSA, and IRS can be found in the section Anti-Communism and the Intellegence Agencies. Fawn M. Brodie (entry 558) and Garry Wills (entry 569) have written perceptive studies of Richard M. Nixon. The president's memoir (entry 563) reveals much about this most controversial of anti-communist politicians. Jonathan Schell (entry 565) explains how the war in Southeast Asia led to government lawbreaking at home which culminated in Watergate. The best of a spate of books on the Watergate scandal is by J. Anthony Lukas (entry 562).

557 Becker, Theodore., and Murray, Vernon G., eds. *Government Lawlessness in America.* New York: Oxford University Press, 1971.

558 Brodie, Fawn M. *Richard Nixon: The Shaping of his Character.* New York: Norton, 1981.

559 Chester, Lewis, Hodgson, Godfrey, and Page, Bruce. *An American Melodrama: The Presidential Campaign of 1968.* New York: Viking, 1969.

560 Chevigny, Paul. *Cops and Rebels.* New York: Pantheon, 1972.

561 Luce, Phillip A. *The New Left Today: America's Trojan Horse.* Washington: Capital Hill Press, 1971.

562 Lukas, J. Anthony. *Nightmare: The Underside of the Nixon Years.* New York: Viking, 1976.

563 Nixon, Richard M. *R.N.: The Memoirs of Richard Nixon.* New York: Warner, 1979.

564 Rips, Geoffrey. *UnAmerican Activities: The Campaign Against the Underground Press.* San Francisco: City Lights, 1981.

565 Schell, Jonathan. *The Time of Illusion.* New York: Vintage, 1975.

566   Stark, Rodney. *Police Riots.* Belmont, CA: Wadsmorth, 1972.

567   Wasserstein, Bruce, and Green, Mark J., eds. *With Justice For Some.* Boston: Beacon, 1972.

568   Widener, Alice. *Teachers of Destruction: Their Plans for a Socialist Revolution.* Washington, D.C.: Citizens Evaluation Institute, 1971.

569   Wills, Garry. *Nixon Agonistes.* Boston: Houghton Mifflin, 1969.

570   Wolfe, Alan. *The Seamy Side of Democracy: Repression in America.* New York: David McKay, 1973.

The New Right

The neoconservative movement is the latest and perhaps the final stop for a group of anti-communist intellectuals who began their ideological odysseys as Marxists (or leftists) in the 1930s and moved right toward liberalism in the 1950s and right again in the 1970s toward the New Right. Peter Steinfels (entry 584) examines their ideas critically in a book which provides a good overview. The neoconservative obsession with answering the New Left can be seen in Bell and Kristol (entry 572) and Nathan Glazer (entry 573). The most important writers among them are sociologist Daniel Bell (entry 571), editor Irving Kristol (entries 574 and 575), historian/politician Daniel P. Moynihan (entries 576 and 577), publicist Norman Podhoretz (entries 578 to 580), and optimist Ben Wattenberg (entry 583).

Conservative activist William A. Rusher (entries 581 and 82) reviews the ideas of the New Right favorably. The ambitious Richard Viguerie (entry 585) explains why he is ready to lead. New Right political organizer Paul Weyrich (entry 586) sets the New Right agenda well into the next century.

571   Bell, Daniel. *The Cultural Contradictions of Capitalism.* New York: Basic Books, 1976.

572   _____ and Kristol, Irving., eds. *Confrontation: The Student Rebellion and the Universities.* New York: Basic Books, 1969.

573   Glazer, Nathan. *Remembering the Answers: Essays on the Student Revolt.* New York: Basic Books, 1970.

574   Kristol, Irving. *Reflections of a Neoconservative: Looking Back, Looking Ahead.* New York: Basic Books, 1983.

575   _____. *Two Cheers for Capitalism.* New York: Basic Books, 1978.

576   Moynihan, Daniel P. *Counting Our Blessings: Reflections on the Future of America.* Boston: Little, Brown, 1980.

577 _____. *Loyalties*. New York: Harcourt Brace Jovanovich, 1984.

578 Podhoretz, Norman. *Breaking Ranks: A Political Memoir*. New York: Harper & Row, 1979.

579 _____. *The Present Danger*. New York: Simon & Schuster, 1980.

580 _____. *Why We Were in Vietnam*. New York: Simon & Schuster, 1982.

581 Rusher, William A. *The Making of the New Majority*. New York: Sheed and Ward, 1975.

582 _____. *The Rise of the Right*. New York: Morrow, 1984.

583 Scammon, Richard, and Wattenberg, Ben. *The Real Majority*. New York: Coward-McCann, 1970.

584 Steinfels, Peter. *The Neoconservatives*. New York: Simon & Schuster, 1979.

585 Viguerie, Richard A. *The New Right: We're Ready to Lead*. Falls Church, VA: The Viguerie Company, 1980.

586 Weyrich, Paul M. *Future 21: Directions for America in the 21st Century*. Greenwich, CT: Devin-Adair, 1984.

Religious-based Anti-Communism

The far right has always had its religious allies in the fight against atheistic communism. Leo P. Ribuffo (entry 594) examines what he calls the Old Christian Right by focusing on the lives of three right-wingers active from 1920 to 1950: William D. Pelley, Gerald B. Winrod, and Gerald L.K. Smith. David H. Bennett (entry 143) covers Christian anti-communism during the Great Depression. Fulton J. Sheen (entry 597), chief anti-communist prophet and philosopher of the Catholic Church long before and after Joe McCarthy, warns of the perils of "red fascism." Donald Crosby (entry 342) and Vincent DeSantis (entry 343) discuss Catholicism and McCarthy. Fred Schwarz (entry 596), founder of the Christian Anti-Communist Crusade of the 1960s, sold millions of copies of his book warning Americans about the evils of communism. More recently, the Moral Majority and other media-based fundamentalist organizations have drawn the attention of a number of scholars and journalists. See Conway and Siegelman (entry 587), Gabriel Fackre (entry 589), and Liebman and Wuthnow (entry 593) for surveys of politically active religious right groups. A leader in the secular humanism movement, Edward L. Ericson (entry 588) fights back against charges that he is part of the communist conspiracy. John L. Kater, Jr. (entry 592) and Perry D.

Young (entry 598) focus on the Moral Majority. Jerry Falwell (entries 590 and 591), founder of Moral Majority, sets his political agenda as does another anti-communist electronic preacher, James Robison (entry 595).

587 Conway, Flo, and Siegelman, Jim. *Holy Terror: The Fundamentalist War on America's Freedoms in Religion, Politics and Our Private Lives.* Garden City, NY: Doubleday, 1982.

588 Ericson, Edward L. *American Freedom and the Radical Right.* New York: Frederick Ungar, 1982.

589 Fackre, Gabriel J. *The Religious Right and Christian Faith.* Grand Rapids, MI: Eerdmans, 1982.

590 Falwell, Jerry, ed. *The Fundamentalist Phenomenon: The Resurgence of Conservative Christianity.* Garden City, NY: Doudleday, 1981.

591 _____. *Listen America!* Garden City, NY: Doubleday, 1980.

592 Kater, John L., Jr. *Christians on the Right: The Moral Majority in Perspective.* New York: Seabury, 1982.

593 Liebman, Robert C., and Wuthnow, Robert, eds. *The New Christian Right: Mobilization and Legitimation.* New York: Aldine, 1983.

594 Ribuffo, Leo P. *The Old Christian Right: The Protestant Far Right From the Great Depression to the Cold War.* Philadelphia: Temple University Press, 1983.

595 Robison, James. *Save America to Save the World.* Weaton, IL: Tyndale House, 1980.

596 Schwarz, Fred. *You Can Trust the Communists (...To Do Exactly as They Say!).* Englewood Cliffs, NJ: Prentice-Hall, 1960.

597 Sheen, Fulton J. *Communism and the Conscience of the West.* Indianapolis and New York: Bobbs-Merrill, 1948.

598 Young, Perry D. *God's Bullies: Native Reflections on Preachers and Politics.* New York: Holt, Rinehart & Winston, 1982.

Contemporary Anti-Communism

For the views of the political moderates who governed in the immediate post-Vietnam/Watergate period, see memoirs by Gerald Ford (entry 603) and Jimmy Carter (entry 600). Journalist Clark Mollenhoff (entry 610) has produced an extremely critical examination of Carter which some will find useful. Laurence I. Barrett (599), Robert Dallek (entry 601), and Garry Wills (entry 615) do the same for Ronald Reagan. Paul D. Erickson (entry 602) analyzes the Reagan rhetoric for clues to his character. Leslie Gelb (entry 604) looks at Reagan's beliefs while Madeleine Kalb (entry 606) explains why Reagan has not been able to bring back the old foreign policy consensus. Robert Scheer (entry 612) delves into the loose talk about fighting nuclear wars which emanated from the Reagan White House. Charles Tyroler (entry 614) brings together position papers from the influential Committee on the Present Danger. Reagan's autobiography (entry 611) predates his entry into politics but contains much material on his fight against communism in Hollywood.

Leftist John Judis (entry 605) issues a warning about a new Red Scare. Andrew Kopkind (entry 608) sees a parallel between the early 1950s when liberals moved to the right and the 1980s while Christopher Layne (entry 609) is careful to differentiate between the conservatives of the fifties and those of today. David K. Shipler (entry 613) offers a portrait of American anti-communism in the 1980s. George F. Kennan (entry 607) offers a vision of anti-communism which has room for both realism and morality as do Destler, Gelb, and Lake (entry 259).

599 Barrett, Laurence I. *Gambling With History: Ronald Reagan in the White House*. Garden City, NY: Doubleday, 1983.

600 Carter, Jimmy. *Keeping Faith: Memoirs of a President*. New York: Bantam, 1982.

601 Dallek, Robert. *Ronald Reagan: The Politics of Symbolism*. Cambridge, MA: Harvard University Press, 1984.

602 Erickson, Paul D. *Reagan Speaks: The Making of an American Myth*. New York: New York University Press, 1985.

603 Ford, Gerald. *A Time to Heal: The Autobiography of Gerald R. Ford*. New York: Harper & Row, 1979.

604 Gelb, Leslie. "The Mind of the President." *New York Times Magazine*, 6 October 1985.

605 Judis, John. "Setting the Stage for Repression." *The Progressive* 45 (April 1981): 27-30.

606 Kalb, Madeleine G. "Where Consensus Ends." *New York Times Magazine*, 27 October 1985.

607 Kennan, George F. "Morality and Foreign Policy." *Foreign Affairs* 64 (1985-86): 205-18.

608 Kopkind, Andrew. "The Return of Cold War Liberalism." *The Nation* 236 (April 1983): 495, 503-12.

609 Layne, Christopher. "The Real Conservative Agenda." *Foreign Policy* 61 (1985-86): 73-93.

610 Mollenhoff, Clark R. *The President Who Failed: Carter Out of Control.* New York: Macmillan, 1980.

611 Reagan, Ronald, with Richard G. Hubler. *Where's the Rest of Me? The Ronald Reagan Story.* New York: Duell, Sloan & Pearce, 1965.

612 Scheer, Robert. *With Enough Shovels: Reagan, Bush and Nuclear War.* New York: Random House, 1983.

613 Shipler, David K. "The View from America." *New York Times Magazine,* 10 November 1985.

614 Tyroler, Charles, II, ed. *Alerting America: The Papers of the Committee on the Present Danger.* Washington, D.C.: Pergamon, 1984.

615 Wills, Garry. *Reagan's America: Innocents Abroad.* Garden City, NY: Doubleday, 1987.

Fiction

Novels About Anti-Communism

See Kenneth Davis (entry 416), Charles I. Glicksburg (entry 417), and George Lipsitz (entry 420) for analysis of anti-communism in literature. Sherwood Anderson's "Red Decade" novel (entry 616) centers around the murder of a Communist party member by the National Guard during the Gastonia strike. Alvah Bessie (entry 617), one of the "Hollywood 10," portrays the tribulations of communists who fought in the Spanish Civil War. E.L. Doctorow (entry 618) has written a fictionalized account of the Rosenberg children. Although set in Colonial America, Arthur Miller (entry 619) plainly had the second Red Scare in mind. Loyalty oaths are the subject of a novel by Abraham Polonsky (entry 620). Radio actors are pitted against an anti-communist magazine in Irwin Shaw's work of fiction (entry 621).

616 Anderson, Sherwood. *Beyond Desire.* New York: Liveright, 1932.

617 Bessie, Alvah. *The Un-Americans.* New York: Cameron, 1957.

618 Doctorow, E.L. *The Book of Daniel.* New York: Random House, 1971.

619 Miller, Arthur. *The Crucible.* New York: Oxford University Press, 1971.

620 Polonsky, Abraham. *A Season of Fear.* New York: Cameron, 1956.

621 Shaw, Irwin. *The Troubled Air.* New York: Random House, 1951.

Anti-Communist Novels

Many great writers sympathized with the Communist party and the Soviet Union in the 1930s at a time when capitalism no longer seemed to work, only to become disillusioned. A profound sense of anger and betrayal is reflected in their work. John Dos Passos (entries 622 and 623) became a staunch anti-communist, as John P. Diggins (entry 461) explains in his excellent study of disenchanted leftists. Ralph Ellison (entry 624) and Richard Wright (entries 631 and 632) portray Communist party activities among blacks unfavorably in their fiction. Wright (entry 445) explains his change of heart in a wartime magazine article. James T. Ferrell (entry 625) chose an autobiographical format to make a strong anti-communist statement. See also anti-communist novels by John Steinbeck (entry 629) and Lionel Trilling (entry 630). Willa Gibbs (entry 626) and Chester B. Himes (entry 627) produced anti-red novels during the period of "Trumanism." A character resembling Senator McCarthy is prominent in a hard-boiled novel by Mickey Spillane (entry 628) although, in the end, he turns out to be a murdering communist.

622 Dos Passos, John. *Adventures of a Young Man*. New York: Harcourt, Brace, 1939.

623 _____. *Most Likely to Succeed*. New York: Prentice-Hall, 1954.

624 Ellison, Ralph. *Invisible Man*. New York: Random House, 1952

625 Farrell, James T. *Yet Other Waters*. New York: Vanguard, 1952.

626 Gibbs, Willa. *The Tender Men*. New York: Farrar, Straus, 1948.

627 Himes, Chester B. *Lonely Crusade*. New York: Knopf, 1947.

628 Spillane, Frank Morrison [Mickey Spillane]. *One Lonely Night*. New York: Dutton, 1951.

629 Steinbeck, John. *In Dubious Battle*. New York: Viking, 1936.

630 Trilling, Lionel. *The Middle of the Journey*. New York: Viking, 1947.

631 Wright, Richard. *Native Son*. New York: Harper, 1940.

632 _____. *The Outsider*. New York: Harper's, 1953.

Author Index
(Indexed by citation number)

Aaron, Daniel, 141
Abbott, Roger S., 223
Acheson, Dean G., 230
Adams, Graham, Jr., 54
Adams, John G., 339
Adler, Leslie K., 199, 297
Alexander, Robert J., 142
Allen, Gary, 530
American Friends Service
    Committee, 16
American Historical Association, 1
Anders, Roger M., 400
Anderson, Jack, 332
Anderson, Sherwood, 616
Andrew, William D., 164
Andrews, Bert, 280, 312
Andrews, Peter, 312
Arendt, Hannah, 427
Avrich, Paul, 42

Bacciocco, Edward J., Jr., 499
Bailey, Percival R., 200
Bailey, Thomas A., 74
Baker, Liva, 108
Baker, Roscoe, 531
Barnard, John W., 165
Barrett, Edward L., Jr., 251
Barrett, James R., 182
Barrett, Laurence I., 599
Barth, Alan, 281-282
Basen, Neil K., 55
Basler, Roy P., ed., 2
Bayley, Edwin R., 390
Beal, Fred E., 166
Beck, Carl, 283
Becker, Theodore, ed., 557
Beier, Norman S., 401
Belfrage, Cedric, 381
Belknap, Michael R., 201
Bell, Daniel, 571, ed., 532, ed., 572
Bellamy, Edward, 43
Bennett, David H., 143
Bennett, Edward M., 144
Benson, Ezra Taft, 473
Bentley, Elizabeth, 428
Bentley, Eric, 298
Bentley, Eric, ed., 284

Berman, Jerry J., ed., 503
Bernstein, Barton J., ed., 202
Bessie, Alvah, 299, 617
Beth, Loren P., 340
Biberman, Herbert, 300
Biddle, Francis, 190, 285
Biskind, Peter, 415
Blum, John Morton, 56, ed., 191-
    192
Bohlen, Charles E., 256
Borosage, Robert L., 504
Bouscaren, Anthony T., 533
Brodie, Fawn M., 558
Brody, David, 167
Brown, Ralph S., Jr., 224
Brown, Thomas M., ed., 17
Broyles, J., 548
Bruce, Robert V., 44
Bruhn, Alfred W., 369
Buckley, William F., Jr., 286, 313,
    370
Budenz, Louis F., 429-430
Buhite, Russell D., 231
Buhle, Mary Jo, 57
Burner, David, 481
Burnham, James, 371
Burns, James MacGregor, 145, 193
Burns, Richard Dean, ed., 3-4
Byrnes, James F., 232

Cade, Dozier C., 391
Cahn, Bill, 58
Calomiris, Angela, 511
Candeloro, Dominic, 109
Caridi, Ronald J., 341
Carleton, Don E., 396
Carr, Robert K., 287
Carter, Jimmy, 600
Caughey, John, 288
Caute, David, 203
Celler, Emanuel, 373
Ceplair, Larry, 301
Chaffee, Zechariah, Jr., 99, 360-361
Chalmers, David M., 537
Chamberlain, Lawrence, 122
Chambers, Whittaker, 314-315
Chaplain, Ralph, 59

Charney, George, 431
Chester, Lewis, 559
Chevigny, Paul, 560
Clemens, Diane Shaver, 194
Clubb, O Edmund, 382
Coan, Blair, 100
Coben, Stanley, 101, 110
Cochran, Bert, 168
Cohen, Warren I., 257
Collier, Peter, 482
Conquest, Robert, 534
Conway, Flo, 587
Cook, Blanche Wiesen, 474
Cook, Bruce, 302
Cook, Fred J., 316, 333, 392
Cooke, Alistair, 317
Corker, Charles, 5
Coser, Lewis, 27
Cotter, Cornelius P., 362
Crosby, Donald F., 204, 342
Crossman, Richard, ed., 432
Curry, Richard O., ed., 17
Curtis, Charles P., 383

Dallek, Robert, 258, 601
David, Henry, 45
Davis, David B., ed., 18
Davis, Elmer H., 393
Davis, Kenneth C., 416
Davis, Lenwood G., 6
Decter, Moshe, 355
Delaney, Robert Finley, 7
DeSantis, Hugh, 146
DeSantis, Vincent P., 343
Destler, I M., 259
DeToldedano, Ralph, 318, 535-536
Diamund, Sigmund, 512
Dies, Martin, 289
Diggins, John P., 19, 461
Divine, Robert A., 205, 475, ed., 483
Doctorow, E L., 618
Donner, Frank J., 505
Donovan, Robert J., 233-234
Dos Passos, John, 622-623
Douglas, Paul H., 374
Dowell, Elbridge F., 169
Draper, Theodore, 20
Drinnon, Richard, 111
Dubovsky, Melvyn, 170
Dugger, Ronnie, 484
Dunn, Robert W ed., 102

Dyson, Lowell K., 147

Eastman, Max, 433-435
Edwards, Jerome E., 363
Egbert, Donald E., ed., 21
Eisenhower, Dwight D., 476
Elliff, John T., 513
Elliott, Russell R., 60
Ellison, Ralph, 624
Ellsworth, R E., 538
Engelhardt, Carroll, 446
Englund, Steven, 301
Epstein, Benjamin, 549-551
Erickson, Paul D., 602
Ericson, Edward L., 588
Ewald, William Bragg, Jr., 344

Fackre, Gabriel J., 589
Fairbank, John K., 384
Falwell, Jerry, ed., 590-591
Farrell, James T., 625
Faulk, John Henry, 385
Feis, Herbert, 260
Ferrell, Robert H., 75, ed., 235-236, 477
Ficken, Robert E., 76
Fiedler, Leslie A., 402
Filene, Peter, 88
Finch, Phillip, 539
Fite, Gilbert C., 85
Fitzgerald, Frances, 261
Fleischman, Harry, 148
Fleming, D., 262
Fogarty, Robert S., 46
Foner, Philip S., 61
Ford, Gerald, 603
Forster, Arnold, 549-551
Fox, Richard Wightman, 62, 447
Freeland, Richard M., 206
Freeman, Josh, 171
Fried, Albert, ed., 48
Fried, Richard M., 345-346, 375
Friedel, Frank, ed., 8
Friedheim, Robert, 123
Fulbright, J., 485

Gaddis, John Lewis, 263-265
Gambs, John S., 77
Garrow, David J., 514
Gates, John, 436
Gelb, Leslie H., 259, 604
Gelhorn, Walter, 364, ed., 397

Gellerman, William, 290
Gibbs, Willa, 626
Gillers, Stephen, ed., 527
Ginger, Ray, 112
Gitlow, Benjamin, 437
Glazer, Nathan, 573
Glicksberg, Charles I., 417
Goldberg, Robert A., 540
Goldman, Emma, 113
Goldstein, Alvin H., 403
Goldstein, Robert J., 22
Goldwater, Barry, 486
Golin, Steve, 63
Goodman, Walter, 291
Goulden, Joseph C., 172, 207
Graves, William S., 89
Green, George N., 398
Green, James R., 64
Green, Mark J., ed., 567
Griffith, Robert, 208, 347-350, 368
Griffith, Winthrop, 487
Gutfeld, Arnon, 78
Gutman, Herbert G., 47
Guttmann, Allen, 23, 149
Gwertzmann, Bernard M., 489
Halberstam, David, 394, 488
Halle, Louis J., 266
Halperin, Morton H., ed., 503
Hamby, Alonzo, 24, 209
Hanson, Ole, 114
Harper, Alan D., 225
Harris, David J., 49
Harris, S M., 538
Hawley, Ellis W., 79
Haynes, John E., 9
Haywood, William D., 115
Hellman, Lillian, 304
Herring, George C., 267
Hicks, Granville, 116, 150, 438
Higham, John, 25
Hillquit, Morris, 117
Himes, Chester B., 627
Hiss, Alger, 319
Hodgson, Godfrey, 559
Hofstadter, Richard, 26
Hook, Sidney, 448
Hoopes, Townsend, 478
Hoover, J., 515-516
Horowitz, David, 482
Howe, Irving, 27, 173
Hunt, R N., ed., 10
Hyfler, Robert, 28

Hyman, Harold M., 226
Hyman, Sidney, 376

Ingalls, Robert P., 334
Irons, Peter H., 124, 210
Isserman, Maurice, 195

Jackson, Kenneth T., 130
Jacobs, Dan N., 541
Jaffe, Julian F., 125
Jaffe, Philip J., 29
Jensen, Joan, 80
Johnson, Claudius O., 196
Johnson, Haynes, 489
Johnson, Lyndon B., 490
Josephson, Harold, 439
Joughlin, Louis,., 131
Jowitt, William Allen [Earl Jowitt],
    320
Judis, John, 605

Kahn, E J., Jr., 386
Kahn, Gordon, 303
Kalb, Madeleine G., 606
Kampelman, Max M., 174
Karnow, Stanley, 268
Kater, John L., 592
Kearns, Doris, 491
Kebabian, John S., 50
Keeran, Roger, 175
Kemper, Donald J., 377
Kempton, Murray, 151
Kendrick, Alexander, 395
Kennan, George F., 90, 237, 269,
    607
Kennedy, David M., 81
Kimball, Penn, 211
Kintner, William R., 542
Kipnis, Ira, 65
Klehr, Harvey, 152, 177
Koen, Ross Y, 270
Kolarz, Walter, ed., 11
Kolkey, Jonathan Martin, 543
Kolko, Gabriel, 66
Kopkind, Andrew, 608
Koppes, Clayton R., 82
Kristol, Irving, 572, 574-575
Kutler, Stanley I., 30

LaFeber, Walter, 271
LaGumina, Salvatore J., 292
Lake, Anthony, 259

Larrowe, Charles P., 178
Lasch, Christopher, 31, 91-92
Lasky, Victor, 318
Laslett, John H. M., ed., 32
Latham, Earl, 153
Lattimore, Owen, 387
Layne, Christopher, 609
Leab, Daniel J., 176, 418-419
Lee, R., 365
Leffler, Melvyn P., 272
Lens, Sidney, 33
Leuchtenburg, William E., 154
Levenstein, Harvey, 179
Levin, Murray, 34
Levin, N Gordon, Jr., 93
Levitt, Michael, 321
Levitt, Morton, 321
Liebman, Marcel, 35
Liebman, Robert C., ed., 593
Liebowitz, Nathan, 449
Lipset, Seymour Martin, 544, ed., 32
Lipsitz, George, 420
Lisio, Donald J., 155
Little, Douglas, 132
Livesay, Harold C., 180
Longaker, Richard, 366
Lora, Ronald, 212
Loth, David, 462
Lowenthal, Max, 517
Luce, Phillip Abbott, 500, 561
Lukas, J Anthony, 562
Lyons, Eugene, 156
MacDonald, Dwight, 238
MacDonald, J Fred, 421
MacNeil, Neil, 463
Markowitz, Norman D., 215, 239
Martin, Joe, 464
Martin, John Bartlow, 451
Massing, Hede, 322
Matusow, Allen J., 492, ed., 335
Matusow, Harvey M., 440
May, Ronald W., 332
McAuliffe, Mary S., 213
McAuliffe, Mary S., 450
McClurg, Donald J., 133
McConnell, Frank D., 422
McNall, Scott G., 552
McWhiney, Grady, 67
McWilliams, Carey, 214
Meeropol, Michael, 404
Meeropol, Robert, 404

Meier, August, 181
Merkley, Paul, 452
Messer, Robert L., 273
Meyer, Frank S., 372
Miller, Arthur, 619
Miller, Merle, 305
Miller, Robert Moats, 134
Millibrand, Ralph, 35
Milton, Joyce, 407
Miroff, Bruce, 493
Mock, James R., 83
Mollenhoff, Clark R., 610
Morgan, Edmund M., 131
Morgan, Richard E., 507
Morlan, Robert L., 126
Moynihan, Daniel P., 576-577
Murphy, Paul L., 84, 103, 135
Murray, Robert K., 104
Murray, Vernon G., ed., 557

Naison, Mark, 157
Nash, George, 465
Navasky, Victor, 306, 323
Nelson, Harold, ed., 36
Nelson, Steve, 182
Nevins, Allan, 378
Niebuhr, Reinhold, 240, 351
Nixon, Richard M., 479, 563
Nizer, Louis, 405
Noggle, Burl, 105
Noyes, John Humphrey, 51
Nuechterlein, James A., 453

O'Brien, David J., 158
O'Brien, Michael, 399
O'Neill, William L., 216, 494
O'Reilly, Kenneth, 324, 518
Ogden, August Raymond, 293
Orr, Oliver H., Jr., 12
Oshinsky, David M., 183, 336
Ostrander, Gilman M., 367
Overstreet, Harry, 519

Packer, Herbert L., 441
Page, Bruce, 559
Pally, Marcia, 423
Parenti, Michael, 37
Parmet, Herbert S., 480, 495
Parrish, Michael E., 406
Paterson, Thomas G., 199, 274-275
Patterson, James T., 241
Pells, Richard H., 159, 454

Pelzel, Sophia R., 94
Perkus, Cathy, ed., 520
Perrett, Geoffrey, 136
Persons, Stow, ed., 21
Peterson, F., 242
Peterson, H C., 85
Philbrick, Herbert A., 521
Podhoretz, Norman, 578-580
Polonsky, Abraham, 620
Potter, Charles E., 294
Powers, Richard Gid, 522-523
Preston, William, Jr., 106
Propas, Frederic L., 137
Purifoy, Lewis M., 217

Quint, Howard H., 52

Raab, Earl, 544
Rader, Melvin, 252
Radosh, Ronald, 184, 407, 466
Reagan, Ronald,, 611
Rees, David, 243
Reeves, Thomas C., 337, 352-353
Reinhard, David W., 467
Renshaw, Patrick, 68
Reuben, William A., 408
Reuther, Victor, 185
Ribuffo, Leo P., 594
Richmond, Al, 442
Rips, Geoffrey, 564
Robison, James, 595
Rogin, Michael Paul, 354
Root, Jonathan, 409
Rorty, James, 355
Rosenberg, Ethel G and Julius, 410
Rosenstone, Robert A., ed., 545
Rossiter, Clinton, 455
Rovere, Richard, 338
Rowe, Frank, 388
Ruck, Rob., 182
Rudwick, Elliot, 181
Rusher, William A, 581-582

Sale, Kirkpatrick, 501
Salvatore, Nick, 118
Sand, Leonard B., 401
Sanders, Jane, 253
Santos, Michael W., 138
Sayre, Nora, 424
Scammon, Richard, 583
Scheele, Henry Z., 468
Scheer, Robert, 612

Scheiber, Harry N., 86
Schell, Jonathan, 565
Schlesinger, Arthur M., Jr., 276, 456
Schmidt, Karl M., 244
Schneir, Miriam, 411
Schneir, Walter, 411
Schoenberger, Robert A., ed., 546
Schomp, Gerald, 553
Schwartz, Nancy Lynn, 307
Schwarz, Fred, 596
Seidman, Joel, ed., 13
Selcraig, James Truett, 254
Seth, Ronald, 325
Shadegg, Stephen C., 469
Shain, Russell E., 14
Shain, Russell E., 425
Shannon, David A., 38-39
Shaw, Irwin, 621
Sheen, Fulton J., 597
Shipler, David K., 613
Siegelman, Jim, 587
Sigal, Clancy, 308
Sims, Robert C., 186
Sims-Wood, Janet L., 6
Skinner, James M., 426
Skolnick, Jerome H., 502
Smith, A., 379
Smith, Geoffrey S., 160
Smith, John C., 326
Smith, Malcolm, 362
Smith, Margaret Chase, 380
Smith, Richard N., 245
Snell, John L., ed., 197
Sobell, Morton, 412
Solberg, Carl, 496
Spillane, Frank Morrison [Mickey Spillane], 628
Spolansky, Jacob, 508
Stark, Rodney, 566
Starobin, Joseph, 218
Steel, Ronald, 457
Steinbeck, John, 629
Steinberg, Alfred, 470
Steinfels, Peter, 584
Stern, Phillip M., 389
Stone, Isadore F., 219
Stormer, John A., 547
Stouffer, Samuel A., 40
Straight, Michael, 356
Strakhovsky, Leonid I., 95
Stripling, Robert E., 295

Strong, Bryan, 69
Strout, Cushing, 413
Suber, Howard, 309
Superintendent of Documents, 15
Szajkowski, Zosa, 127

Taft, Philip, 87
Tanner, William R., 368
Taylor, Telford, 296
Theoharis, Athan G., 198, 220-222,
    227, 357, 509, ed., 327-328
Thomas, Norman, 458
Thompson, Francis H., 228
Toy, Eckard, 471
Trani, 96
Trilling, Lionel, 630
Truman, Harry S., 246
Trumbo, Dalton, 310
Turner, William W., 524
Tyler, Robert, 70
Tyroler, Charles, II., ed., 614

Ungar, Sanford, 525
Unterberger, Betty M., 97
Utley, Freda, 443

Van Tine, Warren, 170
Vandenberg, Arthur H., Jr., ed., 247
Vaughn, Robert, 311
Viereck, Peter, 472
Viguerie, Richard A, 585
Villard, Oswald Garrison, 119
Voros, Sandor, 444

Waldman, Louis, 187
Walker, J., 248
Walker, John T., 128
Walton, Richard J., 249, 497
Waltzer, Kenneth, 526
Warren, Earl, 459
Warren, Frank A., 161
Warshow, Robert, 414
Warth, Robert D., 107
Wasserstein, Bruce, ed., 567
Watkins, Arthur V., 358
Wattenberg, Ben, 583
Watters, Pat, ed., 527
Webber, Everett, 53
Wechsler, James, 229
Weinstein, Allen, 329
Weinstein, James, 71-72
Welch, Robert, 554-556

West, Rebecca, 330
West, Thomas R., 481
Wexler, Alice, 120
Weyrich, Paul M., 586
White, Jon Manchip, 534
White, William S., 250
Whitehead, Don, 528
Whitfield, Stephen J., 460
Whitney, Richard M., 139
Whittemore, L., 188
Whitten, Woodrow C., 129
Widener, Alice, 568
Widick, B., 173
Williams, David, 529
Williams, T., 162
Williams, William Appleman, 98,
    277
Wills, Garry, 498, 569, 615
Wilson, Edmund, 41, 163
Wilson, Joan Hoff, 140
Winters, Donald E., 73
Wise, David, 510
Wolfe, Alan, 278, 570
Wright, Richard, 445, 631-632
Wuthnow, Robert, ed., 593

Yarnell, Allen, 255, 359
Yergin, Daniel, 279
Young, Art, 121
Young, Perry D., 598

Zeligs, Meyer A., 331
Zieger, Robert H., 189

Subject Index

Accuracy in Academia, 165
Acheson, Dean, 70, 72, 82, 84, 91, 92, 104, 109
American Civil Liberties Union (ACLU), 35, 36, 41, 47, 95
Adams Chronology, 95
Adamson, Ernie, 60
Afghanistan, 164, 166
Africa, 125, 147, 164, 171
Agnew, Spiro, 136, 137
Albertson, William, 108
Algeria, 125
Alien Registration Act—See Smith Act
Alliance for Progress, 114
Alsop brothers, 95, 110
Amerasia, 55, 81
American Alliance for Labor and Democracy, 18
American Christian College, 116
American Committee for Cultural Freedom, 154
American Federation of Labor (AFL), 5, 8, 9, 17, 18, 22, 36, 38
American Legion, 21, 24, 31, 35, 54, 82, 84, 89, 95
American Nazi Party, 101, 122
American Opinion, 119
"American Plan", 36
American Protective League (APL), 14
American Relief Administration, 37
Americans for Democratic Action, 59
Anaconda Copper Company, 15
Anderson, Jack, 71
Anglo-Iranian Oil Company, 103
Apocalypse Now, 167
Appeal to Reason, 7, 9
Arbenz Guzman, Jacobo, 103

Army-McCarthy Hearings, 94-97
Aryan Nations, 166
Association of Catholic Trade Unionists, 55
Attorney General's List, 59, 102, 112

Baker, James, III, 165
Baldwin, Margaret, 153
Bell, Daniel, 108, 154
Bellamy, Edward, 5, 6
Benet, Stephen Vincent, 92
Bentley, Elizabeth, 56
Benton, William, 82, 83, 85, 86
Berger, Victor, 7, 13, 26
Berrigan, Philip, 141
Big Jim McClain, 89
Birch, John, 118
Black, Hugo, 153
Black Legion, 42
Black Panther party, 130, 139-142, 146
Blacklists, 61, 89, 90
Blacks, 23, 58, 101, 106, 112, 113,, 121, 129, 130, 135, 136, 139
and Red Scare, 23
civil rights movement, 106, 112, 113, 121, 129, 130
Bohlen, Charles E, 38, 91, 92, 112
Bolshevik Revolution, 15, 17-19, 22, 28, 56, 118, 146, 172
Bonus Expeditionary Force (BEF), 40, 41
Boorstin, Daniel, 154
Borah, William E, 12, 23
Boston Police Strike (1919), 22
Bowman Gum company, 73
Boy Scouts, 45, 108, 112
Boy Spies of America, 14

Bradley, Omar, 77
Brandeis, Louis D, 8
Brave New World, 176
Brennan, William J, 103
Bridges, Harry, 40, 48
Bridges, Styles, 84
Bridgman raid, 36
Browder, Earl, 49, 76, 96
Brown v. *Board of Education*, 105
Brownell, Herbert, 93
Buckley, William F., Jr, 109, 119, 137, 151
Budenz, Louis, 62, 71
Buford, S.S. 25
Bullitt, William C, 51
Bureau of Investigation, 31, 36
Burleson, Albert Sidney, 13
Burnham, James, 109
Burns, William J, 36
Bush, George, 148, 157, 170
Butler, John Marshall, 76

Cain, Harry P, 85, 102
California Un-American Activities Committee, 88
Camp Fire Girls, 45
Carter, Jimmy, 146, 149, 150, 152, 155-158, 166, 169
Castro, Fidel, 124
Catholic War Veterans, 55, 89, 98
Catholics, American, 5, 46, 47, 55, 57, 173
Celler, Emanuel, 40
Central Intelligence Agency (CIA), 88, 94, 103, 105, 106, 126, 130, 131, 140, 143, 148, 150, 154, 163, 165, 170
Centralia Massacre, 24, 35
Chafee, Zechariah, Jr, 63
Chamber of Commerce, 54-56
Chamberlain, Neville, 125
Chambers, Whittaker, 56, 61, 62, 92, 109
Chamorro, Edgar, 164
Chiang Kai-shek, 55, 63, 71, 77, 78, 81, 83, 84
"Chicago 7", 141
Chicago Tribune, 46, 98
China, 33, 55, 63, 66, 71, 73, 77, 78, 81, 83-85, 91, 93, 99 106, 110, 125, 133, 143, 145, 164, 166, 170

China Lobby, 63
China White Paper, 82
Christian Anti-Communist Crusade, 117, 156
Christian Crusade, 120
Christian fundamentalists, 115, 116, 169
Church, Frank, 149
Churchill, Winston, 53
Citizens Protective League, 15
Civil Service Loyalty Boards, 57
Coast Federal Savings and Loan Association, 119
Cohn, Roy, 92, 94, 96, 97
Collier, Peter, 162
Colson, Charles, 144
Columbia University uprising, 128, 154
COMINFIL program, 106
Commager, Henry Steele, 138
Commentary, 154
Committee for the Survival of a Free Congress, 151, 165
Committee of Fifteen, 20
Committee on the Present Danger, 148, 155
Communist Control Act, 98
Communist International (Comintern), 37, 39, 44, 50
Communist Labor Party, 21, 25, 103
Communist Manifesto, 3, 118
Communist Party (CP and CPUSA), 21, 25, 33, 36, 94, 104, 108, 112, 119, 128, 131, 153, 163
    moderation During World War, 49-52
    "Red Decade" and, 39-40, 43-46, 48
    Red Scare (1919-1920), 25
    Red Scare (1947-1954), 54-66, 70, 98
    harrassed by FBI, 106, 107, 112-113
Communist Political Association, 51
Communist Workers Party, 36
Conant, James B, 91
Congress of Industrial Organizations (CIO), 40, 45, 51, 59
Conquest, 153
Conscription Act, 20

Conservative Caucus, 152, 165
Conservatives, 9, 42, 46, 56, 67,
  75, 83, 148, 151, 165
  role in ending Red Scare (1919-
  1920), 26, 28, 66
  role in ending Red Scare (1947-
  1954), 66, 93-98
  conspiracies, belief in, 4, 16, 23,
  34, 35, 36, 72, 80, 81, 83, 88,
  99, 117-119, 124, 143, 153, 165
"Contra" rebels, 163, 164, 167
Contragate", 167
Coolidge, Calvin, 22, 36, 37, 38
Cooper, Gary, 60
Cooperative Commonwealth
  Federation, 39
Coors, Joseph, 151
Coplon, Judith, 62
Coughlin, Charles, 42, 44
Counter-intelligence Program
  (COINTELPRO), 107, 108, 112,
  128-130, 139, 144, 150
Crail, Joe, 119
Cronin, John F, 55
Cuba, 112, 114, 125, 143, 163,
  164
Culbertson, Charles, 12

Daily Worker, 49
Daley, Richard, 135
Dangerous Moves, 168
Das Kapital, 3
Daugherty, Harry, 36
Daughters of the American
  Revolution, 35
Davies, Joseph, 51, 56
Davis, Edward, 142
Davis, Elmer, 95
Davis, Forrest, 81
Deer Hunter, The, 167
Debs, Eugene V, 7-9, 17, 19, 33, 34
  arrest for sedition, 17
  on Bolshevik Revolution, 19
DeLeon, Daniel, 6, 7, 9
Democratic party, 47, 66, 67, 68,
  70-72, 74, 76, 80, 86, 92, 94,
  97, 111, 136, 145, 149, 163,
  165
  "Commiecrats", 82
  McCarthyism of conservative
  wing, 75, 80
Dennis, Lawrence, 42

De Pugh, Robert, 122
Détente, 146, 148, 149, 157, 158
Dewey, John, 92
Dewey, Thomas E, 52, 60
Dies, Martin, 41, 45, 46
Dirksen, Everett, 76, 95
Disney, Walt, 112
Dodd, Thomas, 117, 126
Dolan, Terry, 152
Domestic Intelligence Division, 150
Domino theory, 115, 125
Dos Passos, John, 109
Douglas, Helen Gahagan, 76
Douglas, William O, 138
Du Bois Clubs, 126
Dulles, Allen, 103, 119
Dulles, Foster Rhea, 92
Dulles, John Foster, 86, 90-93,
  103, 111, 114, 119, 135, 165
Dumbarton Oaks Conference, 61

Eagle Forum, 166
Eastern Europe, 6, 18, 19, 52, 53,
  55, 56, 101, 149
Eastman, Max, 51, 109
Edwards, Willard, 95
Einstein, Albert, 56
Eisenhower, Dwight D, 66, 84-86,
  92-95, 97, 99, 101, 105-109,
  111, 115, 118, 124, 136, 158,
  165, 170
  accused of being a Communist,
  119
  CIA and, 103
  loyalty program of, 93, 102, 112
  military-industrial complex, 110,
  174
  McCarthy and, 90, 92
  panders to GOP far right, 85
Eisenhower, Milton, 119
Elitcher, Max, 79
Ellsberg, Daniel, 144
Engels, Friedrich, 3, 62
Equal Rights Amendment, 151
Ervin subcommittee, 141
Espionage Act, 1, 12, 13, 16, 20,
  34, 74
Estonia, 48
Evans, Hiram Wesley, 34
Everest, Wesley, 24
Everett massacre, 10
Executive Order 9835, 58

Executive Order 10241, 80
Executive Order 10450, 93
Executive Order 11905, 150
Executive Order 12036, 150

Fair Deal, 55
Falwell, Jerry, 153, 154, 165
Farrell, James T, 51
Fascism, American, 42, 43
Federal Bureau of Investigation
    (FBI), 37, 51, 55, 56, 60-63, 74,
    88, 89, 93, 94, 101, 105, 112,
    130, 131, 138, 143, 150, 156,
    161, 163, 166
    destroys CPUSA with
    COINTELPRO, 106-108
    Martin Luther King and, 112,
    113, 129, 130
    New Left and, 128, 129, 139, 140
    Rosenberg case and, 78, 80
    Warren Court and, 104
Federal Emergency Management
    Agency, 160
Fish, Hamilton, 41
Fisher, Fred, 97
Fitzgerald, Frances, 125
Flanders, Ralph, 95, 97
Flynn, Elizabeth Gurley, 47
Flynn, William J, 21
Foley Square Trial, 62, 63
Ford, Gerald R, 146-150, 169
Ford, Henry, 35
Ford Motor Company, 31
Foreign Agents Registration Act
    (the McCormack Act), 46
Foreign Intelligence Surveillance
    Act, 150
Fortune, 49, 109
Foster, William Z, 23, 56
Fourier, Charles, 2
Fourteen Points, 18, 22
Franco, Francisco, 46, 47, 55
Free speech campaigns, 9, 10
Freedom-In-Action, 120
Freedom of Information Act, 149
Fuchs, Klaus, 78
Fulbright, J, William, 82, 127, 128
Fundamentalist Christians, 150,
    153-155

Gainesville 8, 141
Garwood, Ellen, 167

Gavin, James, 110
General Electric, 120, 156
General Intelligence Division, 20,
    24, 25
Geneva Summit (1955), 101, 102
Germany, 44, 46, 47, 49, 52, 53
Gillette, Guy, 82, 83, 97
Glazer, Nathan, 154
Gold, Harry, 78
Goldwater, Barry, 117, 119, 124-
    127, 132, 137, 151, 156, 158
Gompers, Samuel, 5, 22, 36, 108
Gorbachev, Mikhail, 164
Graham, Billy, 152
Graham, Frank P, 75
Graham-Sterling Bill, 26
Grand Alliance, 51, 53
Great Britain, 14, 48, 53, 57, 110
Great Depression, 32, 39, 46, 52,
    109, 172
Great Society, 123, 124, 155
Green Corn Rebellion, 14
Green, William, 36
Greenglass, David, 78, 79
Gregory, Thomas, 12, 14
Guatemala, 103, 106, 174
Gulf of Tonkin Resolution, 147

Haig, Alexander, 164
Hall, Gus, 51, 128, 153
Hampton, Fred, 139
Handlin, Oscar, 108
Hanson, Ole, 20
Harding, Warren G, 26, 28, 33, 36,
    37
Hargis, Billy James, 116, 120, 152
Harriman, Averell, 53
Harvey, Paul, 115
Hatch Act (1939), 46
Hayden, Tom, 136, 139
Haymarket Riot, 4
Haywood, William D, 7, 9, 10, 17,
    23
Hearst syndicate, 46, 71, 98
Helms, Jesse, 151, 165
Helsinki agreements, 149
Heritage Foundation, 151, 165
Hess, Stephen, 136
Hillquit, Morris, 7
Hiss, Alger, 61, 62, 82, 85, 86, 91,
    136, 144, 162
Hitler, 47-50, 57, 122, 125, 174

Ho Chi Minh, 125, 134
Hollywood, 50, 60, 61, 64, 89, 155, 170
"Hollywood Ten", 61, 89, 90
Holmes, Oliver Wendell, 13, 103
Hook, Sidney, 51, 87, 154, 162
Hoopes, Townsend, 111
Hoover, Herbert C, 37, 41, 106
Hoover, J, Edgar, 36, 37, 44, 45, 51, 80, 101, 106, 107, 112, 128, 135, 138, 139, 143, 149
    Red Scare (1919-1920), 24, 27
    Red Scare (1947-1954), 56, 71, 72, 99
    obsession with Martin Luther King, 112, 113, 129, 130
    on collapse of CPUSA, 108
    Roosevelt's instructions to, 44, 45
Horowitz, David, 162
House Appropriations Committee, 70
House Civil Service Subcommittee, 57
House Committee on Un-American Activities (HCUA), 45, 51, 55, 56, 59-62, 64, 65, 71, 76, 83, 87-90, 92, 97, 104, 105, 107, 116, 122, 126, 155, 157
House Judiciary Committee, 26
"How the Reds Made a Sucker Out of Me", 90
Howe, Quincy, 95
Hughes, Charles Evans, 26, 37
    on recognition of Soviet Russia, 37
Huk rebellion, 73
Hull, Cordell, 44
Humphrey, Hubert H, 127, 133, 135, 136
Hunt, H, L, 119
Hurley, Patrick, 41, 84
Huston Plan, 143-145
Huston, Tom Charles, 142, 143
Huxley, Aldous, 176
HYDRA, 130

Ickes, Harold, 45
Illuminati, 118
Immigrants, 1, 4-6, 11, 13, 21, 25, 27, 29, 34, 75
Immigration Act (1917), 11
Immigration Act (1918), 20, 27
Immigration Act (June 1920), 28
Immigration and Naturalization Service, 20, 25, 27
Industrial Workers of the World (IWW), 9-11, 14, 15, 22-25
    and Red Scare (1919-1920), 22-25, 28
    persecuted during World War I, 15-17
Institute of Pacific Relations (IPR), 83, 84
Inter-Racial Council, 35
Internal Revenue Service, 140, 150
Internal Security Act--See McCarran Act
International Information Agency (IIA), 92
International Jew, The , 35
International Working People's Association (IWPA) , 4
Invasion USA, 168

Jackson, Donald, 105
Jackson, Henry, 86
Jencks v. United States, 105
Jenkins, Ray, 96
Jenner, William, 78, 85, 92
Jessup, Philip C, 82, 111
Jews, 35, 42, 46, 76, 165
John Birch Society, 101, 115, 117-123, 137, 156, 166
Johnson, Hiram, 10
Johnson, Lyndon B, 102, 105, 123-129, 132, 134-138, 144, 158
Johnston, Eric, 60
Jones, Thomas K, 160
Judd, Walter, 117

Kaufman, Irving, 79
Kellogg, Frank B, 38
Kelly, Robert F, 38
Kennan, George, 59
Kennedy, John F, 85, 101, 108, 110-115, 122, 124, 127, 131, 134, 135, 158
    Martin Luther King and, 112, 113
Kennedy, Joseph P, 85
Kennedy, Robert F, 85, 112, 113, 122, 127
Khrushchev, Nikita, 114, 158
Killing Fields, 168

King, Martin Luther, Jr, 112, 113, 129, 132
Kissinger, Henry A, 134, 141, 145-148
Knights of Columbus, 55
Knowland, William, 92
Kristol, Irving, 154
Ku Klux Klan, 21, 31, 34, 35, 42, 101, 121, 137, 166

LaFollette, Robert, 32
LaFollette, Robert, Jr, 68
Landis, Kenesaw Mountain, 13
LaRouche, Lyndon, Jr, 165
Lattimore, Owen, 71
Laurell, Ferdinand, 5
Lawrence Strike, 10
"Lee List", 70
Legion of Justice, 142
LeMay, Curtis, 120
Lend-Lease, 48
Lenin, V. I., 15, 18, 25, 35, 37, 62
Lever Act, 23
Levering Oath, 87
Levi, Edward, 149
Levison, Stanley, 113
Lewis, John L, 23, 36, 40
Liberals, 39, 43, 46, 56, 58, 64, 71, 122, 127, 148, 151, 169
  anti-communism of, 72, 111, 114, 154, 162
  accused of communism, 118, 121, 152, 156
  redbaiting Henry Wallace, 60, 162
  role in Red Scares, 66
Liberty Federation, 165
Liberty League, 43, 118
Library of Congress, 60
Life, 50, 51
Lipset, Seymour Martin, 108, 154
Lippmann, Walter, 56, 95
Listen, America!, 153
Little, Frank, 15
Lodge, Henry Cabot, Sr, 16
Lodge, Henry Cabot, Jr, 85, 124
Long, Huey P, 42
Looking Backward, 5
Lourie, Donald B, 91
Loyalty Review Board, 80, 81, 104
Lucas, Scott, 76
Luce, Henry, 82
Lusk, Clayton R, 22

Lustron Corporation, 69, 83

MacArthur, Douglas, 41, 50, 73, 77, 78, 81, 84
Madison Capital-Times, 69
Mailer, Norman, 110
Mao Tse-tung, 55, 63, 81, 114, 134, 145
Marshall, George C, 85, 90, 118
Marshall Plan, 59, 81
Martin, Joe, 77
Marx, Karl, 3, 4, 7, 62, 119, 174, 176
Masons, 173
Masses, 13
Mathews, Joseph B, 45, 71, 83, 94
Matusow, Harvey, 102
McCarran, Pat, 64, 66, 73, 76, 83, 84, 88, 92, 98, 99, 169
McCarran Act, 74, 75, 87, 102, 112, 139
"McCarranism", 75, 83
McCarthy, Eugene, 127, 131
McCarthy, Joseph R, 64-73, 76, 78, 81-87, 90-99, 102, 109, 115-118, 136, 137, 157, 169, 176
  and 1950 election, 75, 76
  and 1952 election, 84-86
  and Tydings Committee, 71
  Army hearings, 96,97
  as the "Pepsi-Cola kid", 69
  attacks George Marshall, 81
  contribution to Red Scare, 99
  Salt Lake City speech, 70
  Senate condemnation of, 98, 102
  Wheeling speech, 65, 69, 70
McCormick newspapers, 76
McDonald, Larry, 151
McFarlane, Robert C, 163, 166
McGovern, George, 145
McIntire, Carl, 116, 152
McLeod, Scott, 91
McNamara, Robert, 114, 125
Media, Pa. break-in, 140
Medina, Harold, 62
Mike Hammer, 98
Minutemen, 101, 122
Mission to Moscow, 51, 60
Mitchell, John, 138, 144
Modern Times, N.Y., 2
Molly Maguires, 4
Molotov, V. M., 53, 54, 57

Moral Majority, 153, 154, 165
Morgan, Thomas, 7
Morgenthau, Henry, Jr, 57
Mormonism, 173
Moss, Annie Lee, 94, 95
Mossadegh, Muhammad, 103
Motion Picture Alliance for the
    Preservation of American Ideals,
    89
Motion Picture Producers
    Association, 60, 61
Moynihan, Daniel P, 154
Mundt, Karl, 94, 96
Mundt-Nixon Bill, 59, 73, 74
Munich syndrome, 125
Murrow, Edward R, 95
Muskie, Edmund, 145
My Son John (1952), 88

National Association for the
    Advancement of Colored People
    (NAACP), 36, 108
National Association of
    Manufacturers, 21, 35, 117
National Civic Federation (NCF), 8,
    9, 21
National Commission on the Causes
    and Prevention of Violence, 135
National Conservative Political
    Action Committee, 152
National Education Association, 87
National Endowment for the
    Preservation of Liberty, 166
National Founders Association, 35
National Industrial Recovery Act, 43
National Institute Survey, 8
National Lawyers Guild, 97
National Mobilization Committee,
    141
National Origins Act, 34
National Popular Government
    League, 27
National Review, 109
National Security Act (1947), 105-
    106
National Security Agency (NSA),
    140
National Security Council (NSC),
    72, 124, 163
National Security League, 21, 35
National Textile Workers Union, 32
Nationalist Clubs, 5

Naturalization Act of 1906, 11
Nazi-Soviet Pact, 47, 48, 51, 64,
    171
Neoconservatives, 146, 147, 150,
    154-156, 164, 167
New Deal, 39-45, 51, 52, 61, 108,
    124, 155, 172
New Freedom, 9, 172
New Harmony, Ind., 2
New Left, 127-131, 136-140, 144,
    155, 172
New Republic, 162
New Right, 135, 146, 151-159,
    164-170
New York City Writers Project, 46
New York Times, 50, 143, 144, 162
New York Tribune, 3
Newsweek, 162
Nguyen Van Thieu, 146
Nicaragua, 38, 163-166, 170
Niebuhr, Reinhold, 50, 108, 175
Nitze, Paul, 148
Nixon Doctrine, 134
Nixon, Richard M, 61, 65, 71, 76,
    78, 83-86, 94, 96-99, 110, 117,
    131, 135-139, 141-151, 169, 176
    and 1950 election, 76
    "madman theory", 133, 134
    modifies anti-communist mission,
    146
    vice presidential nominee, 84
Norris, George W, 23
North, Oliver, 163, 176
NSC-68, 72
Nuclear Freeze movement, 161, 170

O'Connor, Sandra Day, 164
O'Dell, Jack, 113
O'Donnell, Kenneth, 115
O'Hare, Kate Richards, 13
Office of Strategic Services (OSS),
    55
Omega Group, 166
Operation CHAOS, 130, 140
Operation MERRIMAC, 130
Operation Midnight Climax (1955),
    106
Operation RESISTANCE, 130
Operation Secret (1952), 88
Oppenheimer, J., Robert, 111
Order, The, 166
Oumansky, Constantine, 44

Overman, Lee S, 22
Overseas Library Program, 92
Owen, Robert Dale, 2, 3

Palmer, A, Mitchell, 19, 21-28, 48, 67, 176
Palmer Raids, 24-27, 87, 144, 170
Panama Canal, 119, 149
Parent-Teacher Association, 118
Paris Commune (1871), 4
Paris peace agreement, 147
Parker, Cedric, 69
Passaic, N.J. strikes, 32
Paterson, N.J. strike, 10
Peace Corps, 111, 114
Peace Links, 161
Pearson, Drew, 71, 82
Pennsylvania v. *Nelson*, 104
Pentagon Papers, 125, 144
Pepper, Claude, 75
Pepsi-Cola , 69, 83, 149
Peress, Irving, 94
Peters v. *Hobby*, 104
Phalansteries, 2
Phillips, Howard, 152
PHOENIX program, 126
Pike, Otis, 149
Pipes, Richard, 160
Playboy, 165
Podhoretz, Norman, 154, 164
Poindexter, John M, 163
Poland, 47, 48, 52-54, 81, 91, 164
Politician, The, 118
Popular Front, 39, 45, 47, 49, 51, 64
Populist party, 6, 7
Post, Louis F, 27
Pound, Roscoe, 26
Prager, Robert Paul, 16
Progressive, The, 162
Progressive Labor party, 126
Progressive party (1924), 32
Progressive party (1948), 60, 108
Progressives, 1, 7-9, 19, 23, 28, 171
Project Democracy, 163, 166
Public Interest, The, 154
Purtell, William A, 86
Pyle, Christopher, 141

Quaker Oats company, 91

Railroad strike (1922), 36
Rambo: First Blood, Part II, 167
Rand School, 22
Randolph, A., Philip, 51
Rather, Dan, 165
Readers' Digest, 161
Reagan Doctrine, 158, 160, 163, 164
Reagan, Ronald, 119, 135, 146-151, 155-167, 169, 170, 176
   early career, 60, 156
   on détente, 149
   on "evil empire", 160, 169
   on fighting Hollywood reds, 155, 156
   on McCarthy, 156
   unites New Right, 151, 156
   use of McCarthyism, 161
Red Dawn, 168
"Red Decade", 32, 39-43
"Red fascism", 54-57, 148, 168
Red flag laws, 26
Red Scare (1919-1920), 2, 19-29, 31, 33, 34, 40, 48, 63, 65, 66, 103, 109, 141, 171
Red Scare (1947-1954), 54-63, 64, 65, 70-103, 108, 112, 174
   compared to 1919-1920, 66
   education, 87, 88
   effects on Hollywood, 89, 90
   state boards, committees and oaths, 87
   Supreme Court and, 103, 104
   victims recognized by JFK, 111
   winds down, 97, 98
Red Squads, 142
Report on Russia, 51
Republican party, 31, 33, 54, 57, 60-64, 67-70, 72, 75, 76, 80, 82-86, 91-93, 96, 102, 110, 115, 117, 124, 136, 137, 148, 150, 156, 164
   Red Scare (1947-1954), and, 54, 57, 62-64, 67-70, 75, 84-86, 90, 102
   rise of right wing to prominence, 115-123, 149-152, 157-167
Reuther, Walter and Victor, 122
Robertson, Pat, 152, 154
Robinson, Edward G, 90
Robison, Jim, 152
Rockefeller Commission, 150

Rockwell, George Lincoln, 122
Rocky IV, 168
Roosevelt, Elliott, 57
Roosevelt, Franklin D, 32, 39, 42-45, 47-53, 56, 58, 73, 91, 118, 172
Roosevelt, Theodore, 8, 9, 12, 15, 133
Rosenberg, Julius and Ethel, 72, 73, 75, 77-80, 163
Rostow, V.D. Eugene, 148
Rousselot, John, 156
Rumania, 53
Rusk, Dean, 127
Russian Orthodox Church, 50
Russian Soviet Bureau, 22

Sacco, Nicola, 32
Saxbe, William, 149
Saypol, Irving, 79
Scales, Julius, 111
Schafly, Phyllis, 166
Scheer, Robert, 157
Schenk, Charles T, 13
Schenck v. United States (1919), 103
Schine, G. David, 92, 93, 96
Schlesinger, Arthur, Jr, 92, 108, 127
Schultz, George, 165
Schwarz, Fred, 116, 117, 142, 156
Scott Paper Company, 31
Screen Actors Guild, 60, 155
Seale, Bobby, 141
Seattle general strike, 20, 21
Secular humanism, 153
Sedition Amendment, 1, 16, 17
Sedition laws, 16, 17, 34, 40, 74
Sedition Slammers, 14
Senate Internal Security Subcommittee (SISS), 76, 83, 88, 90, 92, 102, 105, 117, 126
Service, John Stewart, 81
Service v. Dulles, 104
Sheen, Fulton J, 55
Silverthorne Lumber Company v. United States, 27
Sinclair, Upton, 39
Singlaub, John K, 167
Slochower v. Board of Regents, 104
Smathers, George, 75, 76

Smith Act, 32, 48, 51, 59-62, 86, 104, 107, 108, 111
Smith, Al, 26
Smith, Gerald L. K., 42, 76, 122
Smith, Margaret Chase, 72
Smith, William French, 164
Smith, Willis, 75
Sobell, Morton, 78, 79
Socialist Labor Party, 4, 6, 7
Socialist Party of America (SPA), 1, 7-9, 21, 26, 28, 33, 39, 43, 56, 171
Socialist Workers Party, 51, 112, 126
Soldier of Fortune, 166
Sontag, Susan, 162
South Africa, 159, 170
Southern Christian Leadership Conference (SCLC), 112, 113
"Soviet Ark," 25
Soviet Union, 2, 18, 28, 31-33, 37-39, 46-57, 64, 72, 73, 78, 101, 103, 110, 117, 128, 134, 145, 148, 149, 158-161, 164, 167-169, 171, 175
Spanish Civil War (1936-1939), 46, 47
Spargo, John, 18
Sparkman, John J, 82
Spellman, Francis Cardinal, 55
Spillane, Mickey, 98
Stalin, Joseph, 32, 44, 47-53, 55, 57, 62, 75, 79, 81, 91, 102, 175
Stallone, Sylvester, 167
Stettinius, Edward, 53
Stevens, Robert, 94, 95
Stevenson, Adlai, 84-86, 96, 98, 109
Stone, Harlan Fiske, 36, 44
Stouffer, Samuel, 101
Strasser, Adolph, 5
Strategic Defense Initiative, ("Star Wars"), 160, 162, 165, 170
Stripes, 168
Students for a Democratic Society (SDS), 127, 128, 137, 139
Subversive Activities Control Board, 102, 107
Sullivan, William, 113, 129
Sweezy v. New Hampshire, 104
Syndicalists (See Industrial Workers of the World)

Taft-Hartley Act, 112
Taft, Robert, 70, 84, 92, 118
Taft, William Howard, 133
Taiwan, 73, 164
Tax Reform Act (1976), 150
Teamsters Union, 51
Temple, Shirley, 45
Temporary Commission on
  Employee Loyalty, 58
Terrible Threateners, 14
Them (1954), 89
Thomas, J. Parnell, 60
Thomas, Norman, 39, 42, 43, 51
Time, 82
Tonkin Gulf Resolution, 124
Torcaso v. *Watkins*, 153
Tower, John, 119
Townsend, Francis, 42
Trading-With-the-Enemy Act, 14
Trilateral Commission, 155
Trotsky, Leon, xii, 25, 32
Truman Doctrine, 58, 59, 73
Truman, Harry S, 33, 53-68, 70-74,
  80, 82-87, 90-93, 99, 109, 118,
  124, 131, 135, 158, 162, 169
  and Harry Dexter White, 93
  belief in "red fascism", 57
  compared with McCarthy, 66
  denounces Eisenhower, 86
  dismissal of MacArthur, 77, 78
  loses communist issue, 63
  election of 1948, 60
  loyalty program, 58, 70, 86, 93,
  102, 112
  on Alger Hiss, 61
  on McCarthy, 71, 82, 83
  on Soviets and Yalta, 53
  prosecutes CPUSA hierarchy, 62
  vetoes McCarran Act, 74
Trumbo, Dalton, 90
Twentieth Century Reformation
  Hour, 116
Tydings, Millard, 71, 72, 76, 81,
  96

Uncommon Valor (1983), 167
Ungar, Sanford J, 112
Union of Russian Workers, 24, 25
Union Party, 43
United Auto Workers Union, 123
United Fruit Company, 103
United Mine Workers Union, 40

United Nations, 53, 61, 73, 77, 82,
  118
U.S. Army, G-2 , 19, 41, 58, 141,
  142
U.S. Department of Commerce, 37
U.S. Department of Defense, 144
U.S. Department of Justice, 25, 27,
  31, 59, 62, 63, 141
U.S. Department of Labor, 25, 27,
  40
U.S. Department of State, 31, 37,
  38, 55, 61, 65, 70, 71, 81, 83,
  91, 92, 116, 133, 157, 161
U.S. News and World Report, 98
U.S. Supreme Court, 101, 107, 131,
  153, 164
  and Red Scare (1919-1920), 27,
  103
  and Red Scare (1947-1954), 103
  Warren Court and civil liberties,
  103-105
  World War I, 13
Utt, James B, 121

Vanzetti, Bartolomeo, 32
Veterans of Foreign Wars, 82
Vietnam, 102, 110, 111, 114, 115,
  120-128, 130-136, 138, 140-150,
  155, 158, 167-170, 171
Viguerie, Richard A, 151, 165
Vinson, Fred, 103
Voice of America, 92

Wagner Act, 43
Walker, Edwin, 119, 120
Wall Street Journal, 22, 49
Wallace, George C, 120, 136, 137,
  150
Wallace, Henry, 50, 60, 108, 111,
  162
Walsh, Frank P, 36
War Powers Act, 147
Warner Brothers, 156
Warren, Earl, 103-105, 119
Warren, Josiah, 2, 3
Washington Post, 38, 63, 161, 162
Washington Times, 46
Watergate affair, 145, 146, 148-
  150, 155, 158, 170
Watkins, Arthur, 97
Watkins v. *United States*, 104
Watt, James, 162

Wayland, Julius, 7
Wayne, John, 89
Weather Underground, 139, 140,
    142, 143, 146
Webb, Edwin, 12
Webster, William, 163
Welch, Joseph, 96-98
Welch, Robert, 115, 117-123, 128,
    142, 156, 166
Western Federation of Miners
    (WFM), 7-9
Weyrich, Paul, 151-154
White Citizens Councils, 121
White, Harry Dexter, 93, 95
White House "Plumbers", 145
White Nights (1985), 169
White, Theodore H, 124
White, Walter, 92
White, William Allen, 35
White, William L, 51
White, William S, 99
Who'll Stop the Rain, 168
Why Not Victory?, 124
Wills, Garry, 114, 135, 158
Wilson, Edmund, 51
Wilson, William B, 27, 28
Wilson, Woodrow, 2, 9-18, 22-24,
    31, 33, 37, 67, 111, 123, 133,
    138, 172
    civil liberties and, 18
    offers remedy to Leninism, 18
    on Boston Police Strike, 22
    on recognition of Soviet Russia,
    33
    on Red Scare, 24
    on war, 12, 17
    orders investigation of IWW
    (1915), 11
Women's International League for
    Peace and Freedom, 162
Women's Liberation Movement, 139
Workers Party, 32
Workingmen's Party of the United
    States, 4
Works Progress Administration, 46
World Anti-Communist League
    (WACL), 166
World Peace Council, 161

Yalta, 53, 56, 61, 85, 86, 91
Yates v. *United States*, 104, 112

*You Can Trust the Communists (To
    Be Communists)*, 117

Zwicker, Ralph W, 94, 95